'This is a very important book and is a rare event in media and cultural studies since its conclusions are based on extensive empirical work. It shows very convincingly the processes which underpin the production of television fiction and the powerful impacts which such programmes can have on public understanding.'

Greg Philo, Professor of Communications,
University of Glasgow

'At last a book that bridges the gulf between the study of political communication and television fiction, and between research into media production and audience responses. Lesley Henderson is both original and illuminating.'

James Curran, Professor of Communications at Goldsmiths,
University of London

For Simon and Louis

Social Issues in Television Fiction

Lesley Henderson

Edinburgh University Press

© Lesley Henderson, 2007

Edinburgh University Press Ltd
22 George Square, Edinburgh

Typeset in 11/13 Ehrhardt
by Servis Filmsetting Ltd, Manchester, and
printed and bound in Great Britain by
Antony Rowe Ltd, Chippenham, Wilts

A CIP record for this book is available from the British Library

ISBN 978 0 7486 2531 4 (hardback)
ISBN 978 0 7486 2532 1 (paperback)

Contents

Figures

Acknowledgements

I would like to thank all of those who took part in my research - programme makers, script-writers, story editors and consultants, and other television industry personnel who spent valuable time with me reflecting on their decision making. Thanks also to all of those who represented different charities, organisations, and activist and campaign groups and were willing to engage with my research questions. Thanks to everyone who helped organise or took part in my focus group sessions and who discussed difficult issues in an open and reflexive way. Without your help this book would not exist.

I would also like to thank Greg Philo, Bob Franklin and James Curran for their continued generous support. Thanks as well to Sarah Edwards, James Dale and Máiréad McElligott at Edinburgh University Press.

Much of the research discussed here was conducted during my time spent at the Glasgow Media Group and I owe a debt to my colleagues there: Jacquie Reilly, David Miller, Jenny Kitzinger, Greg McLaughlin and John Eldridge. I would also like to thank Bridget Fowler and David Frisby in the Department of Sociology at Glasgow University. Thanks to my postgraduate students and colleagues in sociology, media and communications at Brunel: Julian Petley, Clive Seale, John Tulloch, Sanjay Sharma, Monica Degen, Alan Irwin, Michelle Peters and Ian Hutchby. I am very grateful to my parents, my sister Lorna and friends for their continued support: Caroline Dover, Mike Michael, Kate George, Charlie Davison, Klara Ekevall, Gill Green, Donna Miller, David Westwater, Emma Miller, Ursula Jenkinson and Denise Goddard. Finally, my love and thanks go to Simon Carter and Louis Uisdean.

Part I Mapping the Field

CHAPTER 1

Television Fiction in Context: Education and Entertainment

Introduction

I want to begin by discussing a recent episode of the prime-time US medical drama *ER* (USA, NBC, 1994–). At the time of writing, this drama series continues to be extraordinarily popular. It remains the top rated show for the channel and US audiences are estimated at around 12 million. In an episode titled 'There Are No Angels Here' (series 12, May 2006), the narrative moved from the emergency room of a Chicago hospital to the humanitarian disaster in the Darfur region of Sudan. Audiences watched as characters Dr John Carter and Dr Gregory Pratt spent time working in a refugee camp, trying to protect their patients from the brutality of Janjaweed militia and struggling with scarce resources. Pratt, on his first visit to the region, functions as the 'audience's eyes' and the central theme of American non-intervention in the bitter conflict is interwoven through-out the story. Pratt tells the local doctor confidently that sometimes it is best to 'Step back and wait for it to end'; the doctor retorts, 'Sounds like an excellent foreign policy' (Channel 4, 22 May 2006). Indeed the intended message of the programme is put simply in the words of one character: 'If the US does not lead the way, who will?'[1] This episode of *ER* was clearly designed to stimulate social action, with online links from the programme website directing fans to petition US president George Bush, urging inter-vention to help 'save Darfur'.

In so doing the fictional drama brought this story to American and indeed global audiences who had seen little attention paid to the same issue in television news (reportedly only ten minutes' coverage from the three main US evening news bulletins in the previous five months; Burkeman and Goldenberg 2006). The programme makers invested considerable resources in the scenes, with costs estimated at around $7 million. On the assumption that audiences knew as little as the production team, advice was explicitly sought from a number of organisations including Médicins Sans Frontières. Meanwhile actor George Clooney, formerly Dr Doug Ross in *ER*, addressed public rallies and appeared on talk shows to try to raise the profile of the disaster. Clooney along with other activists and Christian conservatives is regarded as having successfully kept the issue in the headlines. The programme represented, in the words of one critic, 'an intriguing deployment of prime-time fiction in the cause of consciousness raising' with Clooney providing 'celebrity firepower' (Sutcliffe 2006). Although the actual conditions are believed to be far worse than those portrayed – the conflict has been described by the European Parliament as 'tantamount to genocide' – *ER* was considered to have captured a sense of the 'viciousness' of the government-backed Janjaweed militias. As one academic familiar with the area commented, 'it was prime-time television, and you can't do Darfur [on prime time]. But you can give a suggestion. It gave a good-faith suggestion' (Burkeman and Goldenberg 2006). The producers admitted openly that they had decided to use their unique platform to tackle a topic which they believed was of tremendous social significance. In so doing they had, temporarily at least, disregarded their usual constraints of 'what audiences want to see'.

I want to begin with this example because it provides a useful illustration of some of the issues that are of concern in this book. It raises important questions about the relationship between television news and television fiction. Why might this topic find a place in a popular prime time drama but fail to attract the same commitment from the news media? How and why do certain fictional events attract significant media coverage? How are boundaries between fact and fiction negotiated between creative personnel and source organisations? How are otherwise 'unpalatable' stories packaged for audiences? The *ER* production team reportedly assumed very little knowledge on the part of the audience, especially given the lack of commitment to the story through the news media. But what about other stories – those that already circulate in the public domain? How are 'everyday' issues, for example concerning health and illness, relayed to us through fictional formats? Can television fiction make an impact on audience understandings?

The material that I present in this book is concerned with the same territory – 'public issues' in television fiction. For reasons that will become clear in the chapters that follow, I focus mainly but not exclusively on television serial drama and in particular on the role of soap opera. In so doing I hope to contribute to our understandings of how 'issue' storylines are produced, presented and received. I am therefore using this particular format as a lens in order that we might examine more closely how power is distributed and mediated via television fiction.

Here I want to turn away from the glossy, high octane world of US medical drama to the domestic world of the everyday. Others have highlighted how television serials convey an often claustrophobic world of the domestic. Indeed the television soap opera is frequently characterised as a format in which, unlike other television formats, the personal is privileged over the public. Here are the plots of three storylines in their simplest forms: 'Mandy' finally leaves her abusive husband, but he tracks her down and seems to have changed. Should she trust him? 'Peggy' goes to hospital and receives a devastating diagnosis – she has breast cancer. How can she tell her family? 'Gail's' nanny tells her she has been having an affair with her husband. He denies it. Whom should she believe?

Although at first glance these examples seem to embody the painful reality of everyday life for some women – an abusive relationship, a health problem, the testing of fidelity in marriage – these storylines do more than present dilemmas for the viewer. The construction of these story arcs, and the public response to them, can act as a way of touching upon wider issues which are of interest to media sociologists. As I will argue throughout the book, stories such as these may reveal and embody wider questions concerning media power and society.

On a personal note, my interest in social issues, television fiction and public knowledge developed over a number of years. During the 1990s I was a researcher with the Glasgow University Media Group and involved with a study of child sexual abuse reporting in British media (Kitzinger and Skidmore 1995). Around the same time, late February 1993, a British television soap opera began a powerful fictional storyline of sexual violence and abuse, thus bringing the topic to new and different audiences.

The programme in question was Channel 4 television soap opera *Brookside* and the storyline was played out through a new family that was introduced to 'the Close' – the Jordaches. As the story progressed, viewers discovered that Mandy and her two daughters were living in a safe house. The family were in hiding from Trevor, who had a history of domestic violence (subjecting Mandy to repeated assaults) and sexual abuse (he raped older daughter Beth). As the plot unfolded, audiences were gripped by Trevor's pursuit of his family and watched him charm his way back into their lives. Within a few weeks he had resumed his violent ways and in one episode, after viciously beating Mandy, he was seen to climb into bed with his younger daughter. The implication was clear: Trevor had raped Rachel. This assault had a profound effect on Mandy. In the midst of a violent attack, Mandy reached for a kitchen knife and fatally stabbed him. Rather than risk going to the police, she and Beth decided to bury the body in the garden, where it lay undiscovered for two years.

The Jordache story has been described as 'British soap opera's greatest achievement' (Lawson 2002b). The storyline was certainly a major cultural event and the fictional plot attracted extensive attention in the British media. A deluge of press and magazine features reported and debated each new plot twist (see Sutcliffe 1993). Scenes of sexual violence, unprecedented for a pre-watershed soap opera, were investigated by the regulatory board, the Broadcasting Standards Council (BSC 1993). Further controversy was generated when British soap opera saw its first lesbian kiss – Beth renounced men and began an affair with friend Margaret (see Bindel 2006; Burchill 1998; Culf 1995; Taylor 1995). Meanwhile the actors were invited to lend publicity to public awareness campaigns on behalf of Zero Tolerance (a feminist campaign designed to challenge public attitudes towards domestic violence). Women's refuges reported a marked increase in telephone calls from women in similar situations seeking support. Telephone help lines which ran after key episodes revealed an unusually high response from young people (compared to the response to documentaries) (BSS 1994). Beth and Mandy were finally tried and found guilty of Trevor's murder two years later (Lawrence 1995; Purnell 1995b). These scenes gripped viewers to the extent that Channel 4 managed to capture their greatest ever audience share (28 per cent of the available audience) and nearly 20 million people watched the trial – for the first time in British soap history the episodes were transmitted across five consecutive nights (Rose 1995; Purnell 1995a). Spinoff merchandise from the story included *The Journals of Beth Jordache* (1994), in which the character confides her emotional response to her father's sexual violence and her growing feelings for her close female friend.

The background to this development and the consequences for public understandings seemed worthy of serious consideration. The social problem of child sexual abuse was certainly not new but it was a topic whose public profile had dramatically increased because of media attention over the previous fifteen years. Public awareness that child sexual abuse exists, that it is more widespread than previously thought and that it has damaging consequences has been attributed to media coverage (Kitzinger 2004). But the framing of the issue in TV fiction provokes a series of questions. Do these portrayals simply rework the same themes as news media? Is it possible that the genre of soap opera, with its unresolved narrative structure, might be able to present audiences with more challenging and critical themes? What are the motivations of the production team in deciding to tackle a presumably risky topic in terms of audiences? Does the substantive topic itself present problems for TV soap opera production teams which are distinct from those encountered by media professionals working in other arcas of television? How do audiences respond to this material in what has been traditionally perceived as a 'safe' viewing space – the early evening soap opera? Finally, to what extent can we address these questions fully by exploring just one substantive area or just one programme? This book presents a number of cases (sexual violence, breast cancer and mental distress) which are designed to explore diverse topic and production contexts. In so doing I hope to answer at least some of these questions and generate others.

This book reflects more broadly on the function of television fiction in contemporary culture, positioning it as culturally charged. The television serial drama is a media product which has considerable public visibility and has proved to be an enduring popular format with significant economic importance. Despite this there has been surprisingly little academic attention focused on the production context of these programmes. Yet television fiction has a role to play in what James Curran terms the 'democratic functioning' of the media (Curran 1991). After all, media entertainment facilitates public engagement at an 'intuitive and expressive level in a public dialogue about the direction of society' and is in this respect an integral part of the media's 'informational' role (Curran 1991: 102).

In comparison with a well-developed sociology of news production, there are surprisingly few accounts of how the production process operates in relation to television fiction. The soap opera has not been examined from a political economy perspective. Indeed this is not an approach associated with television fiction (Brunsdon 1995; Geraghty 1996). Again in comparison with production studies of the news, the production of non-journalistic content as a whole has been described as an 'underdeveloped and fragmentary field of research' (McQuail 1994: 188). Indeed those working in the area of news production have regretted that comparable studies have not been extended to television fiction (van Zoonen et al. 1998: 2). Put simply, then, television fiction has largely been studied as a site of entertainment and pleasure despite its importance in 'relaying social meanings and cultural forms' (Gripsrud 1995: 21). Television drama formats have been identified as a crucial 'open' space in which more challenging representations may be constructed, in comparison with the relatively 'closed' factual formats of news media (Schlesinger et al. 1983). This empirical 'gap' means that, as Murdock and Halloran surmised nearly thirty years ago: 'Paradoxically, then, we know the least about the production of the very programs that are the most popular with the viewers' (Murdock and Halloran 1979: 274).

There is no simple answer as to why this should be the case, but within what has been described as the 'incoherent' discipline of media studies, two distinct projects have emerged (Corner 1991). First, there is what Corner

(1991) terms the 'public knowledge' project, a concern with the definitional power of the media. Second, there is the 'popular culture' project,
which has been traditionally concerned more with taste and pleasure.
Despite some interconnections, the research which has been conducted in
the two projects is distinct in both emphasis and genre. Thus studies which
might fall into the category of 'public knowledge' have tended to take news
and current affairs as their central focus, whereas the investigation of
media as a source of entertainment and pleasure has focused on popular
television forms (Corner 1991).

As I explained earlier, my own interest and approach to this field of
research developed out of my involvement with the Glasgow University
Media Group. The GUMG is largely associated with substantive studies
of 'balance and bias' in television news, with more recent research exploring links between media reporting and public beliefs (GUMG 1976, 1980,
1982, 1985; Philo 1990, 1999; Philo and Berry 2004).[2] The overriding
concern here is with the power of the media to shape public attitudes and
beliefs about public issues. This approach can be characterised as 'being
empirical, problem based, alert to questions of power and keen at points to
inform policy and public debate' (Corner 2001: 152). The studies I draw
together in the book can thus be situated at the intersecting point between
these two distinct projects – analysing television fiction not simply as a site
of pleasure but also as a site of definitional power.

Feminism and Everyday Pleasures

As Charlotte Brunsdon writes 'It is arguably feminist interest that has
transformed soap opera into a very fashionable field for academic inquiry'
(Brunsdon 1995: 50). Indeed the study of television soap opera is most
closely associated with the work of feminist writers who see the cultural
form as having a role to play in women's empowerment. This strand of
research has been important in theorising pleasure and seeking to understand and account for women's uses of television serials, magazines and
romance novels (Brunsdon 1981, 2000; Brunsdon et al. 1997; Hobson
1982; Modleski 1982; Radway 1984). The relationship between text and
'female spectator' is of central concern here (Ang 1985; Geraghty 1991).
The feminist approach sought deliberately to carve out a distinctive
research agenda:

> If the traditional leftist critique of the media, with its structuring sense of class
> conflict, was drawn to the reporting of the public world – to industrial dis-
> putes, to the interaction of state and broadcasting institutions, to international

patterns of ownership and control – emerging feminist scholarship had quite another focus. The theoretical impulse of feminism pushed scholars not to the exceptional but to the everyday. (Brunsdon 1995: 59)

As Brunsdon admits, in some ways it seems obvious that television fiction and the format of soap opera in particular should have attracted feminist attention. Here was a genre which was largely for and about women and in which, unlike other parts of the media, strong women were highly visible (see Gaye Tuchman on 'the symbolic annihilation' of women by the media; Tuchman et al. 1978). Crucial to the development of a feminist tradition were Dorothy Hobson's research into women and their identification with the British soap opera *Crossroads* (Hobson 1982); Ien Ang, who studied fans of American prime-time series *Dallas* (Ang 1985); and Tania Modleski on mass-produced women's fiction (Modleski 1982). This work prioritised the text-spectator female experience and highlighted specific cultural competencies brought to bear by women on media texts which were often ignored or denigrated (for discussion see Brown 1990; Fenton 2000; Livingstone 1990). Yet as noted earlier this research was primarily focused on audience activity rather than the macro-structures of production.

Developing a Model

While there is no obvious model to follow in developing a production study of television fiction, the numerous studies of news production do prompt a series of questions. Television soap opera is a very different format, arguably more open than news, targets different audiences and occupies a distinctive place in the public domain. Clearly it would seem impossible to argue reasonably, as news journalists sometimes do of their area, that material is self-evident – the television drama writer has the whole world of imagination to choose from. But we can surely ask how story choices are made. Why do some issues feature in such programmes whereas others are overlooked? In what ways do wider social and cultural values shape storyline development? How do commercial imperatives influence such decisions? The production team operates within a larger broadcasting organisation; how then does the institutional culture influence the nature of storylines? The role of source organisations has been identified as important to understanding news content as a site of struggle. To what extent might production team members similarly be influenced by external forces? Television soap opera attracts extraordinarily large audiences, but how does this 'imagined' diverse audience play an implicit role in developing different storylines?

The cases presented in this book build upon a valuable body of work which has developed within the often overlapping fields of media and cultural studies and the sociology/anthropology of the media. I do not include a comparative, in-depth, ethnographic study of the organisation in which media is 'made'.[3] But here I want instead to use a series of snapshots or case studies to examine television production from the perspectives of those involved in making programmes and thus to allow comparisons to be made where possible (across and within different programmes as well as diverse substantive topics). Such an examination is designed to shed light on the production processes and explore the extent to which these processes are shared or distinct. In so doing I hope to address the phenomenon of controversial social issues in television fiction, extending discussion beyond the production or reception of a specific programme to illuminate the role of such programmes in contemporary culture (see Alasuutari 1999: 15–17).

Those rare but valuable studies which have considered the production of fictional television tend to investigate a single programme, for example studying the production factors of US prime-time series *Dynasty* (Gripsrud 1995), day-time soap opera *Guiding Light* (Intintoli 1984) or Australian drama *A Country Practice* (Tulloch and Moran 1986). Research has focused on the style of US television producers (Cantor 1971), power relations in the US industry (Gitlin 2000) and the symbiotic relationship between powerful medical organisations and US medical drama (Turow 1989). Kathryn Montgomery has contributed to an understanding of the 'rules of the game' which govern relations between advocacy groups and US prime-time television (Montgomery 1989). John Thornton Caldwell integrates theory and practice in his fascinating account of how the threat of cable led to new and exciting modes of production in the US industry (Caldwell 1995). In a British context, David Buckingham has addressed how audiences were broadly envisaged by *EastEnders* creators and senior BBC broadcasting management (Buckingham 1987), and, although most closely associated with studying soap opera audiences, Dorothy Hobson did also interview production team members working on *Crossroads*, in relation to programme direction and audience (Hobson 1982). More recently she has explored industry perspectives on the economic importance of the genre (Hobson 2003). But in the British context particularly, we know less than might be expected about how TV fiction is produced.

This book is based partly on my own empirical research with television industry professionals working in different television formats and occupying different points in the institutional hierarchy.[4] This material is organised in relation to three 'social issues' in particular which were chosen to reflect different dilemmas for production team members, namely sexual violence, breast cancer and mental distress. I have been involved in a number of research studies over the past few years and these too have inevitably helped shape and contextualise my analysis. In brief, these include: taking part in 'behind the scenes' discussions between the medical profession and the BBC drama *Casualty* in a study of hospital drama and its impact on health-seeking behaviour (Philo and Henderson 1999a, 1999b); a study of breast cancer and public understandings (Henderson and Kitzinger 1999; Henderson 2000); charting the rise in PR strategies around health issues (Hastings et al. 1999); exploring how science stories are 'made' (Henderson and Kitzinger 2007); and examining the 'framing' of professional groups and health-related behaviour in popular television (Henderson and Franklin 2007; Henderson et al. 2000).

This book allows me the opportunity to draw together diverse strands of work in different areas and across several television formats in the hope that this breadth of approach will shed light on the 'circuit of communication' that surrounds television fiction. In addition to discussions of the production process (and the role of sources) I also consider broad story themes alongside their possible impact on public knowledge. Adopting a holistic research model of the 'circuit of mass communication' is not that common in media and cultural studies, but it is a useful analytical frame because it accepts the process of communication as 'a complex interaction of unequal relationships of power' (Fenton et al. 1998; Fenton 2000; Hall 1980).

In the following sections of this chapter I outline some of the reasons why studying television serial drama and in particular the format of television soap opera provides us with a useful index of the changing direction of society.

Social Issues and the Importance of TV Fiction

The ways in which social issues are framed in television fiction are arguably worthy of serious study. In particular here I wish to highlight the potential of studying television soap opera. Storylines in television soap opera reach large audiences and are discussed across different media formats (from television news and press to magazines and internet sites). The genre has infiltrated other media formats (for example, the prime-time drama series, the social documentary) ensuring that its role within the current broadcasting climate has never been so heavily debated. The soap opera plays a central role within current debates about the blurring of 'hard' and 'soft' news. As the news media currently faces criticism over 'dumbing down' in terms of content and presentation, the soap opera has emerged as a format within which controversial or socially sensitive issues are played out. In some ways we might argue that this format has replaced the 'quality' play, a space where in the past British audiences were confronted with 'boundary-pushing' fiction. Television soap opera has always played a part in social education, as has been observed elsewhere (notably developing countries, where the soap opera has been used explicitly for social education purposes), and the British soap opera has from time to time been developed in order to modify public behaviour (particularly in relation to health issues). Finally, I would argue that while the format has long been associated with controversy, over recent years this became more publicly visible with a swathe of previously 'safe' programmes altering their ethos to take on increasingly controversial topics. This direction has generated explicit criticism from different organisations (from activists in the field to 'official' organisations such as the British Medical Association). At the same time, however, the format has never been so keenly lobbied by campaigners to aid in public awareness campaigns and to reinforce government policy (Franklin 1999). In the following sections I develop these points in more detail.

Everyone's Talking About It: The Reach of Soap Opera
In a digital age, soap operas may not deliver the much-envied audiences of the 1980s. Famously, over 30 million people watched the Christmas Day episode of *EastEnders* in 1986 – more than watched the wedding ceremony of Princess Diana and Prince Charles (BARB 2006). But nonetheless soaps do still consistently attract the largest audiences for any fictional or factual programming across most broadcast channels.[5] As one critic describes it, 'The days of 25 million viewers for anything is long gone. That mass viewing experience has passed. But even in the fragmented, depleted market, soaps remain *the most-viewed things*' (emphasis added) (McLean 2006). These programmes are traditionally trivialised by academics and media commentators, but they have captured larger audiences in more countries over a longer time span than any other form of television fiction (Allen 1995: 3).

Indeed these extraordinarily high audiences mean that soap opera remains firmly at the forefront of a channel's economic success in contemporary broadcasting. We can therefore mark changes in a national broadcasting culture by tracking the domination of soaps in television schedules. In a British context, we have witnessed a significant expansion, in which the five main television channels, which had been producing eleven and a half hours of soap opera per week, increased output to fifteen hours per week in the 2001 autumn schedules (Brown 2001b). This growth has been ascribed to intensified competition for large audiences at a low cost and, the domination of the soaps has been viewed very negatively as marking a departure from programming diversity to bland and homogeneous broadcasting (Brown 2001b). There has also been an increase in the frequency of transmission, from two episodes per week to three or more plus accompanying weekend omnibus editions. BBC1 soap opera *EastEnders* now transmits four episodes per week, *Emmerdale* is screened every week day on ITV. New soaps have tried and failed; for example, *Footballers' Wives* (ITV, 2002–6) attempted to move away from the traditional formula offered by British soaps and emulate the glossy US soap world of excess and celebrity with 'exploding boobs, a hermaphrodite baby, catfights, affairs and fake tan aplenty' (Byrne 2006). The proliferation of 'cheap television' has generated considerable debate amongst critics (Moreton 2001). Indeed a report by the Independent Television Commission criticised ITV in particular for showing too much soap opera at peak time and stretching the boundaries of what could be considered to be current affairs television (Hodgson 2003).

Simple counts of viewing figures and programme episodes underestimate the global popularity and potential reach of the genre. Numerous publications (US: *Soap Opera Digest and Soap Opera Weekly*; UK: *Inside Soap* and *Soaplife*) and specialist magazines devoted to specific programmes can be added to many internet sites which ensure continual cross-genre obsession with gossip around characters and future storyline 'spoilers' (an online Google search on 'soap opera' will typically generate about 5 million 'hits'). Fans share their favourite scenes from current and past programmes (see www.youtube.com). They also exchange highly critical and often sophisticated analyses of character and plot online (Baym 2000). Indeed a brief glance at any web forum will demonstrate that messages are being typed through the duration of the programme – an indication of the global community facilitated by new technologies and arguably offering fresh challenges to research on audience-text relations (see Livingstone 2004). Online communities do not just provide academics with 'evidence' of audience activity, they also provide production teams with a vital instant connection to their audiences – the affective response to current storylines can be measured by the sheer number of posts devoted to a particular character.

A major event such as the death of a programme 'favourite' now traditionally draws comments from programme personnel discussing the impact of this upon viewers' lives. Indeed deaths in the radio serial *The Archers* (BBC Radio 4) are typically also discussed in detail on the *Today* programme.[6] Journalists attempt to disentangle just why fiction can have such an impact on 'real' people. Most of these rehearse the usual arguments about our increasingly fractured modern lives in which fictional characters appear more 'real' than neighbours or relatives (Hilpern 1998). The level of social 'talk' generated by storylines is noted not just by academics but by the industry. Indeed a recent marketing campaign for *EastEnders* depicted groups of office colleagues, builders and friends excitedly discussing the latest plot twist, and closed with the strap line '*EastEnders*: everyone's talking about it.'[7] Soap actors' celebrity means that their personal and fictional lives are endlessly covered in the daily press, magazines and other associated media. This is due in no small part to the slick PR of the BBC's press office. As a spokesperson from the *EastEnders* office describes it, 'If people ask me when was the last time an actor from *EastEnders* was in the news, my answer is usually the same: today' (Hilpern 1998). Indeed the rise in celebrity and magazine interview culture has meant that the personal lives of actors have become a rich source of programme publicity, but that they are also publicly available in ways that may detract from traditional audience engagement with TV serial drama. Contemporary audiences are believed to be more aware of the artifice of soap opera, with the result that programme makers are constantly challenged to ensure that viewers become 'lost' in their viewing in ways that they could once take for granted (McLean 2006). The soap opera format thus pervades our wider media and social culture, providing storylines with a reach far beyond their immediate audiences.

Perhaps unsurprisingly, diverse groups seek to replicate this unique power to communicate with large audiences. Episodes of *Neighbours* and *EastEnders* are reportedly studied by the Anglican clergy as tools to facilitate discussion of ethical issues, and many groups in society are keen to learn 'the key to their success' (Dignan 1998). Yet the relationship between the daily press and these formats is not always positive. John Yorke, head of drama serials at the BBC and a former executive producer of *EastEnders*, was compelled to respond to stinging criticism led by mid-market tabloid newspaper the *Daily Mail*. The programme was described as a 'morally void cess pit', a 'sick soap' in which 'the married family was vilified as a nest of violence and sinister secrets' and 'the educated middle-class and religious believers were dismissed as victims, idiots or crooks' (Yorke 2002).

Soap Infiltration

The soap opera as a continuous serial has become less easily defined as it has infiltrated other genres. Indeed some have questioned whether television soap opera is still a useful defining category of TV format. Creeber

(2004) refers to a swathe of programmes under the broad term 'soap dramas', including popular imports to the UK such as the US channel HBOs *Sex and the City* (1998–2004) and *Six Feet Under* (2001–6). These programmes, he argues, have moved TV drama from social realism to 'social surrealism', which in his view better represents the social and moral uncertainty of contemporary life. Indeed Creeber challenges the perception of a decline in 'quality' programming and argues that we should not lament the death of the single play but should instead 'celebrate the generic hybridity of television drama' (Creeber 2004: 15).

Medical and police drama series (commonly termed 'cops and docs') similarly dominate television viewing schedules and here too we can observe the characteristics and influence of the television soap opera. Although strictly defined as within the genre of drama series (produced as self-contained episodes to be watched, in theory, in any order), they do now share many of the characteristics of soap opera – interweaving multiple plots with a continuous core cast and concluding with 'cliff-hanging' plot twists (for classic definitions see Holland 1997: 113–17; Hobson 1982: 29–35). Such drama rescued falling ratings by transforming into soap opera. For example, the revamped version of *The Bill* (ITV) has seen 'stories spill over between episodes and the private lives of the characters eclipse their adventures in uniform' (Moreton 2001). Few would disagree that medical programme *ER* is at heart a soap opera. Viewers are gripped by the personal lives of the doctors and nurses as much as if not more than by the stories of the patients, who are fleeting guests in the programme and provide a vivid backdrop to the unfolding drama of the staff who tend them. The narrative conventions of the soap opera have breathed life into hybrid programmes (*Ally McBeal*, *Sex and the City*, *Desperate Housewives*) to the extent that, as Norwegian sociologist Jostein Gripsrud suggests, 'almost all US TV series are effectively soap operas, since storylines stretch across several episodes and there is a sense of a long story being slowly unfolded as seasons go by' (Gripsrud 2002: 301).

This proliferation of soap opera and what might be termed the 'soap-isation' of other television dramas has been matched by the relentless rise of the 'docu-soap', now broadened into the landscape of reality television. These programmes were structured to chart the minutiae of everyday life, with early examples including *Airport*, *Driving School*, *Model Behaviour* and *Hotel*.[8] Reality television has since proliferated in multiple directions, with game-show programmes such as *Survivor* (where cameras record a group of men and women stranded on a desert island, competing for a large cash prize), *Temptation Island* (where the fidelity of couples is tested) or *Joe Millionaire* (a dating show where women compete for the affections of an ostensibly wealthy bachelor) representing just a few of the diverse formats. Swapping lives (*Faking It*) or even wives (*Wife Swap*) and watching forgotten celebrities try to revive their career by enduring hardship (*I'm a Celebrity, Get Me Out of Here!*) provide audiences with new twists on the genre. The global phenomenon of game show *Big Brother* (continuous coverage of young adults living for several weeks in a purpose-built set, with their every move, not least in the bathroom, captured on camera) has been described as 'a soapie where the characters get to write the script as they go along' (Roscoe 2001: 480).[9] Indeed the links between soap and reality TV narratives are fairly explicit – both are constructed to build audiences for the channel and enhance the public visibility of the product by attracting controversy and associated media coverage (Turner 2005; Roscoe 2001).

These programmes have provoked hot debates about the appetite of programme makers and the public alike for cheaply produced, voyeuristic television at the expense, it is implied, of more challenging programming. In the British context the evoking of a 'golden age' of television drama has been contested as more of a nostalgic construction than a reality. Nevertheless, it is precisely the 'soap-like' qualities of reality television that form the basis of accusations of 'dumbing down' and that trigger repeated pessimistic reviews of the state of British television (Lawson 2002a). Implicit in these debates is an important concern – that the ability of British television to continue fulfilling a public service function is under threat. Indeed it has recently been argued that the impact of these programmes has been felt across the wide spectrum of mass media (Schlesinger 2006).

It seems clear that in part the extraordinary infiltration of the soap opera is linked to commercial imperatives. Advertising slots in soap opera intermissions remain among the most frequently sought by advertisers, a fact due not simply to the scale of audiences but to the unique demographics – soap opera attracts the notoriously elusive and advertising-friendly 18-35-year-old viewer. The former BBC director-general (2000–4) Greg Dyke has admitted that increased production of TV soap opera is a sign that the industry at large is experiencing the strain of advertising slowdown and is opting for cheaper soaps at the expense of prestige drama (Brown 2001a).[10] The point I am making here is that the role of the soap genre is thus firmly at the heart of debates which have accompanied alleged changes in fictional and factual television. These debates have cited the rapid rise in reality television shows, the decline in resource allocation to documentary programming, and the alleged 'feminisation' of news media to suggest that British broadcasting is in crisis and becoming audience-led to the detriment of challenging programming. The soap opera form is thus subject to extended and frequent critical debate.

Entertainment and the News: The Blurring of 'Hard' and 'Soft'

At the same time as other television genres are blurring with soaps, the terrain of the soap opera appears to have shifted. In fact the genre has been criticised for moving into the 'fact-based' domain of 'hard news' – taking on subjects more usually dealt with in the television news bulletin or documentary. Indeed some have argued that soap opera can be described as approaching the genres of *information* (Gripsrud 2002: 218). Journalists and media sociologists distinguish between 'hard news' and 'soft news' to describe the value and substance of media content: however, the meaning of the terms is often assumed rather than explicitly defined.[11] 'Soft' news has been described as light or human-interest, interpretation-based stories and is associated with both the feminisation and sexualisation of the media (see Holland 2004). John Tulloch observes that 'hard news' in professional media discourse is considered to be "important" as against "offbeat". In the eyes of academics and soap opera critics they have traditionally been contrasted as "serious" (and healthy) versus "impoverished" (and noxious)' (Tulloch 1990: 44). Hard news concerns traditional front-page and headline stories in which the important issues of the day, related to 'matters of state' or 'hard science' for example, are reported, using elite sources such as politicians or scientists. By contrast, soft news encompasses 'lower-status' lifestyle issues on social aspects of life. These 'soft' stories are believed to attract a predominantly female or youth audience, which is now being targeted by all sections of the media.

The breaking down of the traditional divisions between 'hard' and 'soft' news has been viewed as a process of 'dumbing down'. Bob Franklin observes how contemporary British news media has retreated from investigative journalism to what he describes as the 'preferred territory of "softer" or "lighter" stories' (Franklin 1997: 4). This move towards consumer-led news media means that the 'hard news' values which traditionally governed news-media editorial policy have all but been abandoned in favour of 'homogeneous snippets' which make few demands on audiences. News media have thus all but become part of the 'entertainment industry', and Franklin suggests that traditional news values have been undermined by new values – 'infotainment' is rampant. This has been mapped to far-reaching changes across the entire British news media (regulatory, technological and financial as well as changes to journalistic culture and pressures from increased competition to become more audience-led). This moving of news media from the 'public' to the 'private' realm is considered to have serious repercussions for the role of journalism, with some concern about the implications of a media in which the 'raw testimonies of experience' replace expertise (Murdock 1999: 14). Parallel ongoing debates concern the changing role of documentary programming (Corner 2002; Kilborn 1994). The drive within news media to target new audiences (younger people, women) and accusations that television as a whole is becoming advertiser- and focus-group-led have implications for the occupational practices of news production personnel, but not all agree that this is necessarily to the detriment of 'quality' (McNair 1998).[12]

These are significant debates which tend to be fairly marginalised in traditional analyses of the television serial. But it is important that we do not assume that the soap opera is a cultural product isolated and immune from these wide-ranging pressures. Fictional representations have become the focus of lay public, lobbying and regulatory organisations' attention in ways which prompt critical questions: why is this shift towards increasingly controversial material taking place? What might the role of the media organisation or personnel be in this process? What influence might source organisations exert over programme content? What might be the impact on audiences? These are questions which seem particularly salient at this time. Yet as I discussed earlier there is a scarcity of empirical data with which we can fully address these questions.

The Soap as Social Education

The use of the television soap opera as a tool for social change is a common feature of humanitarian work in many countries (for specific campaigns see Shapiro et al. 2003; Rogers et al. 1999; Tufte 2001). The production process which lies behind these programmes is firmly established within a health promotion model. In this respect the ethos and aims of such productions are unusually visible in comparison to most popular TV fiction. Perhaps the most widely known educational soap opera is *Soul City* (1992-), a soap opera shown at 8 p.m. on SABC, a popular South African broadcast channel. The programme was developed as part of a multimedia 'edutainment' strategy and designed explicitly to harness the potential of drama to communicate with audiences. The aim is to empower individuals and communities, and the production team work closely with an NGO to produce highly researched storylines. Field studies identify key social problems such as TB, smoking, HIV and AIDS; researchers work through scripts with writers, and episodes are tested on target audiences both before and after transmission (Carlin 2003). In the words of the head of research, 'the secret is to make sure that the drama remains recognisably real, while subtly redefining reality in such a way as to alter perceptions of what is normal and good' (Carlin 2003). Television fiction forms part of a wider approach to eliciting change in social attitudes and health behaviour (alongside radio drama, booklets, newspapers, PR, advertising, advocacy and education packages).

Educational *telenovelas* have also been successfully developed to a strict formula in other countries, such as Mexico. 'Entertainment–education' telenovelas, written and produced by Miguel Sabido according to a theory-based formula, were structured to bring about social change in relation to reproductive and other social issues such as family planning, drug abuse and AIDS prevention (Nariman 1993). But overt use of soap opera narrative as a tool for communicating explicitly educational or social messages is mainly confined to developing countries and closely connected at the point of production to government literacy and reproductive health programmes. From their inception such radio/television serials have had the aim of modifying behaviour, and this means that their production ethos is markedly different from equivalent UK or USA prime-time counterparts. Indeed similar attempts have failed in a UK context. A soap opera funded by the Department of Health, *Kismet Road*, was designed to target the health behaviour of the 'difficult to access' British south Asian population. Using *Soul City* as a model, the programme makers canvassed local residents to help construct storylines which would be salient to this population (coronary heart disease, diabetes); for example, a 'hapless' consultant is depicted warning Asian patients to 'stay off the fatty curries'. Despite these efforts to construct a 'relevant' programme, the makers failed to generate interest from television companies. The producer was clearly bemused: as he notes, 'we were following the strict Reithian principles of educate, entertain and inform. It is a realistic drama. We went for an unglamorous look – many scenes are set in an inner city GP surgery' (Coombes 2003: 110). But this suggests that such programmes require more than good intentions or simple formulae to work within this fiercely competitive industry.[13]

Social anthropologist Andrew Skuse (2002, 2005) discusses the production of Afghan radio soap opera *New Home, New Life*, modelled on *The Archers*. Skuse highlights rightly that for these social education programmes to fulfil their role they must be read by audiences in the way that programme makers intend. Thus pathways from poverty must be shown to be successful – offering positive models of new agricultural and animal husbandry practices. Similarly, a character that leaves his animals without winter fodder must be viewed as incompetent (Skuse 2005: 417). These interventions are frequently informed by the fields of health communication or public health and offer a linear model of communication which allows for no disruption in the transmission between programme and audience. There is often little recognition in these social education productions that audiences may not respond in the way that producers expect or would wish.

Despite offering a prototype of how radio serials might 'inform–educate' in the context of reaching rural and often illiterate populations, the BBC Radio 4 soap opera *The Archers* has itself shifted recently in tone and ethos. This programme was originally conceived over fifty years ago as a vehicle to re-educate farmers and the British public on post-war food issues. Indeed the serial has become subject to significant cultural comment because of the inclusion of the type of 'gritty', socially realistic storylines more commonly associated with its television counterparts. Stories of domestic violence and breast cancer represent a significant move away from its original agenda, and initial controversies prompted cultural commentators to ask 'Are there story lines that soaps shouldn't touch?' (Arnold 2000). A recent plot involving a paternity dispute between two brothers attracted 2.44 million listeners, and current issues include the dilemma of whether a gay character should father a child. As editor Vanessa Whitburn explained in a recent newspaper article, 'I think *The Archers* has got a reputation of touching the zeitgeist, of touching what's affecting people in the real world.' The programme aims to continue with hard-hitting issues such as drug abuse and homelessness rather than 'the adventures of the plough horses Blossom and Boxer' (Sharp 2006).

To continue this theme of the shifting terrain of the serial drama it is worth also briefly considering the longest-running and still hugely popular television serial *Coronation Street* (ITV, 1960–). The programme emerged at a crucial moment in British cultural history and was seen to capture 1950s working-class life in a unique way. In 1998, *Coronation Street* was credited with 'defining modern TV soap' when reality and fiction blurred in a storyline. Character Deirdre Rachid was sent to prison for credit card fraud and became the focus of campaigning led by The *Sun*, a 'red top' newspaper. In a populist gesture this extraordinary campaign received the support of newly elected British prime minister Tony Blair (Moreton 2001). The programme was considered to symbolise changes in television soap opera culture at large when the first transsexual character in a British soap was introduced. This prompted comments that *Coronation Street* was finally giving up its traditional identity as a soap opera which 'steered clear of the more controversial subject matters of incest, child abuse, and lesbian love affairs which have been *Brookside*'s meat and drink' (Ahmed 1998). Despite acknowledging that audience loyalty is built on the continuity and familiarity of such serials, producers of these programmes are now expected to stay abreast of changing socio-cultural mores. As *Coronation Street* producer Steve Frost, commented in an interview:

> Coronation Street has been there for 45 years and there's a real danger in that . . . People need to see something that is recognisably Corrie but also something they've never seen before – I feel at the moment, its moving out of the 1990s five years too late. What is entirely new? What is the 21st century character? What does 21st century Corrie look like? I don't think we've seen it yet. That's my big challenge. (McLean 2006)

Increase in Controversy

In delivering 'something [audiences have] never seen before' Frost openly acknowledges a serious point. Taking over an industrial product such as the soap opera is akin to managing a brand – *Soul City* is reputedly as recognisable a brand name in South Africa as Coca-Cola (Carlin 2003). Astute branding and marketing bring established audiences but also expectations. As the acceptability of hitherto taboo topics shifts so too must the television serials – working ahead, taking their audiences with them but maintaining an ethos that is distinct and does not compromise the loyalty of long-term viewers. In a British context we can look to the example of the controversy which greeted schoolgirl Michelle Fowler's 'teen pregnancy' in *EastEnders* (1985), and at how a story such as this has become eclipsed by fictional treatments of heavily stigmatised social problems (alcoholism and schizophrenia), potentially fatal disease (AIDS and various cancers), and physical and sexualised violence (violence towards women, incest and date or acquaintance rape). Indeed when *EastEnders* revisited the same topic of teen pregnancy fifteen years later, Sonia Jackson received nothing like the social opprobrium awarded Michelle (Smith 2000). The ways in which long-established characters such as Sonia have developed over time also illustrates how we might look to the television serial as a barometer of shifting cultural values. Currently, Sonia has left her marriage to embark upon a lesbian affair (*EastEnders*, 2006). If teenage pregnancy symbolised controversy and outrage for audiences in 1985, then in the year 2000 what some might have considered a 'final' soap taboo was breached when the 'teenage' soap *Hollyoaks* (Channel 4, 1995–) became the first to tackle male rape. The act occurred in a special late-evening transmission, but subsequent storylines developed the impact of this experience on Luke and his close relationships, particularly those with his girlfriend and his father. This development was cited as explicit evidence that 'popular drama's need to address spurious "big issues" is getting out of control' (Peretti 2000).

At the same time as the daily press and other media have enjoyed a vicarious pleasure in condemning the unpalatable material offered up for audiences, the genre has continued to be criticised on perhaps more serious grounds – for its inability to represent marginalised groups adequately. Among numerous controversies is the case of *EastEnders*, which was criticised by both the Irish ambassador to the United Kingdom and the Commission for Racial Equality for cultural and racial stereotyping – depicting Irish characters as 'drunken, dirty and feckless' (Harnden 1997). Recent debates concern an apparent lack of commitment to disability – there have been very few (permanently) disabled characters in a television soap opera and they rarely become part of the established community (Atkinson 2006). These criticisms hark back to that of earlier attempts in the 1980s to broaden the traditionally white, heterosexual landscape adequately and include ethnic minority, gay and lesbian characters (Geraghty 1995).[14] This attention to visibility and representation has sparked numerous content analyses of entertainment/serial programmes and brings me to a central point – the contested relationship between television fiction and 'the material world'. In associated media coverage we can identify a relationship that is undoubtedly synergistic. News reports frequently borrow from current storylines to add a 'hook' or 'peg' for a story. Particularly controversial issues attract press and television coverage and are clearly designed to do so. Production teams frequently generate storylines on the basis of specific events. Yet can we describe or predict when and how particular storylines move between material and fictional worlds? The ways in which stories reflect upon and reference events 'outside' the realm of television fiction, the arguably shifting boundaries between these two worlds, and the way these are negotiated seem a legitimate concern.

A Site of Struggle

Drama with a social message has developed a unique position in British broadcasting culture – we need only look to the play *Cathy Come Home*, which is firmly associated with the subject of homelessness in the UK. Such programmes demonstrate how fictional programmes may themselves become events with social and material consequences (Tulloch 1990: 124). However, the routine portrayal of 'hard' subject matter in prime-time 'entertainment' slots and the impact of this on audiences have sparked repeated discussions about the cultural role of the soap opera.[15]

Television soap operas are subject to intense lobbying by diverse groups keen to have their issues incorporated into storylines to increase public awareness and also of course to increase the visibility or branding of an organisation. The explosion in PR concerning health and illness issues in particular means that there is significant competition between charities to place information posters and leaflets in background shots. In this context the billboard standing amidst the parade of shops in Channel 4 soap opera *Brookside* became a coveted place for posters which reflected ongoing campaigns. The placing of such posters, leaflets or mugs within fictional settings is not just beneficial to the charity which receives wider exposure, but arguably adds authenticity and realism to the hospital scene or the local GP surgery. In other words I would argue that these details function as crucial visual referents, just as Geraghty has noted the care taken over domestic details in characters' homes such as dishes in the sink or photographs on a mantelpiece (Geraghty 1991: 38). Health charities, lobbying groups and the government now consider television fiction as a useful conduit for policy messages. Storylines designed to support the National Year of Reading Initiative were featured in *Brookside*, *Coronation Street*, *Hollyoaks* and *Grange Hill* (Franklin 1999: 17). The first National Childbirth Trust baby-friendly award was given to *Brookside* for portraying breastfeeding positively, very unusually for British television showing a baby suckling at his mother's breast (Henderson et al. 2000).

However, there is an ambiguous relationship between seeking the public profile which a drama storyline can confer and simultaneously policing these storylines. Indeed production teams are frequently criticised for the negative impact of their storylines on the public. A story involving the termination of a pregnancy when antenatal screening identified that the fetus had spina bifida drew hundreds of telephone calls of protest to the *EastEnders* office and sparked numerous personal testimonies in sympathy with the dilemma (Davies 1997). A terminally ill character depicted as begging her family to end her suffering because a GP failed to provide sufficient pain relief featured in *Brookside*. The British Medical Association and the director-general of the Cancer Research Campaign were swift to criticise the portrayal of cancer carers (forced to buy drugs on the street and perform euthanasia) as 'not only unreal, but irresponsible' (Laurance 1997).

Resisting the efforts of medical organisations, charities, lobby organisations and indeed the government to promote policy initiatives seems to have become an established part of the role of soap opera producer. Former executive producer of *Coronation Street* David Liddiment recalls government pressure to insert a storyline which presented a positive role model for teachers to complement an ongoing campaign. Liddiment resisted this move and comments that 'Television, and ITV in particular, has a sterling record of social action campaigns on- and off-air. But soap, corporate agendas and politicians make a heady mix best avoided' (Liddiment 2005: 1).

Familiar Discourses?

The discourses which surround the genre of television soap opera are surprisingly familiar. Indeed in her vivid account of lobbying groups and American prime-time television, Kathryn Montgomery (1989) identifies the main approaches of these diverse groups to the field of entertainment television. It is useful just to highlight these here:

> To **minorities, women, gays, seniors,** and the **disabled,** television is a cultural mirror which has failed to reflect their image accurately. To be absent from prime time, to be marginally included in it, or to be treated badly by it are seen as serious threats to their rights as citizens . . . To **conservative religious groups,** television is a threat to traditional values, too often a dangerous intruder in the home . . . **Social issue groups** believe television is an electronic class-room, in which lessons are taught by the heroes of prime time . . . **Anti-violence groups** see television 'murder and mayhem' as a toxic substance. They fear that continued exposure to this poison will produce a more violent society. (emphasis in original) (Montgomery 1989: 8–9)

These approaches and their resulting discourses can be easily identified in the contours of the debates discussed above. Television soap opera is perceived by diverse groups in society as a 'mirror' which unproblematically reflects and shapes audience understandings and confers or withholds cultural legitimacy from particular groups. For conservative religious groups, the world of television soap opera with its depiction of marital affairs, teenage sex and lesbian and gay relationships represents society in crisis, in moral decline. For groups who wish to promote particular social issues, the power of the television soap opera to influence positively is unlimited. For those who campaign against violence, television fiction is responsible for generations of children, desensitised to casual interpersonal violence and easily influenced and corrupted by the routine violence which has become a feature of early-evening drama.

Organisation of the Book

This book aims to address the concerns that have been highlighted above and to build on other work in the area of TV fiction and of 'public issue' television. My main concern here is to investigate how social meanings about the world circulate within and around the format of the television soap opera. I address how what we might term public issue storylines are produced with a view to articulating the values and priorities of the media personnel working in this area. As I have already discussed, the relationship between television fiction and 'the material world' is subject to considerable debate. Arguably the boundaries between facts and fiction are constantly negotiated and drawn/redrawn (Michael and Carter 2001). Let me make it clear that I do not assume that television soap opera, regardless of its commitment to social realism, can offer a 'mirror' of society. Others have highlighted that it is not social or literal realism that these programmes offer viewers but rather 'emotional realism' and high levels of personal involvement (Ang 1985; Livingstone 1988). Yet television fiction tells us about our social world and, despite the often exaggerated situations and condensed time scales of the television soap opera, this format offers a useful lens through which wider power struggles can be viewed.

The book is divided into five parts. Part I, 'Mapping the Field', has traced some of the debates concerning television fiction and its entertainment and educational role. The format of television soap opera has become the focus of significant debate by both academic and lay commentators, yet, as I have identified, there is a scarcity of research into how specific storylines are produced. Part II, 'Inside the Industry', addresses the perspective of industry professionals and draws on interviews with different members of production teams where they reflect 'in theory' upon their decision making. Here different programmes are situated in their institutional context and television industry producers, script writers and others discuss their self-image, professional ethos and creative philosophies. Part III, 'Struggles over Television Production', briefly introduces the main cases of sexual violence, health and illness, and mental distress before discussing how production team members make decisions 'in practice' and under specific circumstances (Chapters 3, 4 and 5). These chapters address how storylines were originally generated and how these were brought to the television screen, thus highlighting commonalities and differences across programmes and substantive story topics. As a point of further comparison, I address the production values of television personnel working in areas of television other than soap opera (documentary, drama series) and explore decision making concerning mental distress (Chapter 6).

In Part IV, 'Social Issues and Television Audiences', I explore how audiences interpret and respond to 'issue' storylines. This allows us to reflect on possible links between the intentions of programme makers and audiences specifically in relation to a study of sexual violence. Finally, Part V, 'Television Fiction and Public Knowledge', revisits some of the key arguments in the book and concludes by addressing contemporary debates concerning television and cultural citizenship.

Notes

1 I invited a group of international postgraduate students on the MSc in media and communications programme at Brunel University to watch and discuss this episode in October 2006. None of the (mainly North European) students were aware of the specific situation in Darfur, but they considered that the programme merely served up familiar images of Africa (depicting poverty and disease, passive 'victims', corruption). There was no identifiable support for American intervention to 'help resolve' the situation. Indeed American intervention under any circumstance appeared to be viewed negatively (students discussed this in relation to the ongoing American presence in Iraq). This suggests that the programme makers cannot assume that the message was explicit to or indeed accepted by all audiences.

2 For discussion see Quinn (2006).

3 There are useful ethnographic studies of the BBC (Born 2004; Schlesinger 1987).

4 The core data set comprises tape-recorded interviews which I conducted with sixty-four television production personnel (commissioning editors, heads of drama, producers, story consultants, script editors and script writers). These professionals were involved in production decisions concerning different programmes (television soap opera, medical drama, single plays and documentary series). I also interviewed programme personnel from children's television and different medical drama programmes. Interviews were conducted with source organisations which collaborated on or lobbied against different storylines (mainly in relation to mental distress, breast cancer and sexual violence, but also concerning race, ethnicity and other issues). Additional data were collected from those who compiled industry reports and supervised telephone help lines. Most of these interviews were conducted in person and they were sometimes followed up by a tape-recorded telephone interview. These were fully transcribed and then responses were cross-tabulated.

5 The exception to this is Channel 4, which relies on reality television formats such as *Big Brother* to deliver similar audiences.

6 This programme is considered to set the British political news agenda for the day and to reach an 'elite' audience (politicians, opinion formers).

7 The same tag line was most recently appropriated by reality programme *Big Brother* for its website (Channel 4, 2006) (www.channel4.com/bigbrother).

8 The origins of the genre date back to earlier documentary series (see Kilborn 2003).

9 Programmes such as *Pop Idol* and *Popstars* (LWT) have merged elements of reality television and soap opera in charting the search for a new pop star, with the public voting by telephone each week. In *Soapstars*, Yorkshire Television made a deal with the actors' union Equity to film the search for a new family in the soap opera *Emmerdale* (Brown 2001b). As these formats become 'tired' new

twists are offered, as in the recent series of *Survivor* in which teams were organised to compete along racial lines, or by the inclusion of celebrity contestants.

10 Dyke in his post-BBC career agreed to head a six-part Channel 4 show *Get Me the Producer* (based on *The Apprentice*), in which twelve contestants compete for a contract with a television production company. The programme recruited on the website www.beonscreen.com/uk, alongside adverts for participants in other shows which pose questions such as 'Are you a compulsive masturbator?', 'Are you killing your kids with kindness?' and 'Are you unemployed and ready to dump the dole?' These give a sense of the spectrum of shows within the reality television format.

11 The nature of the event being reported, positioning of the story, the sources and the status of the journalist covering it are all factors in 'hard' or 'soft' stories. Philip Schlesinger observed in his BBC study that hard news gathering was considered to be 'a man's job'. He describes soft stories assigned to female journalists as 'abortions, lost babies, the Royal Family, fashions, the Cruft's dog show' (Schlesinger 1987: 155). Allan references soft stories as 'relationships, fashion, beauty and childcare' (Allan 1998: 132–4). Tulloch describes soap opera as 'soft news' and argues that soap operas are defined by their relationship to other television genres including news, documentaries and even advertisements (Tulloch 1990).

12 McNair refutes the idea that 'tabloidisation' is necessarily negative. In his view, 'quality' relates to 'a particular set of news values, a particular style and presentation of the world which focuses on the worthy issues of politics, economic and foreign affairs, while paying less attention to the unworthy concerns of human interest and trivia' (McNair 1998: 121). For some members of the audience, he argues, 'the genres of "true crime", real-life rescue and celebrity lifestyle coverage are as much broadcast journalism as is needed' (McNair 1998: 121). The 'true crime' genre is one which is certainly not unproblematic (Schlesinger et al. 1992), but others have argued that inter-genre formats such as audience discussion programmes (for example *Donahue*) break down traditional distinctions between public and private and challenge authority and expert knowledge, thus making important contributions to an 'emancipatory public sphere' (Livingstone and Lunt 1994).

13 The culturally specific contexts of production and reception contribute to the success or failure of such 'educationally driven' initiatives. Martín-Barbero (1995) relates the phenomenal success of the telenovela in Latin American countries to its unique ability to connect with oral culture. This exploits 'the universe of legends, scary stories, and tales of mystery, which have travelled from the countryside to the cities' (Martín-Barbero 1995: 276). In a useful extension of the cultural imperialism thesis explored by Ien Ang (1985), telenovelas are considered to have made a significant impact on US day-time soap opera, a process described as 'telenovela-ization' (Bielby and Harrington 2005). Telenovelas have also been identified as a valuable source of 'information' on how the world of politics works (Porto 2005: 343).

14 Recent figures suggest that *EastEnders* attracts 250,000 black viewers, which is higher than for any other British-produced programme (Armstrong 2006). This does not of course mean that the programme has necessarily become more successful in depicting the lived experience of black viewers.

15 The television play *Cathy Come Home* (1966), produced by Tony Garnett and directed by Ken Loach, is a classic example of the impact of socially realistic drama on social policy and public attitudes. Steve Platt provides a useful critique of how the programme raised awareness and public intolerance of homelessness and led to the formation of housing charity Shelter within two weeks of its first transmission (Platt 1999). There have also been recurrent debates concerning fictional storylines and controversial issues, from special reports in *Woman's Hour* (Radio 4, May 1997) to numerous newspaper features and magazine day-time programmes.

Part II Inside the Industry

Making 'Good' Television: Creative Philosophies, Professionalism and Production Values

Introduction

The ways in which diverse social issues are represented in prime-time television are frequently the focus of attention for a range of groups. As I pointed out in Chapter 1, activists, policy makers, lay audiences and media commentators have criticised and debated how contemporary issues are presented to audiences, with concerns frequently coalescing around the television soap opera. The underlying assumption seems clear – these images matter. There is, however, often a tendency to discuss television 'soaps' and serial drama as a homogeneous entity. Yet this assumption is both wrong and unhelpful. Furthermore, in assuming homogeneity the opportunities for creating different sorts of representations and influencing representation at the point of production may be lost. The aim of this chapter is to demonstrate the importance of differentiating between programmes in terms of production philosophies – these underpin how members of the team approach their role. Accordingly, audiences too bring different expectations to their viewing experience. In short, just as the substantive topic of storylines should be positioned within a wider socio-cultural landscape, I argue here that so too should the programmes in which these storylines appear.

This chapter seeks to place a number of different programmes in their institutional and commercial context. We see how the distinct production philosophy and ethos may influence the development of social issue storylines, both opening up and closing down possibilities for representation. We also begin to see the complex nature of the production process; for example, how the team process operates, how different production personnel perceive their role, the ways in which the storyline is above all, an industrial product. This chapter acts to set the scene for the case studies which follow (Chapters 3, 4 and 5). It aims to identify how the production process functions 'in theory' and contextualises the later discussion of how specific storylines were produced and developed 'in practice'.

The Same but Different: Programme Diversity

As noted above, before looking at the production context of specific issue storylines, in the areas of breast cancer, sexual violence and mental distress, it is useful first to give an overview of the diversity of programmes within this genre. Soap opera production team members may all work within the same format and adopt the same narrative conventions, but there are central differences in terms of production ethos and philosophy which are strongly tied to programme identity. In the British context, both *EastEnders* (BBC1) and *Brookside* (Channel 4) have been popularly assumed to pursue the same aims – social messages intertwined with entertainment. In contrast, *Coronation Street* (ITV1) has traditionally eschewed social controversy in favour of a blend of 'comedy and drama'. Certainly, *Brookside* and *EastEnders* have been assumed to share a 'public issue' agenda explicitly, and both productions have remained at the forefront of 'issue' drama, dealing fairly consistently with controversial material. These programmes have competed to push British soap opera in the direction of social issue drama, dealing with issues overtly and moving social problems from the personal plight to the public sphere. In so doing, the programmes have sought new audiences of young people and male viewers, thus challenging the traditional image of the soap opera audience made up of female housewives.[1]

Family Entertainment

The ITV soap opera *Coronation Street* was first transmitted on December 1960 to the Granada region and networked in 1961. The programme increased output from two to three episodes a week in 1989 and is currently screening four episodes per week. In the early 2000s viewing figures were 15.29 million (BARB, week ending 2 December 2001). The programme typically occupies the top five places in audience ratings for the channel and currently attracts audiences of 12.15 million for a single episode (BARB, week ending 26 March 2006). An indication of the central importance of the soap genre to ITV can be seen in the fact that nine of the ten top-rated programmes for a single week are in fact soap opera episodes (BARB, week ending 26 March 2006).

Coronation Street has been positioned as a 'critics' soap'. Indeed the programme was awarded best drama by *The South Bank Show* in January 2005 and its high-quality writing was praised by arts broadcaster Melvyn Bragg (Teeman 2005). The television serial is regarded as embodying the values of a 1950s working-class culture and was seen to reflect on aspects of the influential *Uses of Literacy* (Hoggart 1959), not least in its focus on 'strong' women and the powerful theme of nostalgia. These themes, it was argued, defined the fictional world of *Coronation Street* (Dyer et al. 1981: 4). Although it has become somewhat of an orthodoxy to perceive the British soaps as offering a distinctively 'working-class' outlook, in fact, as O'Donnell (1999) argues, it is not the 'working class' proper that is represented here but the 'petit bourgeoisie' (with many characters owning small businesses). Regardless of how representative this working-class life is, *Coronation Street* has, along with *EastEnders* and *Brookside*, successfully conveyed a sense of commitment to a working-class world. Audiences are presented with an unglamorous lifestyle, 'grubby housing', 'run-of-the-mill' clothes and regional accent – a traditional marker of the British 'working class' (see O'Donnell 1999: 208). Certainly, as Geraghty (1991) points out, the northern soap opera was developed at a time when 'working-class culture' was emerging as the focus of a 'new wave' in British film (see *Room at the Top, A Kind of Loving* and *Look Back in Anger*) as well as theatre and novels. There are a number of extended analyses of social realism in British film (see Hill 1986) and I wish here simply to point out that the programme represented part of a wider shift in the representation of social class within British culture, although I would agree that this is an imagined, mythic, working-class world – as seen from the perspective of the middle-class writer.[2]

The programme is not just of considerable importance nationally but was one of the world's first prime-time TV soap operas. *Coronation Street* has influenced international soap opera, finding an export audience in Australia and New Zealand from 1964 and offering other programmes a template of community. As Dunleavy points out:

> As a conceptual blending of British 'Northern realism', an equally distinctive 'Northern humor', and soap's characteristic melodrama, the fictional Weatherfield and its colourful characters were open to universal readings and appeal. The combination of characteristics that Coronation Street's community pioneered for the genre – the 'ordinariness' of Weatherfield people, their almost claustrophobic close-knittedness, their unwritten code of shared values, and their ears terminally cocked for neighbourhood gossip – lent itself to considerable imitation and adaptation in soap operas subsequently developed. (Dunleavy 2005: 372)

The programme agenda of *Coronation Street* has been typically perceived as in marked contrast with other programmes and their social message agendas. Rather than purposely inserting 'issue' storylines, *Coronation Street* producers have routinely insisted that future story development is generated simply by the *realistic* concerns of characters. This is a discourse which permeates every discussion with production team members. For example, the producer told me that the programme had not excluded gay or lesbian characters but simply 'we have not yet had a character who *could* be gay'. Indeed it was not until 5 October 2003 that the programme included the first gay kiss – *EastEnders* did so in 1989 (Press Association 2003). The argument above is somewhat circular, however, since the sexual identity of characters and indeed which 'issues' the fictional characters will find 'important' or 'concerning' depend entirely on how their character has been constructed (that is, by those in 'control', the production team). This circularity notwithstanding, the programme producer explains that programme development must continue to be generated organically, through the 'natural' development of characters, and that the production should resist lobbying from pressure groups:

> The interesting thing about 'The Street' is that people feel comfortable with it and people can watch it as a family. All our stories are generated by the characters in the programme. We are not issue led. We don't sit around and say 'Let's have a story about rape.' Many people write to us and say 'Would you debate this issue? And would you please let everyone know it is national breastfeeding week?' and I have to write back and say 'No' to everybody because we just then become a political machine. It would become propaganda that we were churning out and we are supposed to be entertaining people, not brainwashing them.

In this sense *Coronation Street* promotes a self-image of using the power of the soap opera medium to offer 'message-free' enjoyment in direct contrast to other popular programmes:

> *EastEnders* and *Brookside* have chosen to use that power to give a message to the British public. What we have done is chosen to use that power to entertain the British public. In other words give them good television. We aren't thrusting issues down their throat because they get enough of that with news and documentaries. We just want people to relax and enjoy themselves.

Programming for Change

The soap opera *Brookside* was first transmitted on 2 November 1982, the first day of Channel 4. Jeremy Isaacs, chief executive of Channel 4, reportedly saw how ITV used *Coronation Street* to build budgets and audiences for 'quality' drama such as *Brideshead Revisited* and considered that soap opera could function as 'viewer glue' (Lawson 2002a). Isaacs recalls meeting *Brookside* creator Phil Redmond at a meeting of potential independent producers in London. As he recounts:

> I'd never met him before but he struck up a conversation with me by asking me if I objected to strong language on television. I said that I didn't and he said he thought he might have something for me. At that stage, I don't think I was looking for a soap opera but I was certainly looking for strong drama which would hold an audience. (Tibballs 1998: 9)

For much of its twenty-one-year life span, the continuous drama was screened thrice weekly and repeated in a weekend omnibus edition. The programme was 'axed' in 2003 and final storylines were played out in a weekend transmission slot (a time when serials generate extra viewers via repeats of the weekday shows). Viewing figures fluctuated at around 5 million and a single episode typically attracted just 4.01 million viewers (BARB, week ending 2 December 2001). However, in the final months of transmission, audiences fell perilously low, to around just 1 million. Yet the success of *Brookside* could never be measured simply in terms of statistics – the programme certainly could not directly compete for the large audiences of BBC or ITV. It was nonetheless important economically to Channel 4 and consistently attracted the highest ratings of any programme screened by the channel. An indication of shifts in current broadcasting are represented by the fact that this position is now occupied by reality show formats (*Jamie's Kitchen*, *Location Location*, and *Big Brother*, which attracts up to 6.1 million viewers; BARB, week ending 18 June 2006). Importantly *Brookside* also attracted young audiences, the 'gold dust' for advertisers, with 50 per cent of viewers aged under 35 years.

Over time *Brookside* dealt consistently with topical and controversial social issues, addressing homosexuality, HIV and AIDS, drug misuse and both 'stranger' and 'acquaintance' rape. The programme may have had fewer viewers than other soap operas but, as numerous journalists lamented on its demise, it was *Brookside* that frequently attracted the media coverage and controversy. The programme commonly tackled issues before other soap operas and was responsible for groundbreaking representations such as the first lesbian kiss. *Brookside* also developed new formats now commonly observed in other soaps (the 'spinoff' show, the long story arc). The programme thus had an influence which extended far beyond its relatively meagre viewing figures. Actors who left continued to work in more 'serious' television and film, and writers such as Jimmy McGovern developed their own series (including his psychological thriller series *Cracker*, which has proved popular with US audiences) while still maintaining a *Brookside* sensibility and commitment to 'gritty' human drama. The programme creator, Phil Redmond, oversaw both *Brookside* and BBC1 drama *Grange Hill*, which ran simultaneously for twenty years. Redmond has proved a powerful figure in British broadcasting, consulting on other programmes and launching the now firmly established early-evening soap opera *Hollyoaks*.

Mal Young became the programme producer in the early 1990s before moving to the BBC as controller of continuing drama series, where he oversaw *EastEnders* and created the daily medical soap *Doctors* and *Holby City*, a spinoff from the medical drama *Casualty*. At the end of 2004 he joined Simon Fuller (creator of *American Idol*) as head of drama at *19TV*, an independent company, with reported plans to develop new drama formats for the UK and US markets. In other words, despite transmitting on a niche channel to relatively small audiences, the team at *Brookside* have had considerable influence in British broadcasting as a whole. Indeed the production team members were always conscious of their ability to influence other programmes and considered themselves responsible for shifting the boundaries for British soap operas, which were once 'cosy affairs'. In the book which accompanied the programme, *Total Brookside* (Tibballs 1998), the production is conceptualised as a powerful force for change:

> Then along came *Brookside*. Never afraid of controversy, *Brookside* led the way in tackling such topics as drug abuse, unemployment, rape and lesbianism, and, more recently, domestic violence, incest and euthanasia. As the goal posts were moved, other soaps were forced to become grittier. Without *Brookside*, *EastEnders'* Kathy Beale would never have been raped, Deirdre Rachid from *Coronation Street* would never have ended up in prison and Emmerdale's Zoe Tate [a lesbian character in the programme] would have been chasing every man in the village. (Tibballs 1998: 189)

Redmond proposed that by taking up social and political topics, the soap opera format might balance what he describes as 'the dramatic requirements of modern, small-screen entertainment with a real sense of depth, concern and insight' (Kilborn 1992: 170). His personal agenda very much determined the programme remit; as he described it, 'I have always argued for socially strong drama and it has always proved to be popular' (Redmond 1985: 41). As we shall see in the chapters that follow, in comparison with other production teams that I interviewed, the *Brookside* team members were unusually open about the way in which potential storylines were selected. An explicitly 'issue-led' agenda meant that while writers could propose ideas in meetings it was also routine for storyline developments to come directly from 'the top'. The long-term strategy for the show was mapped out in biannual meetings between executive producer and producer. Statistical trends of unemployment, crime and social problems were used to compose 'demographically correct' plots with textbook characters. This production philosophy changed little over the years from Phil Redmond's original vision, in which representative characters were quite deliberately included in the programme. Indeed Redmond constructed the programme originally around key families which were drawn to represent 'the four elements of society', as he explains:

> When we started out, we had the Collinses, the Grants, the Huntingtons and the Taylors as the four elements of society on the Close. The Collinses represented the management capitalist leg; the Grants represented the trade union movement; the Huntingtons were a young professional couple; and the Taylors represented the black economy. (Tibballs 1998: 8)

Mal Young, reflecting on his role as producer, believed that *Brookside* could offer a far more 'realistic' portrayal of social issues than other drama. As he told me, 'If someone has a breakdown in *Brookside* they never get over it because life's not like that.' However, this focus on social realism was always necessarily balanced with the perceived needs of audiences. Storylines therefore might arise from a well-researched base but for audience enjoyment they must then be 'packaged'. As Young explains:

> The trick is to take all [the research] and not do a documentary on it or people will go 'It's just facts and figures, it's a documentary.' The trick is to package it in a story which has become soap opera because you make it entertainment then. You make people guess and use all the tricks of soap opera, which is 'Will she do this? Will she do that?'

Despite an initially socially realistic approach to subject material, the values of entertainment and acceptability to audiences remain crucial, regardless of programme identity. Programme makers generally do not wish to be perceived by audiences as 'educating' them, particularly in the soap opera genre. This is seen to conflict with the role of that particular format. By 'packaging' stories for audience consumption, *Brookside* could position itself as provoking audience debate rather than providing audiences with clear social messages which could be mistaken for 'education'. As the producer argues:

> [Audiences] are not finding in *Brookside* any answers. That's how you educate, you give people answers. If I started to believe we are educating, God, you know? What have I become? I couldn't!

As noted earlier, *Brookside* has had from the outset a production philosophy which was explicitly 'programming for change' (Tibballs 1998). An indication of the way in which this programme was unashamedly ruthless concerning its 'issue-led' nature in strategy and philosophy is reflected in casting decisions. The programme producer and production team members openly acknowledged that characters were introduced regularly to maintain a constant source of new social problems for the show to address. The role of the programme is outlined neatly by Mal Young:

> *Brookside*'s there to provoke debate, we're there to rattle the cage on life's seedier side, on things that society would prefer to hide under the carpet. That's my brief and that's what I want to do as producer. Make strong drama at a time accessible to everyone.

The programme was described in populist terms as the 'soap for people with brains' and found perhaps unlikely fans in well-respected arts and culture critics such as Mark Lawson, who has written consistently about the legacy of the production for the British drama industry. In his view the demise of the programme was simply explained:

> What happened was greed. All television executives should read the story of the golden goose at least once a week. Channel 4 demanded more and more episodes (three from 1990 with occasional special runs of five a week) with ever darker and wilder arcs to pump the ratings. With BBC1 and ITV using *EastEnders* and *Coronation Street* in the same way, the recurring serials began to trade shocks in the hope of knock-out. Whereas early controversial storylines had seemed planned to educate the audience, titillation now seemed the aim of Beth Jordache's lesbian kiss and Nat and Georgia Simpson's incest. (Lawson 2002a)

Lawson also found it worth noting that the programme's demise was overseen by Mark Thompson, the first Channel 4 boss to have come from a channel (BBC2) which prospered without a soap opera (Lawson 2002a).

Reflecting 'Reality'

EastEnders was launched on BBC1 in February 1985 and is currently screened four times weekly with a repeat weekend omnibus edition. In the early 2000s viewing figures for a single episode were 16.74 million (BARB, week ending 2 December 2001). The programme typically occupies the top three highest-rated programmes for the channel and attracts audiences of around 10.50 million (BARB, week ending 26 March 2006).

EastEnders was designed both to build a crucial mid-evening audience and also to fill a gap in the BBC's drama output. Aiming for a less self-consciously didactic approach to social issues than *Brookside*, the programme nevertheless assembled the requisite characters through which contemporary inner-city life might be examined (see Buckingham 1987). As Julia Smith, who developed the programme along with Tony Holland, describes it:

> We decided to go for a realistic, fairly outspoken type of drama which could encompass stories about homosexuals, rape, unemployment, racial prejudice, etc. in a believable context. Above all we wanted realism. Unemployment, exams, racism, birth, death, dogs, babies, unmarried mums – we didn't want to fudge any issue except politics and swearing. (Buckingham 1987: 16)

The extent to which *EastEnders* was designed as a cynical attempt to recapture the BBC's audience share from ITV or simply to illustrate that public service broadcasting could also be popular without diminishing quality and responsibility is arguable (Buckingham 1987). The fascinating and lengthy debates which surrounded the creation of the programme touch on wider political issues facing the institution at the time (McNicholas 2004). However, it is worth noting that the personal vision of *EastEnders* creators Smith and Holland remains constant twenty years later. For example, it was striking that while production staff from other programmes regarded *EastEnders* and *Brookside* as equally 'issue-led', members of the *EastEnders* production team were keen to dissociate themselves from this perception. Indeed, perhaps surprisingly, the *EastEnders* self-image echoes that of *Coronation Street*, where it is character development rather than contemporary 'issues' that underpin storyline decision making. *EastEnders* production staff in interviews simply rejected accusations that issues could be 'just bolted on' to characters, because, in their view, 'it just won't work' for audiences. This position is exemplified in the words of a senior production member, who outlines his vision of the programme as one in which 'issues' simply emerge 'naturally':

> What we do is create a microcosm of society within Albert Square. Therefore it would, hopefully, naturally reflect the problems and troubles of people of twentieth-Century England. I know we don't deliberately set out to tackle issues.

This perception of 'issues' emerging 'naturally' closely echoes the earlier words of the producer of *Coronation Street* and is, as I have pointed out, in distinct contrast with the *Brookside* vision, where there were no similar attempts to conceal the ethos of the programme as 'issue-led'.

Taking the Production in a New Direction

The ITV soap opera *Emmerdale* was originally transmitted as *Emmerdale Farm* on 16 October 1972 and is currently screened on each weekday. In the early 2000s the viewing figures were 11.33 million (BARB, week ending 2 December 2001). More recently audiences have been typically 9.36 million (BARB, week ending 26 March 2006). The programme has now significantly narrowed the gap and closely follows *Coronation Street* in terms of audiences, but as I discuss later this has not always been the case.

The programme has traditionally been absent from academic study and cultural comment. This absence is perhaps partly explained by its original agenda. In its original form, *Emmerdale Farm* did not include 'issue' story-lines and focused entirely on gentle, meandering stories of rural farming life – there was little material here which would be likely to trigger public debate or the outrage of campaigners. The programme identity was one which did not attempt to incorporate serious contemporary problems. In the following chapter, I address the commercial pressures brought to bear on the programme and the consequences of this for the development of specific storylines. Here, it is simply worth noting that *Emmerdale* changed more than its programme title. The production was entirely rebranded by senior television executives who were concerned that the existing audience did not have sufficient appeal to advertisers. The programme thus sought new and younger audiences. The programme ethos within which story-lines had been developed over the previous twenty years or so was radically altered.

Arguably the story of change in *Emmerdale* provides one of the most interesting examples of how a soap opera may make 'issues' work in economic terms. This particular programme has now effectively increased audience ratings with a series of 'issue' storylines, but the producer who briefly guided the programme through the rocky period of change claimed (despite some evidence to the contrary) that her priority was realistic characterisation rather than a cynical strategy. She argued that increased ratings are an incidental, and indeed welcome, by-product of 'character-led' stories, but that it is entirely possible to retain professional integrity within the intensely competitive soap production world. As she comments:

> Stories [in *Emmerdale*] are character-led. Now if out of that comes a good story about child abuse which raises the ratings then all well and good. I'm fulfilling my brief which is to make a programme appeal to as wide a range of audiences as possible. There is a cynicism in that respect *but I have an integrity as a programme maker*. (emphasis added)

A measure of success is that in 1993, *Emmerdale* achieved audience ratings of 13.5 million (BARB figures). This figure peaked in 1994 to 19.1 million during a dramatic New Year storyline in which a Boeing 747 crashes on the village (neatly killing off older cast members in the process). The plot was instigated by Phil Redmond, who had been brought in to act as story consultant, much to the resentment of existing staff. However, this process of 'spicing up' the programme sparked media controversy – not simply because the unlikely crash story suggested a cynical ratings ploy but because the episode was screened close to the anniversary of the Lockerbie air crash. In fact, the Broadcasting Standards Council upheld complaints about the 'insensitive' episode. The dramatic change in programme agenda did result in some critical audience feedback, but the producer believed that challenging issues in popular drama will always receive a proportion of negative reception. As she recalls:

> There were letters from people who said 'I don't want to watch *Emmerdale* doing stories like sexual abuse, leave it to *EastEnders* and *Brookside*.' But with everything we do we get letters saying 'Give us more farming and give us lots of nice shots of the countryside, we don't want to hear about people's miseries and woes.'

Although the producer defended this new direction on the show, these management decisions were undoubtedly the source of considerable tension within the production team.[3] The rapid nature of change within the programme did not simply result in letters from regular viewers but had a considerable impact on production staff, who were left in no doubt that change would be imposed. Senior management at Yorkshire Television have openly stated that the success of the rebranding in terms of attracting new young audiences means that *Emmerdale* should be considered part of the 'big three' (in other words, on equal terms with *EastEnders* and *Coronation Street*). It would seem that audience figures now support this claim.

Before I go on to discuss commercial imperatives in more detail it is worth noting that, with the exception of *Brookside*, it is common for production personnel to express the organic nature of their storylines. It is particularly interesting that staff working for *EastEnders* should be so keen to dissociate the programme from an issue-led agenda. However, although this professional 'discourse' claims that it is simply character biography which influences the take-up of particular issues, it is clear that soap operas are 'big business' and that economic concerns can and frequently do override a commitment to simply following through on character psychology. The next section examines television soaps and commercial imperatives.

The Commercial Imperative

The production philosophies may differ, but every television drama programme shares a commitment to commercial imperatives. For *Emmerdale*
or *Coronation Street* the economics of the industry are perhaps more overt,
as these programmes are broadcast on commercial television. However, it
would be a mistake to assume that a prime-time programme such as
EastEnders could be free of such concerns, despite being transmitted on
BBC1. While there is no strict correlation between licence fee and ratings,
there has been a long-term concern within the BBC that the 'political and
public will' to support the organisation (and crucially the licence fee)
would be jeopardised if the organisation failed to 'serve majorities as
effectively as it served minorities' (McNicholas 2004: 492). Soap operas
are at the forefront of recent changes within the broadcasting industry,
and commercial concerns can indeed influence the development of
socially controversial stories. This is a point which is rarely made explicit
by production staff. However, one production member told me quite
simply that:

> Every production company on the independent television network would
> like to have its soap because it is the biggest money earner there is.
> [Television soap opera] makes lots and lots of money.

Television soap opera thus forms a major part of British television
industry output, which, as a whole, is under intense commercial pressure.
Jeremy Tunstall noted that while television soap opera is at the bottom end
of the 'drama-prestige scale', it is a crucial part of a channel's image and
economic success. As he describes it: 'Successful soaps, of course, achieve
large, or very large, audiences at a remarkably low cost per audience-hour,
and at a surprisingly low total cost per year' (Tunstall 1993: 114). These
programmes also secure audience loyalty not just for specific productions
but also for the channel. Soap operas remain one of the few points of continuity for viewers in a rapidly changing broadcast world where numerous
channels compete for audience attention. Indeed research undertaken
on behalf of the BBC in 1984 (in other words before the creation of
EastEnders) revealed that audiences 'knew' ITV schedules far better than
those of the BBC. The reason was simple – the presence of the three soaps,
Coronation Street, *Crossroads* and *Emmerdale Farm* (McNicholas 2004).
These programmes do not only attract large audiences in their own right,
they also generate additional audiences for the programmes that follow. As
Jonathon Powell, controller of drama at Carlton television, explains in
interview with Dorothy Hobson:

If you put a good programme that [audiences] really like after a soap you can really increase your audience. You can increase your audience by 25–30 per cent with something very strong. So [soap operas] have a very strong functional purpose. (Powell quoted in Hobson 2003: 55)

Television soap opera thus provides a large, loyal audience, a point of continuity in the schedules, and potential audiences for other programmes and generates income which can be used to develop more 'prestigious' drama. For the commercial channels, economic imperatives play the crucial role of delivering audiences for advertisers. Indeed advertisers are considered to play a vital role in shaping programme content. As the experienced television producer Tony Garnett (who worked with Ken Loach on *Cathy Come Home*) proposes:

The ad buyers are the biggest power in television and indirectly control the content of most of it. Ask yourselves, who do the broadcasters most want – indeed, need – to please? (Garnett 1998)

This point was also underlined recently by Irene Costera Meijer, who was told by the former head of the largest Dutch commercial production company quite simply that, 'What counts are the demands of the advertisers who pay for the commercials. They set the standard, not the viewers' (Costera Meijer 2005: 32). Indeed it is an obvious point, but certainly worth noting, that the soap operas that operate within the commercial sector are required to 'deliver up' audiences for advertisers. All of those I interviewed 'at the top' of the production hierarchy acknowledged that production decisions are made with advertising needs in mind, albeit implicitly.

In the late 1990s *Coronation Street* attracted a £10 million sponsorship deal with Cadbury Schweppes, and this has recently been renewed for two years in a £20 million deal, the largest broadcast sponsorship agreement anywhere outside the USA. This involves sponsorship idents at the beginning and end of each programme as well as within advertising breaks in which new products are marketed. At the time of writing, the media regulator Ofcom is expected to relax product placement regulations concerning the blurring of programme material with advertising. These have been in place for fifty years and it is anticipated that *Coronation Street* will become a key target.

Of course, this brings British commercial television into line with US imports such as *Desperate Housewives*. However, it is likely to create some controversy. Recently, US producers representing the Writers Guild of America voiced concern over the increasing integration of advertising into drama storylines. Marc Cherry (*Desperate Housewives* producer, ABC) discussed a sponsorship deal with an auto company which was then swiftly withdrawn when they discovered that the character associated with their product was to be the 'psycho teenager' Andrew Van der Kamp (Myers 2006). Such constraints have already been felt in medical dramas. Producer of *ER* John Wells is reported as saying that the programme must use generic drug names in order that drug companies are not associated with side effects. When products must only be presented positively this makes storytelling difficult and highlights the conflicting tensions between creative staff and the networks and sponsors. US producers fear that they will ultimately lose the right to deny these requests, and they are seeking a formal agreement with networks. While some view this blurring of content and commerce as an imaginative way of securing funding, there is significant concern that similar possibilities in British television will herald a new era in commercially driven broadcasting.

It would be wrong to assume that these are entirely new pressures. For example, *Coronation Street*, as a brand, brings with it significant problems. Indeed even when I interviewed the programme producer first in the late 1990s, there was an acknowledgement of the necessity of maintaining the programme's market positioning:

> If you are producing a show which regularly tops the ratings, the advertisers want to advertise in the breaks and the pressure is to be consistently good within the parameters.

The team at *Brookside* were also acutely aware that any successful television soap opera must assemble a cast which at least includes the most desirable age range for advertisers, as Mal Young pointed out:

> The advertisers love these 16 to 34 [year olds] because they've got the money. They will spend money on CDs or whatever so the advertisers like that. We never sit down and say 'Right, we're going to target this audience', but you do make sure that you've got a range of characters that reflect the type of stories you want to do and reflect the society that is out there.

Soap opera producers are under intense pressure to develop storylines which maintain existing audiences and of course attract new viewers. Jeremy Tunstall has noted that in comparison with other television producers, soap opera Producers are closer to the organisational hierarchy:

> When the producer of such a programme [the soap] wants to tinker with the script and production formulae he is also tinkering with a prominent piece

of the corporate structure. Soap producers thus tend to get involved in internal corporate negotiations in a way that most producers do not. (Tunstall 1993: 116)

For *EastEnders* (made 'in-house' at the BBC) and *Coronation Street* (Granada, ITV Productions) an additional concern is the inter-genre competition for industry awards. Indeed Mal Young has reflected that *Brookside* felt a surprisingly strong rivalry with *EastEnders* despite being quite unable to match its viewing figures. *Coronation Street* and *EastEnders* have commonly engaged in a series of 'head-to-head' scheduling battles. As soap opera production teams struggle to maintain their position within a changing broadcast industry, advertising concerns can play a significant role in altering soap 'parameters'. This is made explicit in the following statement by a member of one production team:

> Soap is at the forefront for ratings and the advertisers have their requirements. The whole notion about television is that you grab an audience at 7 and it stays with you all night because audiences tend not to switch over. That's a brutal fact of life. No one makes soaps out of a concern for social justice.

The concern here is that commercial pressures demand controversial storylines as a 'hook' for audiences and to fulfil the demands of advertisers rather than on artistic or creative grounds.

The Storyline: A Mediated Product

Over and above the 'identity' of a programme, storylines are the products of a series of negotiations involving production personnel. Underpinning the decision-making process is the constant pressure for audience ratings. This concern can sometimes override other social responsibilities and can under certain circumstances censure portrayals which might convey more challenging messages.

Crucial to understanding how the production process works is the recognition and examination of the often complex *negotiation* process. As we shall see, a single storyline may involve a number of personnel working throughout the organisational hierarchy; script writers, story editors, story consultants, producers, directors, and members of senior broadcasting management such as heads of drama (Chapters 3, 4 and 5). None is autonomous. All are working under a series of competing pressures. Underpinning all of these concerns and implicit in production personnel decision making is the key factor of audience ratings. However, the extent to which these pressures come into play differs depending on the storyline subject matter, the values of the production staff, and the wider social climate at the time of transmission.

The Production Team: A Microcosm of Society?

This industry is populated by a fairly wide cross-section of men and women from different age groups, social classes and educational backgrounds. Certainly with respect to the script-writing team this is likely to be a deliberate strategy on the part of senior management, mixing experienced staff with the fresh ideas of younger colleagues. Here I wish to explore in more detail how one programme, *Brookside*, managed production team meetings.

The first point is that Mal Young was explicit in using team meetings to generate a range of personal responses to storyline material. In short, Young saw his role as one of provocation:

> You try and keep the team as representative of what's going on as possible and as varied. There's no point in me having two of the same type of people in there because suddenly [the storyline suggestion] goes across the room like wildfire and you've got all these different opinions. What we do is basically play devil's advocate and the best meetings are the ones where there's a fight. People are actually passionately fighting each other and that's fabulous because that's all going into the notes and the minutes that form the nucleus of the storyline. You say 'That's a lot of rubbish!' even if you believe them and play them off again. This happens with politics, sexual politics, every storyline we do and the writers all have their favourite characters and they have their own imaginations, they have their own experiences. That's the trick.

The extent to which the production philosophy encouraged 'in-fighting' and personal revelations may be considered to go beyond the usual limits of workplace culture.[4] Writers were specifically played off against one another at story conferences and encouraged to bring all of their previous experiences into play when arguing their case – particularly where storylines involved gender politics. The following quotation concerns how the producer used the writers to develop an acquaintance or 'date rape' plot:

> It's the analyst's couch. I put them all on the analyst's couch and I say 'Why are you saying that?' or 'What are you basing that on?' and they'll go 'I've been there.' 'What?' Everyone goes quiet and we bring it out of them.

Suddenly they say, 'All right you know I've been through it yeah. I thought about hitting this girl.' The date rape [storyline] was an amazing one because the guys were all starting to be very new men, saying 'Woman should be allowed to say no.' Suddenly my female, very feminist writers were saying, 'She's been a stupid bastard. She knows what she's getting into.' I went 'Wow, what have we got here?' You couldn't have predicted that. I couldn't sit down and just think up the storyline. I didn't even know their opinion existed and suddenly you've got opinion, based on your own experiences and your own opinions, but you've got twelve of them.

The above quotation illustrates powerfully how professional loyalties are engendered, confidences exchanged and bonds strengthened, which may be very useful for a drama producer who needs to connect consistently with audiences.[5] As Young continues here:

We have a rule that nothing is ever said outside that room. No arguments are carried on and any personal details are forgotten about. A couple of the writers have said 'I've said stuff in there that my wife doesn't know about me.'

When the writers were asked to reflect on the protocol and conduct of these meetings their responses added valuable insights to the account above. All of the writers I spoke with agreed that the meetings were 'democratic', in that they were all encouraged to air their views. As one writer said '[You argue] until you lose your voice or your cool.' However, the writers were also wary of any attempt by senior production staff to manipulate the direction of arguments. As one writer explained, 'Sometimes there is a hidden agenda but you can smell it a mile off and so it tends to make you react further against it!'.[6]

It is important to remember that production personnel receive high levels of feedback about storylines. This is not simply via audience research commissioned by the programme or broadcasting channel, or via press coverage written by critics, but from members of their existing social network. One writer explained that 'You listen to anyone and you're more likely to glean something from a friend or someone who you just strike up conversation with because they're the people who actually watch it as viewers. Telly critics watch it as telly critics.' Another writer described how friends will often give very frank feedback on specific episodes:

A mate phoned me up a while ago as soon as the programme had finished and [said] 'What was that shit line?' And it wasn't one of mine, it was put in by the producer. The only line he picked out wasn't mine. Now he says 'What was that shit you were writing last week? Oh yeah, it wasn't yours!'

Soap opera producers may encourage their staff to draw upon their personal experiences to develop gripping fictional storylines with strong characterisation. However, sometimes personal experiences or beliefs can jeopardise their commitment to story development. A senior member of the *EastEnders* script team confided that he believed the programme did sometimes 'get it wrong'. The storyline he referred to involved the abduction of a child. Here viewers saw Michelle Fowler in agony as she waited for information about her young daughter Vicky, who had simply disappeared. He explained how this story, in his opinion, sought to engage the audience at the expense of the realistic concerns of any parent:

> We get it wrong when we take the easy route like the kidnap snatch with Vicky. My argument about that was that I am a father but have never had my kids snatched. If I'm just even sitting at home and my children are out late at night and they say they're going to be back at midnight and they don't come back, you immediately think they're dead and you start to worry. If they'd actually been snatched, it would have affected my entire life forever. I would never have recovered from it. I would have been frightened every time one of them left my side. Therefore the consequence of running a storyline like that is immense. If we were being totally responsible about it the fallout on Michelle would have been, well I just don't think she would ever have been the same person again.

Characters who are changed by their experiences and who cannot 'realistically' move on from such storylines do present problems for the production. This may account for why so many characters simply leave the programmes after being involved in a 'big-issue' story. In the case discussed above, it would appear that audience feedback was equally critical. In a coincidence of ill timing, the abduction story was transmitted at the same time as high-profile media reporting of the abduction and murder of a child named James Bulger. His name is now synonymous with public anxiety concerning child violence – two adolescent boys were responsible and the story received both highly sentimental and deeply sensationalist treatment by British media (Franklin 1997: 3). In response to these events, and against a wave of public revulsion, a fictional abduction in popular television soap opera seemed completely inappropriate. The BBC was forced to transmit a 'health warning' prior to the *EastEnders* episodes, assuring viewers that the story would be resolved positively; however, the story was regarded as having 'misfired' badly.

Production team members therefore have their own personal barometer about their commitment to material. For example, whereas the *EastEnders* senior consultant brought his experiences as a father to bear on the

Michelle Fowler story, the producer of *Emmerdale* felt herself to be vindicated by her involvement in a lesbian story when her 'conservative' parents
assured her of their support. As she recalls here:

> My parents are good Scots Presbyterians who live in a very narrow commu-
> nity and vehemently denied to me that Rock Hudson was gay, saying that I
> was scandal mongering. But my father actually rang me after the scene when
> Zoe told her father [that she was gay] and said 'That was a very good episode
> tonight. It was interesting and it made me think. Of course your mother and
> I know that these things exist but we've always turned a blind eye to it. It's
> out of our ken [knowledge] and it's made us think how difficult it must be for
> people who find themselves in that situation to be accepted by their family
> and friends.' I thought if my father can say that, who's approaching seventy
> and a Scots Presbyterian, then we're making headway.

However, it is very important to note that there is a distinct hierarchy in
the production process and in the end, the writers are well aware that their
personal barometer is far less important in influencing story development
than that of the producer. There are thus clearly limits to the 'democracy'
of the team process. As one writer explained, 'The bottom line is if [the
producer] wants it changed then what are you going to do?' Ultimately of
course writers are pragmatic and recognise these constraints of the hierarchy. As the same writer continued, 'You're not going to stand and shout
over one line when the rest of the script might be to your liking and has
your particular stamp on it'.

Conclusion

My aim in this chapter has been to map programme diversity and demonstrate how production philosophies are tied to programme identity and
ethos. This, as we shall see later, has significant consequences for the type
of material which is presented in storylines and how this is packaged. Here
I have highlighted the importance of reputation and production philosophies and have considered the differences between programmes and the
importance of the self-image of the creative team. I have also sought to map
the relationship not only between the programme and channel but also
between producer and writers, the latter often overlooked in studies of the
genre. The relationship between production and audiences and the commercial priorities and pressures which arise from advertisers and channel
hierarchy are vital. Audiences are of course at every turn envisaged through
the production process. However, there is no necessary match between
ratings and influence. Indeed it is possible to argue that producing material

for a niche channel can allow a production to take risks with material that would have been far more difficult for major productions that are under closer scrutiny.

It is possible to describe the production process 'in theory' as I have done here, but there are often gaps between theory and practice. The following chapters (3, 4 and 5) discuss a number of different cases. These develop some of the main points which have been discussed in relation to programme identity, ethos and the team process. These case studies are designed to shed light on how the production process works 'in practice' and under specific circumstances.

Notes

1 These programmes specifically tried to broaden the ethnic mix of characters in popular drama and produce storylines with a strong anti-racism message. The success of these attempts to incorporate black characters into what is considered to be a predominantly white, female-centred narrative has been somewhat limited. Black characters frequently carry 'black issue' storylines and are thus marginalised in the community. The soap opera genre is also more likely to deal with personal rather than institutional racism, which limits how structural inequalities might be addressed in this format (Buckingham 1987; Geraghty 1991). In a recent interview with a new actor in *EastEnders* (who happens to be a black woman), the first question asked was whether this brought a 'special responsibility'. The actor replied that 'the responsibility goes beyond being black; it's being a woman, being a mother, being all those things' (Pool 2006). The fact that this question is still posed suggests that less has changed than we might have expected, and the same article highlights the fact that black characters in the programme are more likely to be men and also to be gangsters.

2 The creator and writer of *Coronation Street*, Tony Warren, was raised in middle-class surroundings near Manchester but drew for inspiration for the programme on inner-city Salford, where his grandmother lived. Warren is quoted nostalgically recalling his childhood memories as follows: 'The fat was just coming on to fry at Parker's (you could smell that) and there was wrestling on the telly. I said "I love it, oh I absolutely love it", and I had this strange feeling that it was all going to change. I wanted to preserve this whole little world like flies in amber' (Dunleavy 2005: 372). Although Dunleavy uses this quotation to underline the concern with working-class culture in the programme, it seems instead to support the view that this is a middle-class depiction of mythologised working-class life.

3 I was fortunate to gain access to production members who had left the programme, in their account, as a direct result of conflicts over the programme direction. Some considered these stories to be entirely exploitative and were keen to reveal the 'behind-the-scenes' tension on the production.

4 The provocation of production personnel certainly provides a powerful point
of contrast with the culture in which news media personnel work. As Philip
Schlesinger observed, it was crucial to their survival that BBC journalists
revealed no personal values or agendas which might be seen to compromise the
'value-free' production of the news (Schlesinger 1987).

5 It seems timely to note here that at no point in my interview sessions did production team members express even mild 'contempt' for audiences or indeed
for their occupational culture. I suspect this reflects the changing nature of
working in television soap opera. Certainly, when Terry Lovell presented the
first feminist defence of *Coronation Street* to industry professionals at the
Edinburgh Television Festival (1977), she was shocked by the ferocity of
response and what she saw as their obvious contempt for 'the punters' and 'for
the product'. Lovell explains that these professionals were caught in 'a situation where they precisely inhabited some of those attitudes of contempt
towards what they were doing and they were compromised in terms of their
livelihood and their whole career development and they were actually only
doing a professional job in the production of soap opera' (Brunsdon 2000: 139).

6 Katja Valaskivi (2000) discusses issues of gender and genre in the production
of Japanese television soap opera *Wataru seken wa oni bakari* ('Living Among
People is Nothing but Trouble'). She emphasises that production staff on the
programme often made a joke about themselves being a 'family', alluding to the
myth of the Hashida Family (named for script writer Hashida Sugako) and
emphasising the useful construction of the soap opera 'family' for PR purposes
(Valaskivi 2000).

Part III Struggles over Television Production

General Introduction

The topics of child sexual abuse, breast cancer and mental illness have been selected as case studies, and these are presented in the following three chapters. Other issues could of course have been chosen and it is possible that these would have yielded different findings. My aim here is not to attempt to provide a definitive guide to how these issues are covered and will be addressed in every prime-time drama. Rather, these storylines can be considered as snapshots through which we might explore the production process, recognising that this will not necessarily remain fixed or static over time or place.

There are a number of reasons why these topics offer a useful platform to discuss complex issues concerning television production processes. The issues are located at very distinct points within the Anglo–US socio-cultural and political context. All are potentially sensitive, involving personal pain and sometimes taboos. However, there are key differences. For example, mental distress is a topic which has traditionally formed the basis of jokes and comedy across all media formats – particularly so with acute conditions such as schizophrenia (Philo 1996a). This is in marked contrast to breast cancer, an arguably 'high-status' disease which is treated with reverence rather than humour by media personnel (Henderson and Kitzinger 1999; Kitzinger and Henderson 2000). Child sexual abuse, or rather, the moral panic concerning paedophilia, was subjected to satirical coverage in July 2001 (Channel 4, *Brass Eye*), and this caused an absolute furore for the channel – the topic was considered to fall outside the bounds of taste and decency. A number of celebrities were duped into taking part in the spoof documentary, including singer Phil Collins, who was furious that celebrity involvement should be parodied in this way. In fact the episode was described as the most controversial television programme 'in living memory' (BBC2 *Newsnight Review*, 21 December 2001).[1] As Kilborn points out, the programme was penalised not for including faked or misleading material but because it had offended against two of the ITC codes relating to taste and decency, causing 'gratuitous offence' (Kilborn 2003: 143).

The relationship between those who lobby around these issues and the mass media is also significantly different. Public awareness of the disease, breast cancer, and the social problem, child sexual abuse, has increased dramatically over the past ten years or so and this has been attributed to media coverage of the issues. Breast cancer has enjoyed a media profile which is frequently out of proportion to its epidemiology (colorectal cancer, lung cancer and heart disease tend to receive less media attention). The lobbying around breast cancer and its prominence in government health policy are a story of success for the PR operations which have nurtured relationships between journalists and other media personnel on behalf of different research and charity organisations (Hastings et al. 1999).

The issue of child sexual abuse/paedophilia has similarly been brought to prominence largely by media reporting (Boyle 2005). There has been some concern that the high profile of the problem could not be sustained, particularly in news media, where saturation point had been reached (Kitzinger 2004). Arguably, in the Anglo-US context at least, this fatigue has been reinvigorated in the 2000s with ongoing concern with identifying and locating risk to children.[2] By contrast, those working in the field of mental health speak frequently of the difficulties in attracting 'positive' media attention and have in the past found it difficult to attract celebrity alignment. Media reporting, particularly of events involving those with acute mental health conditions such as schizophrenia, has been characterised by the use of negative language and is considered to fuel misconceptions about those with mental health problems as violent and unpredictable. Challenging media reporting has therefore been a central function of the organisations working in the field of mental health (Hastings et al. 1999).

It is important to note these differences because TV production personnel do not operate within a social and cultural vacuum and nor do their audiences. Examining these three diverse substantive areas (all in the field of the sphere of social or health and illness problems) allows me to explore the possibilities (and limits) of television fiction within and across different programmes. The main concern of this part of the book is to examine the production context within which storylines are developed. Here I examine the ways in which institutional, organisational, commercial and regulatory pressures interconnect to inform the selection, timing and development of 'issue' story lines. Major story themes are analysed alongside interviews from production personnel who worked on developing the programme scripts, and alongside the perspectives of sources who advised the production. In order to explore commonalities and differences within and across topic areas, I have organised each case around key decisions which were made by production personnel. These include the motivations for developing a specific storyline and decisions made about casting the main roles. I also explore the issues and problems encountered in bringing a social issue story 'to screen' for 'pre-watershed' audiences and the extent to which different story topics are given added suspense and narrative pace to maintain audience interest. The chapter identifies how the same subject can be developed very differently across different programmes and how decisions made over the casting, characterisation and narrative pace contribute to what we might term the overall 'framing' of a storyline.

Chapter 3 addresses the issue of child sexual abuse and sexual violence. Chapter 4 examines the case of breast cancer and explores how health and illness may become 'fictionworthy'. Chapter 5 examines mental distress stories and concludes by comparing and contrasting all three case studies and the values and priorities of television drama personnel.

Notes

1 This was the 'most complained about programme' of 2001, with 922 people lodging complaints with the Independent Television Commission. A total of 1.5 million viewers watched the repeated programme (Channel 4, 13 May 2002). This is 200,000 more viewers than watched the original transmission (Standard Reporter 2002).

2 Recently some British newspapers have campaigned for closer monitoring of paedophiles. This has been sparked by public revulsion following the case of 8-year-old Sarah Payne, who was abducted and murdered in 2000 (see www.newsoftheworld.co.uk/sarah_history.shtml). Criticism of the campaign has come perhaps surprisingly from such diverse organisations as the Association of Chief Police Officers (ACPO), the National Association for the Care and Resettlement of Offenders (NACRO) and the NSPCC (the National Society for the Prevention of Cruelty to Children). This approach borrows heavily from the US 'Megan's law' (1994), which was introduced in response to the murder of 7-year-old Megan Kanka by a known paedophile who lived in her road. The message is simple – knowledge ensures protection. This legislation has been criticised by the American Civil Liberties Union on the grounds that there is no empirical evidence that it actually works (for paedophilia and the press see Soothill et al. 1998).

CHAPTER 3

Family Secrets: Sexual Violence

Introduction

Family loyalty, kinship and inheritance are pervasive themes in television soap opera and drama serials. Storylines concerning secret affairs, concealed births and dubious paternity feature regularly. Plot twists that involve the return of estranged family members mean that incest is a topic which many soap opera storylines are likely to have touched upon, albeit in terms of the threat of brother–sister incest (Stempel Mumford 1995) or the 'para–incestuous relationships' of the US prime-time soap opera (Geraghty 1991: 70). Child sexual abuse within the family arguably takes the programme into different, uncharted territory. This chapter addresses how television soap opera, where narrative revolves so tightly around 'the family', develops storylines concerning child sexual abuse. In this chapter I aim to consider different accounts of sexual violence stories and to unpack the processes by which different production teams confronted and attempted to resolve problems raised by such material.

I want first to examine a recent storyline in *EastEnders*, which attracted praise for its sensitive account of sexual violence and at the same time was severely criticised for symbolising the descent of popular television into distressing and inappropriate material. The festive period remains a time of intense competition for television drama and soap opera in particular. At the close of 2001 millions of viewers sat down to watch the Christmas Day episode of *EastEnders*, and were confronted with the culmination of a long-running domestic violence storyline in which the character known by the Dickensian name 'Little Mo' was viciously beaten by her husband, Trevor. Trevor, incidentally, remains one of the very few Scottish characters to have featured in the programme and at the time was the sole Scottish character, which helped to mark him as a community outsider.[1] Interwoven with this domestic violence story arc was a retrospective story of sexual abuse played out through the character of Kat, who is Mo's sister. Kat is known for her sexually provocative style of dress and her inability to form serious relationships with men. The disclosure is triggered by Zoe, the youngest Slater sister, who is disaffected with life in the Square and reveals her plans to go to Spain and live with their Uncle Harry. In a highly emotive scene it emerges that Kat was raped by Uncle Harry when she was a teenager: Zoe is their daughter, the product of rape.[2] When a distraught Zoe runs away and attempts to contact Mo, Trevor intervenes to keep them apart. It is this discovery that finally provokes Mo to leave her abusive husband. In an episode screened on New Year's Eve Mo retaliates for the first time; she strikes back forcibly, hitting Trevor with an iron and leaving him for dead. With typically cruel irony, this means that Mo faces jail for attempted murder; she is convicted, and is only released when Trevor viciously assaults Kat. Trevor later tracks Mo down and holds her captive in the Slater house. In desperation he douses the house in petrol and, although Mo survives, he dies in the fire. Viewers discover later that Harry, who raped Kat, has also died 'off screen' in Spain from a heart attack.

The programme ran a series of telephone help lines after key episodes (1–5 October 2001) and consulted throughout with the NSPCC and the Samaritans.[3] Programme script editor Jane Perry described doing a pre-watershed story about incest as 'very frightening', and discusses here some of the revisions which were made in the light of advice:

> [The advisors] said you can't have Harry leaving and wandering around Europe, you can't have somebody who's committed a crime going free. So I said OK we'll kill him then and they said how will you do this? Please don't have him committing suicide because children reporting abuse, particularly of their parents are going to associate reporting that abuse leads to their parents killing themselves. I went back to the executive producer and we immediately changed this. The other thing was about Kat's suicide attempt. The Samaritans asked us not to show her afterwards surrounded by her loving and supportive family because that message says if you attempt suicide you immediately get what you want – the love and care of your family. We changed this too. (Cable and Page 2003: 22–3)

In Perry's view, it is not the 'issue' that audiences engage with but the character. She reminds source organisations of what she considers to be their central priority thus: 'I'd work at getting the central message across and not worry too much about the peripherals' (Cable and Page 2003: 22–3). The 'peripherals' are of course often extremely important to those with a special interest in how such material is developed.

The storyline attracted a number of complaints from the public, and in response to the overall increase in complaints specifically around soap storylines, the Broadcasting Standards Commission undertook their first study of sex and violence in television soap opera for twenty years (Millwood Hargrave and Gatfield 2002). The report identifies a number of public concerns about the increase in controversial material in soap storylines (focusing on *EastEnders* and *Coronation Street*). The most important element highlighted by the research participants was that social issue storylines should be 'factually correct' (Millwood Hargrave and Gatfield 2002: 28). The report was front-page news in some papers (Westcott 2002; Conlan 2002) and provoked protests concerning the impact of this material on children. The BBC simply responded that storylines are 'carefully considered and well researched' (Westcott 2002).

This story generated considerable public attention, and I would argue here that by tackling similar material (in far more explicit ways) the Jordache story in *Brookside* provided a template for other programmes. This earlier story of sexual violence also offered viewers a significant story arc (being introduced and revisited over a period of years rather than weeks or even months). In the next section I examine the production background of this storyline and contrast it with another story in a different programme.

Overview of the Stories

It is worth first noting the main features of the two storylines. In February 1993 *Brookside* introduced the Jordache family. Mandy Jordache is living in a safe house in the Close provided by a domestic violence support organisation. She lives with her two daughters Beth (17 years old) and Rachel (13 years old). Mandy resists contact with neighbours and the family are the subjects of gossip and speculation in the community. It gradually emerges that the family are in hiding from Trevor, who is in prison for viciously beating Mandy. Viewers discover that when Beth was 14 years old he raped her, but Rachel does not know about her father's abusive behaviour. Trevor is released from prison, and with the help of well-meaning neighbours he tracks down his family and manages to convince Mandy that he has changed and that she should take him back. Beth refuses to speak to Trevor and is furious with her mother for trusting him. Once installed in their home, Trevor resumes his violence against Mandy. One evening after a vicious assault on Mandy he goes upstairs and climbs into bed with Rachel. Beth arrives home to find her mother badly injured and runs upstairs to discover Trevor asleep in bed with Rachel. A brief shot of his bare arm conveys that he has sexually assaulted her. Mandy and Beth resolve to protect Rachel from further abuse. In the midst of a serious assault on Beth, Mandy, in self-defence, grabs a kitchen knife, and stabs and kills Trevor. The women decide to bury the body and keep this secret from Rachel. It is not until May 1995 (a remarkable two years later) that Beth and Mandy stand trial for his murder. They submit evidence of Trevor's abuse, while Rachel persistently denies in court that her father sexually abused her. Mandy receives a life sentence for murder and Beth five years' imprisonment for conspiracy. A campaign is mobilised by the local community to free the women. Rachel recovers memories of her abuse and an appeal is lodged. Prior to the Court of Appeal hearing, Beth is found dead in her prison cell (of a mystery heart problem). In July 1995, Rachel gives evidence and discloses for the first time that she was raped by Trevor. The new evidence secures Mandy's release. Mandy leaves Brookside Close to begin work for a women's refuge.

The sexual abuse story in *Emmerdale* was introduced via a different route. Troubled teenager Lorraine is the daughter of an existing character, Carol Nelson, whom audiences already know. Lorraine swiftly comes to represent the resident 'wild child' and in October 1992, she discloses the reason for her 'difficult' behaviour – her father had sexually abused her when she was a child. The storyline portrays Lorraine as she comes to terms with her abuse. She first discloses to a supportive neighbour Lynne and then tells her mother Carol. Carol is now divorced from Derek and initially refuses to believe that Lorraine was sexually abused; however, in time she supports her daughter. Lorraine comes to terms with her past through therapy and the storyline is resolved when she leaves the village to begin art college.

This chapter and the next two are organised around some or all of the following sections: generating the story; casting and characterisation; the role of suspense and narrative pace; the issue 'on screen'; advice from outside agencies; language; taking audiences behind closed doors; and finally, source power. These offer a useful point of comparison across different programmes and diverse stories, and allow us to examine more closely the importance of story topic in the following chapters.

Generating the Story

As we shall see in Chapter 4, other programmes were keen to maintain audience loyalties in developing their breast cancer storylines; however, in complete contrast, for *Emmerdale* (Carlton UK, ITV Productions) the inclusion of a sexual violence storyline was part of a deliberate strategy to attract an entirely new audience. The context is very important here, for in the early 1990s the programme had begun the process of changing its image from, as one member of the production team described, 'cosy, farming, country, slow and dozy'. As part of this strategy the programme dropped the word *Farm* from the title, the theme tune was rewritten and the title sequences were reshot. The aim was to signal explicitly to audiences that, as one production team source describes it, '*Emmerdale* is not just about farming. It's part of the contemporary world.'

There had been heavy pressure from Thames Television to take the programme off air. *Emmerdale*'s problem was not simply how many people were watching but their social background and disposable income. As a production source describes it:

> The programme had an imperative over the last few years to change its audience profile, which was fairly old and a C, D, E audience with a strong basis in Yorkshire. The remit was to try to change that audience. To try to get a younger audience, a bigger audience if possible, but a younger audience and an A, B, C audience which had a greater following in London and the south east. Of course all those areas being where the money is and where advertisers are interested. Advertisers are not interested in advertising to 65-year-old D and E audiences who live mostly in Yorkshire. It's simply not of any interest to them, and that's a fact of life.

At the time this child sexual abuse storyline followed a series of measures designed to update the show. As part of this, two Asian characters were introduced and another storyline depicted the dilemma of a teenage mother who abandons her baby. The motivation for introducing social controversy was, in the opinion of a production source, that:

> Controversial stories would buck up that image and encourage people to watch who otherwise wouldn't have thought of watching *Emmerdale*.

Yorkshire Television also engaged *Brookside* executive producer Phil Redmond as programme consultant to help inject some controversy into the programme and increase public interest. Decision making on this particular story was fraught with commercial tensions. The imperative to introduce an incest storyline came from the very top of the organisational hierarchy, according to one source:

> That [child abuse] story actually came about very specifically because the head of programmes at YTV said that he wanted three controversial story lines.

Although the directive did not specify particular issues, it was important that the programme introduce a story with a young protagonist.

Audiences had not yet seen the new teenage character, but the actor had been cast to fill an existing 'age gap' and filmed six months of episodes in which the producer recalls she was cast as 'a bit troublesome, a bit of a rebel'. The team considered several ways in which the character could develop and take on a socially controversial story. Suggestions included a drug storyline, but eventually the decision was made: Lorraine had been sexually abused. The process is described quite simply in the following quotation:

> Three of us were all sitting around a table, the producer, the script editor and myself, and we kind of all clicked at the same time that the story would be that she had been abused.

The programme producer, however, presents a different account of Lorraine's story development.[4] The producer proposed that the sexual abuse story was reasonable as 'it seemed a valid story and fitted her behaviour pattern on paper', and had therefore developed out of the existing character in an organic way. As I have noted earlier, this is seen to confer integrity on such decisions and avoid criticism that production team members simply chase ratings. The programme had utilised the character simply to broaden the age range of the *Emmerdale* cast – at that point the only members under the age of 18 were two infants and a 7-year-old child.

As noted earlier, *Brookside* has always been issue-led. However, the producer admits that in the mid-1980s the programme had lost touch with their audience, who could see little of the reality of Conservative Britain reflected in the socially conscious soap. As Mal Young outlines here:

> In the mid-eighties I don't think we were wrapping [issues] up in good enough stories. That was when people were saying '*Brookside*'s lost its way' and we admitted it did, a little. I can say this because I wasn't producing then. It became issue-led and not story- and character-led. Society was getting fed up with speeches. [Audiences] would accept them in the early eighties when we first started because the unions were fighting back. [By the mid-1980s] people's fight was knocked out of them and to hear it reflected in a drama wasn't realistic to them.

By 1990 *Brookside* was under increasing pressure to maintain fast-dwindling audiences and Channel 4 had actively begun to seek replacement soaps (Bellos 1994). Phil Redmond admitted that he 'killed off' two characters, 'mother and child', in what he describes openly as 'a cynical ratings pulling exercise to get the show talked about' (Bellos 1994: 24). The

Jordache story was introduced as a heavy storyline (domestic violence and incest) quite cynically to 'kick start waning audience interest'.[5]

The incest/domestic violence storyline was devised in late 1991 at the biannual long-term strategy meeting between executive producer Phil Redmond and producer Mal Young. The programme makers aimed to highlight the plight of women who kill abusive partners. In the British legal system at the time, such women could be imprisoned without legal leniency for the years of abuse which they suffered. Although the storyline did tackle incest in conjunction with domestic violence, the sexual abuse element was included *primarily* to drive the formerly passive character of Mandy Jordache to kill her abusive husband. In other words, the rape of Rachel quite simply provided, as one script-writer describes it, 'the impetus finally to take the knife to Trevor'.

The initial inspiration was newspaper reports which Phil Redmond had read about the acquittal of a man who had murdered his 'nagging' wife. The impetus was to run a fictional storyline to challenge the British judicial system. Balanced with this was the fact that the storyline would be innovative as well as novel and gripping for audiences.[6] As one *Brookside* source explained, when the idea was first presented to the writers in a production meeting there was great excitement because:

> It was something that a soap had never done. On a purely televisual level it would be very exciting to do for *Brookside* in story terms.

The Jordache family was introduced to the programme, therefore, as the microcosm through which complex issues around the legal definition of 'provocation' could be played out. These issues were, however, not fully addressed until two years later in the court case surrounding Trevor's death.

Casting and Characterisation

Emmerdale were keen to develop their retrospective story of incest, but this required an actor who could handle what was considered to be a 'heavy' acting role. Production staff saw themselves as fortunate in having discovered Nicola Strong, an older actor who could nonetheless play a teenage school student convincingly. As the producer describes it:

> I was really looking for an actress who was actually probably aged nineteen or twenty [years old] to play fifteen, sixteen [years] because I felt that to be able to talk an actress through the sort of drama that was coming through the script would require someone with a bit of maturity, who also

wouldn't, you know, fight shy of heavy emotional scenes on the subject of child abuse.

The 'look' of the actress was also central to the storyline being convincingly played, and in fact Nicola Strong not only looked younger than her years but was fairly short in stature, and so could portray a teenage girl. Interestingly, the production team did not even attempt to incorporate her abusive father Derek into the storyline. The producer justified this on the grounds that his was a story that they did not want to tell. As she describes it: 'I'd decided from the word go that what we did not want to do is to have a story about child abuse and the abuser, what we were interested in is how the abuse affected the victim and the family.' In other words the story was centred on the psycho-social 'fallout' experienced by the 'victim' and was unconcerned with the perpetrator. It is also worth noting that by dealing with Lorraine's abuse retrospectively the production team were spared any difficulty in interweaving an abuser into the soap community. Arguably it is also possible that the programme identity was not so firmly established in terms of audiences, and the production thus minimised the risks of moving into this type of terrain.

The *Brookside* producers introduced a new character specifically to take on the abuser role, and prioritised audience suspense as a key factor in casting the role of Trevor.[7] The character had to be convincing in a violent and abusive role, and the 'look' of the actor was crucial in maintaining audience suspense. Trevor was written specifically for actor Bryan Murray, who was recognisable to British audiences from previous gentle comedy roles (thus playing against type). The reason was that, according to the producer, audiences would think:

> 'Oh I quite like him, he's a nice guy. Doesn't he usually play the nice guy?' The minute people saw [Bryan Murray] on screen he had a history, and we knew we had to drive this story fast to grab the audience very quickly and keep them held onto a subject that we knew some of them might not normally want to watch.

Perceptions of audience play a central role in casting and developing scripts. A *Brookside* writer commented on the added tension provided by casting Bryan Murray, saying, 'If people just see a psychopath up on the screen then they say "Yeah, he deserves to die" as soon as he walks on screen'.[8] It is clear that drama writers theorise constantly about audiences, and production decisions such as skilful casting require close knowledge of audiences and their cultural references outside the programme, as well as detailed knowledge of character biography and programme history.

The Role of Suspense and Narrative Pace

It is perhaps an obvious point that, as with any other storyline regardless of topic, the issues of suspense and narrative pace were central considerations in how the sexual abuse storylines were developed. In fact it is possible to argue that these conventions were perhaps used more overtly with such a potentially unpalatable storyline. The way in which storylines are 'wrapped up' for audience consumption is central to their success. Issues are therefore introduced and then given the soap 'spin' for audiences. All of the conventions of the soap genre will be employed to engage viewers in such a storyline, and then, as *Brookside*'s producer says:

> If you package into that [issue] a good story with credible characters that people have sympathy for and believe in, you can start to do something with an issue that a documentary can't touch.

The *Brookside* storyline was described as *Sleeping with the Enemy* (20th Century-Fox, 1991) meets *Fatal Attraction* (Paramount, 1987), two popular cinema films in which sexually obsessed and violent protagonists pursue the object of their attraction to the point of (their own) death. Indeed the production team clearly borrowed elements from highly successful cinema releases to develop the story on screen. This is particularly the case in scenes where Trevor pursues Mandy, and also in the 'murder' scene when Mandy stabs Trevor; he appears to be dead but suddenly rises up to lunge at her again. The conventions of cinema also played a crucial role in alerting audiences to Trevor's 'true' nature. In a series of episodes, he maintains a charming front to convince his wife that he has changed and can now be trusted. A common technical device is for the camera to remain on Trevor's face after Mandy has turned away from him. His 'look' signals to audiences that Mandy should not allow him back to the family home. The producer explains how this works:

> You'd see [Trevor] with his back to Mandy and you just see a look on his face, which she couldn't see, and then you're setting up in the audience's mind 'Oh this fella isn't straight.' That's great because that gives a lot of tension for the audience.

An additional concern, over and above 'suspense', was that these camera techniques would build audience support for Mandy. As one of the script writers puts it, 'What you want for us as storytellers is to get the audience really on the side of Mandy. What we kept doing is just coming out of a scene where he tried to persuade her to do something.'

The treatment of the issue in *Emmerdale* was mainly retrospective and in that sense less obviously dramatic than in *Brookside* (where the abusive behaviour of Trevor was ongoing and unfolded over a number of episodes). The programme nonetheless still required dramatic pace. In order for this to work, the production team decided to build a relationship between Lorraine and another 'strong and outspoken' character, Lynne, and to have both characters work side by side in the local wine bar so that the story could build to a dramatic disclosure for audiences. The producer explains here:

> A primary concern is to get a good story which will get people watching the next day, so the first cliff-hanger was when Lorraine first told Lynne about her sexual abuse.

Advice from Outside Agencies

Sometimes soap opera production personnel have a specific commitment to a particular storyline. For example, the researcher working on the incest story in *Emmerdale* had worked with emotionally disturbed children and had contacts in the social services field. The story editor drew on the expertise of friends described as being 'outside television' who specialised in family law, and as the producer describes it:

> We were lucky in that we had a straight line to several people who were in a position to give us a 'cross the board' view of the subject. One of the people concerned was actually a counsellor in the Yorkshire Dales, so we were not only getting accurate stories – we were getting accurate stories for the area.

Production team members working on the Jordache story were given interview material gathered by a programme researcher. Newspaper clippings detailing the experiences of male perpetrators and female survivors of domestic violence/incest were also made available. However, the extent to which these were used differed between writers. For example, one writer described how this can sometimes take up valuable screen time:

> I just like to write from my imagination and we do have a researcher on *Brookside* who picks up any factual or technical things you've got wrong. Even then, sometimes they will come and tell you something which you would have to write down in about five pages, and it's so boring you just forget it and go for the truth of the feelings.

Other interviews with writers revealed that the use of research is clearly linked to ideas about professionalism. Thus the notion of writing as a

creative endeavour (a gifted, skilled, personal and organic process) does not
fit with writing scenes which must draw upon 'real-life' statistics and personal testimonies. As one writer explained:

> I'm not a great fan of research. I wouldn't be writing if I didn't feel I had the
> confidence to be able to transmit whatever it was I think people are feeling.

There were also some differences in terms of how 'research' was used to
help the actors develop their roles on screen. Although the actor who
played Mandy was encouraged to speak with women who had experienced
abuse from their partner, the actors who played Beth and Rachel were
actively discouraged from involving themselves in the 'research' related to
their roles. The producer believed that this type of knowledge would be
reflected negatively in their performance. He explained this decision as
follows: 'I wanted them completely in the dark and unknowing because
children like that are not full of "Hey do you know the stats on abused children?"'

Sometimes, however, despite any amount of 'research', important elements of a character coping with a problem can be absent from a storyline.
In *Brookside* there were a number of controversial scenes, and, as noted
earlier, in one episode Trevor rapes his daughter Rachel – the rape is
implied rather than in any way graphic. Rachel does not discuss her feelings about the abuse for a substantial period of time. A programme source
confided that this time lapse was due to the team having simply 'forgotten'
about the character for some time. As this team member recounted it:

> We've pretended [Rachel] is in total denial at the moment and Mandy can't
> face bringing it up with her because of her guilt, so we can hold off until she's
> ready. It's an entirely false device which luckily turns out to be psychologi-
> cally true!

Indeed, as we shall see later (Chapter 7), the characterisation of the abuse
survivor 'in denial' was well received by those who worked professionally
with sexual abuse survivors. Her apparent confusion, mixed feelings and
challenging behaviour resonated with young women who had themselves
been sexually abused and who recognised something of their own behaviour (as one young woman explained, 'Give her an inch and she takes a
mile').

The characterisation of Beth as a strong and angry survivor has become
iconic in British soap opera history. This is less to do with her role as survivor, perhaps, than the fact that Beth became the first soap opera 'lipstick
lesbian'. The production team members considered that these identities

were distinct (survivor/lesbian), but as we shall see lat
with audience members, who clearly saw her lesbiani:
her having been sexually abused (Chapter 7). Beth e
attributes – consistently challenging her father abou
their home and his description of raping her as 'o
around'. She often tried to warn Rachel subtly al
support Mandy. However, maintaining this level of hi
character is not easy. One of the writers who scripted
reflected on the problem that characters such as this pose to the continuous
format of the serial drama, where characters must always face another day:

> One of the problems is the seriousness of [Beth's abuse] means that some-
> times when, from purely dramatic reasons, you think 'Right we'll lighten
> Beth up now for a bit, just let her be an ordinary teenager', you sometimes
> [wonder] do people think we're being terribly trivial now? But of course it's
> just life and life goes on . . . In a drama [series] you bring it to a climax and
> then you stop, and you never have to face the consequences, like what
> happens the next morning in Elsinore? You know, with all these bodies lying
> about the floor, Hamlet dead and goblets of wine splashed everywhere. I
> mean, what happens the next morning?

Soap opera production personnel frequently justify the way in which
elements of storylines might be condensed, overplayed or simply absent
from the portrayal. The long-term recovery of characters from mental
trauma is rarely seen. The *Emmerdale* production team justified the decision not to portray Lorraine's therapy sessions, where she addresses her
sexual abuse, because 'therapy' lacks 'dramatic interest'. As the story editor
explains it: 'Going to therapy is not dramatically interesting. It's profoundly important but it's not actually dramatically interesting.' This
apparent lack of drama and televisuality is an important and recurrent
theme (see Chapter 4 concerning breast cancer and medical procedures
and Chapter 6 concerning mental distress and therapy).

The Politics of Language

Sexually explicit scenes are also problematic, and scripts were checked
carefully by production teams and organisational management. An additional issue for the *Emmerdale* team was that the abuse storyline was transmitted in England at 7 p.m. but the programme was scheduled even earlier
in Scotland (5.10 p.m.), a prime after-school slot for children.[9] A story
editor gives an example of the way in which explicit description of abuse
might be unsuitable for audiences:

of the lines, which I argued to keep in, because it was so common, and was overruled, was that [Lorraine] said 'Daddy asked me to lick his ice cream.' That phrase was in a first draft version and that was taken out and seen as being too much for a 7 o'clock slot. I personally felt they toned it down a lot so you didn't really know what was happening.

Taking Audiences behind Closed Doors?

Brookside attempted to take audiences behind closed doors in new and challenging ways with the Jordache story, portraying often very graphic physical violence (Trevor was seen slapping, punching and kicking Mandy and Beth in several scenes). However, such scenes of domestic violence and incest within a pre-watershed soap opera provoked controversy. The storyline attracted significant attention across a range of media outlets. Press coverage profiled forthcoming episodes which were to be censored, and a number of complaints were made to the Independent Television Commission and Broadcasting Standards Council. Members of a production team must of course balance the priorities of drama alongside broadcast regulations. At the time this was managed by two key regulatory bodies, the Broadcasting Complaints Commission (a statutory body comprising the Broadcasting Standards Council and Broadcasting Complaints Commission, merged in April 1997) and the Independent Television Commission (which from 1991 combined the Independent Broadcasting Authority and Cable Authority). These organisations monitor broadcast output in terms of taste, decency and violence, and investigate complaints of unfair treatment. The 'super-regulator' Ofcom replaced these organisations and was created in the wake of the Communications Act, December 2003.

Despite this care and attention on the part of the programme makers, the ITC investigated complaints from twenty-four viewers concerning scenes portraying Trevor's violence against his wife (24 April to 8 May 1993). A severe formal warning was issued to Channel 4 for the use of a kitchen knife in the final murder scene (8 May 1993). It was believed that this weapon would be available to children and could be easily imitated, in breach of section 1.7 of the programme code (ITC 1993). However, no complaint regarding the incest storyline was upheld. The Broadcasting Standards Council shared the view of Channel 4 view that:

> The nature of 'Brookside' in its evening placing was well-understood by the audience which had been accustomed to watching equally serious and difficult issues dramatically presented. It took account of research work commissioned by the Council on domestic violence, which suggested that its

victims were willing to confront its graphic presentation in order to convey its real nature. (BSC 1993)

Additional concerns focused on the early transmission time of the Saturday omnibus repeat (5.05 p.m.), when children might watch unsupervised. In order to pre-empt outside intervention, the scenes of physical violence were carefully constructed so that no punch was seen to connect. The key scene in which the sexual abuse of Rachel was 'suggested' was edited for the omnibus repeat at the weekend. The producer and deputy head of drama for Channel 4 viewed the scene and decided to remove a brief shot of Trevor's 'bare arm', which is glimpsed when the character is found asleep in bed with his daughter (thus signifying that he is in bed naked and has abused her). This self- censorship was undertaken, as the producer describes it, because 'You don't want to get your head cut to ribbons the night before transmission by someone who doesn't understand the power of drama. I'd rather do the censoring myself and I'm still telling the story.'[10] Indeed the producer was also concerned that refusing to self-censor might mean losing the entire scene from the repeat edition.[11] It is worth noting that senior management at Channel 4 supported the decision to go ahead with the scene, and Michael Grade personally defended the programme. When I discussed this with members of the production team, all agreed that they had broken the rules 'in black and white' but not 'morally'. However, the ITC continued to monitor the omnibus edition carefully, which meant that the writers were forced to operate under tight restrictions for future storylines. As one disillusioned script writer described it:

> We've had such a big fuss about the knife so we are constrained. We keep trying to push the barriers [but] it's not easy and really the thought police are out in such force at the moment.

An additional area where it was not possible to 'push the barriers' was with respect to Trevor's motivation for abusing his daughters. According to production sources, the Channel 4 'hierarchy' decided that it should be made clear that Trevor had abused his daughter Beth on only one occasion. This decision was made on the grounds that 'if it's once it could be that Trevor had an aberration, a mental aberration. If he does it over a period of time then that's no mental aberration.'

This would also of course have potentially serious repercussions for the other characters. Indeed there was some concern that audiences would be unable to empathise with Mandy – a woman who allowed her daughter's abuser back into the family. If raping Beth had been one incident in isolation then Mandy (and audiences) could assume that it was, as Trevor justifies it to Beth, 'one weak moment'. Presenting the abuse as an isolated incident also arguably removes the need to address wider debates about power structures and why some men abuse their children.

Source Power

Production decisions can certainly go against the desires of groups with a special interest in the storyline. This is perhaps most strikingly illustrated if we examine the controversy which surrounded the decision to sack Anna Friel, the actor who played the role of Beth.[12] The characterisation of Beth Jordache had been praised highly by women's organisations as a rare positive and strong survivor of sexual abuse.[13] Friel had also become a popular television celebrity and appeared in numerous 'youth' magazines – as noted earlier, Beth and her friend Margaret provided the first lesbian kiss in a prime-time British soap opera (Collins 1995; Culf 1995; O'Kelly 1994).[14] When news emerged that she had been sacked there was a media furore (Corless 1995; Moyes 1995). Newspapers announced that the character was to be 'killed off', possibly murdered by a 'prison lesbian' or even 'hanged in her prison cell'. The *Daily Mirror* reported that Beth would commit suicide, under the headline 'Beth us do part', and continued:

> Beth, jailed in the body-under-the patio cliff hanger, can't face a five year sentence. Although an appeal is pending, she decides to end it all. (*Daily Mirror*, 14 June 1995)

Street demonstrations by lesbian groups and incest survivors took place outside Channel 4 offices.[15] These women protested about the negative impact of the decision. As one spokeswoman for incest survivors told me:

> Beth had portrayed this really strong survivor, giving out all these messages saying 'Look, you can do something about it, you can come to terms with it, you can be strong about it.' And then all of a sudden, somebody, somewhere, and I feel very insensitively, decided she would hang herself in prison so they're saying to us as survivors, 'You're always the victim, you never survive.'

Channel 4 officials assured demonstrators that the storyline would not climax with suicide, and audiences eventually saw Beth die in prison from a heart attack (26 July 1995). Despite the efforts of programme makers, her death was framed by media coverage as 'a final tragedy'. The story received front-page coverage in soap opera magazines with headlines which framed her life as 'wasted' (*TV Quick*, 22–28 July 1995). Even the popular tele-vision listings magazine *TV Times* presented her death as an inevitable tragedy: 'Why Beth had to die. There could have been a happy ending – she could even have escaped from jail. But for tragic Beth Jordache there was only one way out' (*TV Times*, 22–28 July 1995).

Such coverage undermined all the positive strengths of the character and placed Beth firmly in the category of victim 'scarred for life'. The above accounts undoubtedly also framed her death as a 'release' from her painful experiences, thus *reframing* the characterisation which had been carefully built within the programme. This highlights the ways in which the availability of actors can effectively influence the development of any social issue storyline.

In this respect it is important also to note that simple technical con-straints are of course an additional factor in relation to producing television soap opera. The availability of actors, the restrictions of sets and other bureaucratic or technical limitations do act as 'significant constraints' (Dyer et al. 1981: 62). As one writer describes it:

> It's not only constraints of the Broadcasting Commission, the watershed and actors you've got to work with, but also really ridiculous things like how many locations you can have, how many houses you can have. For example, you're only allowed to have two houses on the street at a time because there will be other shoots going on using other houses. They haven't got time to light them all. You might have a really important story to tell with, say, the Jordaches, and you haven't got their house.

Conclusion

In this chapter I have addressed some of the factors which influence how sexual violence stories may be dealt with in prime-time drama and the con-cerns which underpin these decisions. These are discussed in the light of other cases in Chapter 5. In Chapter 4, we consider the priorities which influence how breast cancer is depicted in television fiction.

Notes

1   It is not only 'abusers' who are marked as 'outsiders'. A study of social-work professionals in popular British drama (soap opera, police and medical series) found that social workers are not integrated into the community that they serve (Henderson and Franklin 2007). Some of the interview material dis-cussed in this chapter and Chapters 4 and 5 has been discussed elsewhere (Henderson 1999).

2 Key episodes from this story can be viewed online at the BBC EastEnders website, where they are listed under the heading 'trauma' (bbc.co.uk/ eastenders).

3 The actor who plays the role of Kat was awarded a Mental Health Award (2002) for challenging the stigma and silence which surrounds childhood sexual abuse and for powerful scenes in which she contemplates suicide. Such storylines are of course rarely concerned with a single issue (sexual abuse, domestic violence) but frequently spill over into other issues (mental distress, lesbianism).

4 The radical changes imposed on this programme led to significant tensions in the production team, and I have tried to highlight where accounts of decision making differ. As with any research of a qualitative nature, it is important not to mistake 'discourse' for 'truth' (Barker 2003).

5 'Social issues' have clearly been used to harness other audiences. As Kathryn Montgomery has identified, *The Day After* (1983) presented American audiences with a fictional account of a nuclear attack on the US and drew extraordinary audiences of around 100 million, thus paving the way for the 'social issue movie'. The film *Something About Amelia* (ABC, 1984) featured Ted Danson, known as lovable womaniser Sam Malone in *Cheers*. Here he is cast as an abusive father who rapes his daughter. As a senior vice-president of NBC describes it, 'How do the networks fight back against cable? We can't do it by putting on more violence and sex, but we can probe social issues that haven't been explored' (Montgomery 1989: 196).

6 The competition between programmes is intense. All production team members are aware of material in other programmes. To an extent soaps are simply vying with each other to produce more challenging drama. In some respects this can amount to pushing back the line on what can be shown further. It is undeniable that this has an effect on decision making around new characters. The producer of *Coronation Street* discussed how the three main competitors (*Brookside*, *EastEnders* and *Emmerdale*) were all running lesbian storylines, and declared that as a result, '*Coronation Street* will never run a lesbian storyline.' In fact shortly afterwards *Coronation Street* introduced a new character named 'Hayley' – the first transsexual to be featured in British soap opera.

7 There is significant risk in casting existing characters to take on such roles. Former executive producer of *EastEnders* John Yorke has discussed how the production team felt that using existing characters for the 'hidden' abuse story would be difficult but more realistic. In the end audience loyalties (and clearly also viewing figures) cannot be jeopardised (Boyle 2005: 168).

8 I have concentrated on casting issues with one or two characters here, but there were significant problems with audience reaction to Mandy. The producer told me, 'I got letters from male and females saying "Stupid woman, no woman puts up with that, she'd just leave him or she deserves it" and things like "That's mad!", and that's what you're fighting.'

9 The 'to air' time is an important constraint on the imported television serial. I do not discuss the Australian soap opera *Neighbours* here; however, I did correspond with some members of the production team to discuss how they approach 'issue storylines'. One member responded that script writers had been told not to write 'issue-based' stories as a result of the early transmission time in *Neighbours* global markets. As she describes it, 'There are many directives from above to tackle certain stories that as a writer one would not choose to do. In the twenty five years I have worked in the industry I have never known a situation where a writer exploited a story to increase ratings.'

10 Despite careful editing it seems that viewers were convinced that they had seen more. As the producer described it, 'It's funny, you still get letters from people complaining who think they've seen something, and they say "That's dreadful what he was doing to that girl in bed", and we say "What did you see?" So their minds are working overtime.' Viewer imagination was also discussed by other producers in relation to different storylines where there was any suggestion of sexual activity.

11 Several members of the team mentioned in interviews that the mother of the young actor who played Rachel was unhappy with the scene. Other factors may also be important here.

12 There was some 'off-the-record' discussion that Friel had criticised production regulations which prohibit actors from altering their lines in the scripts. She may even have begun to assume that her acting abilities had 'made' the character. The producer discussed the role of actors in the programme as follows: 'We've worked through many drafts, many storylines to get it right and if sometimes they just change a sentence because they feel like it and it can actually change the whole sentiment of a storyline and destroy it.'

13 The producer remarked upon the number of letters received from survivors of sexual abuse who identified with Beth: 'Some of [the viewers] are now in their forties and they say "I've never told anyone, I just want you to know this, I feel that *Brookside* by putting it on screen has made me feel I'm not alone, and actually it's bringing to everyone what I'm going through and I feel good about that, that someone else understands my head." '

14 Despite developing a career in film Anna Friel is still associated in media coverage with her time at *Brookside* and 'that kiss'. For many years an online 'fan' site replayed the scene of Beth and Margaret kissing repeatedly.

15 Mal Young has been reported as saying that the team did not plan for Beth to be a lesbian character and that the decision had been made in order to maintain audience interest while Trevor's body lay undiscovered (Hobson 2003: 151). Interviews with script writers similarly hinted at some dissatisfaction with this twist.

CHAPTER 4

A Woman's Disease: Breast Cancer

Introduction

Health and illness storylines populate prime-time serial drama with regularity. Sometimes these involve familiar illnesses such as cancer (now dealt with by many soap operas), or conversely, extremely rare illnesses, unknown to audiences and medical practitioners alike. Such storylines generate significant dramatic opportunities in television soap opera as characters typically avoid hospital appointments, secretly wait for diagnoses, or begin to come to terms with the impact of serious ill health on their family relationships. Medical problems do not even need to be genuine. Characters may fake illness, sometimes terminal illness, in order to manipulate close relationships, though audiences know that ultimately their secret will be at some point revealed. Medical storylines do come under a lot of scrutiny and have under certain circumstances been considered to have a significant impact on health-seeking behaviour. In this chapter I discuss soap opera treatments of breast cancer, but other 'women's cancers' also feature in television soap opera. A 2001 storyline in *Coronation Street* depicted an older character, Alma Halliwell, who missed two cervical smear tests. When she received the results of the third test, she was diagnosed with inoperable cervical cancer. Her swift screen death triggered a front-page story in the *Sun* newspaper with the headline, 'Alma: I'm so Angry with Corrie', and featured a long interview in which the actor accused the production team of cynically 'cashing in on cancer' (Kay and Bonner 2001). During the period of story transmission there were 300 extra calls per week to cancer charity CancerBACUP. The organisation produced a chart where peaks in calls were matched directly to twists in the storyline. This illustrated that, in their view, the story had been successful in increasing awareness of this form of cancer and also helped the public profile of the charity (Hardyman and Leydon 2003: 498). The same story was, however, criticised severely by public health researchers, who reported that more than 14,000 smear tests were performed as a direct result of the storyline in the north west of England alone (importantly, only 2,000 of these were in women whose test was overdue or who had had no previous smear test) (Howe et al. 2002). Local laboratories were overwhelmed, women's anxieties were arguably increased and scarce health care resources were overburdened (Howe et al. 2003: 498). The storyline was estimated to have cost the NHS around £500,000, with this figure rising to around £4 million if the same pattern was repeated across England (BBC 2003).

As a disease primarily affecting women, it seems perhaps appropriate that breast cancer should be dealt with in the realm of television soap opera. Indeed it is a disease which appears to be accommodated within a diverse range of programmes, including the traditionally 'safe' space of Australian soap *Neighbours*, where audiences saw character Stephanie Scully recently forgo treatment for breast cancer to preserve the health of her unborn child (2006). A diagnosis of breast cancer also allowed the drama series *Sex and the City* to move into 'social issue' territory, when character Samantha Jones discovered a lump in her breast and was forced to renegotiate her identity when treatment caused her to lose her hair and sexual desire (2004).

The metaphorical power of cancer in Western culture has been discussed elsewhere, notably by Susan Sontag (1991). Ien Ang (1985) commented on the relative 'daring' of prime-time drama *Dallas* in bringing breast cancer to the screen at a time when cancer was largely underrepresented in soap opera (Ang 1985: 67–8). Ang is unsurprised that illness features regularly in television fiction, as it is a means to propel the narrative forward in particular ways:

> the phenomenon of illness is liberally surrounded by all sorts of emotionally loaded associations and images. Being ill means not only physically being out of order but also being excluded from the world of the healthy, being overcome by an unknown and uncontrollable force, etc. And some illnesses, such as tuberculosis and cancer, have a uniquely terrifying aura. Being ill therefore has far-reaching cultural consequences extending far beyond the biological fact of illness itself. (Ang 1985: 66)

In the following sections I examine the production decisions which influence how and why breast cancer was selected by two different programmes.

Overview of the Stories

As discussed earlier, the soap opera *Brookside* was groundbreaking and innovative in its approach to social issues. It was the first major British soap

opera to tackle the topic of breast cancer, in 1994. However, the actor who
played cancer survivor Patricia Farnham left the production and the storyline was left unresolved. Two years later, at the end of September 1996,
Brookside reintroduced Patricia in a one-week special – she had discovered
another lump in her breast. Without disclosing this news to ex-husband
Max (who, in her absence, remained a constant character within the
programme), Patricia returns to Liverpool for tests. The revisiting of
Patricia's breast cancer is discussed in the case study.

As is sometimes the case, this *Brookside* storyline (September 1996)
directly competed with a breast cancer story in *EastEnders*, transmitted
around the same time, when Peggy Mitchell discloses to her daughter-in-
law Tiffany that she has found a lump in her breast. Peggy is reluctant to
alert her GP but is finally persuaded to undergo tests. The storyline culminates over Christmas (as noted in Chapter 3, a time of intense competition between the soaps) when Peggy finally agrees to undertake a
lumpectomy. The story is revisited in August 1997 when she receives an
'all-clear' for her followup mammogram.[1] Later, in 1999, the storyline is
revisited and Peggy undergoes a mastectomy.

Generating the Story

The soap opera genre has long been fascinated by medical tragedy, and
health and illness remain a staple fare of storylines. However, the process
of selecting an illness for soap is influenced by production teams' perceptions of their audiences. In choosing breast cancer for inclusion in
EastEnders and *Brookside*, a central concern was that the disease should be
easily and swiftly understood by viewers. In other words, the illness should
first have a resonance with audiences. As one of the writers explains:

> If you say MS, motor neurone disease or ME – what does that mean? We
> would need to set up explaining a whole host of things about the disease
> process for people to understand. [But] you say 'cancer' and the viewers say
> 'Yes, I know what you're talking about.' Cancer is in the language.

In the original breast cancer story, Patricia has a mastectomy and struggles with the psycho-social impact of the disease. Her recovery is made
more difficult by the constant presence of Max's first wife, Susannah, who
has never forgiven Patricia for 'stealing' her husband and plots to drive
Max and Patricia apart. Originally production staff had thought it likely
that the breast cancer storyline would be interwoven throughout Patricia's
biography. However, as with all drama programmes, changes in the cast
inevitably have repercussions for future plotted story arcs. In this case the

actor decided to leave the production and the story remained unresolved in order to allow her to return. A script writer describes here where the story picked up:

> [Patricia] had a mastectomy and as far as breast cancer was concerned it was left at that. Probably those aspects of her story would have been pursued but because the actress wanted to move on, [breast cancer] wasn't referred to again. When Patricia reappeared on the Close, Max was confused. Susannah had moved in at the time and she thought Patricia was coming back to get her man. In fact she was back because she had found another lump and had come for a biopsy.

Soap opera production teams are subject to intensive lobbying by source organisations to promote positive messages. The understanding here is that these in turn will be unproblematically accepted by audiences. Despite dealing with a 'high-status' disease such as breast cancer, and the publicity likely to be generated, the writers deny that they are involved in making 'education' television. One writer cites a common ambivalence towards material of this type:

> At the end of the day you've got to make a programme and you've got to look at entertainment versus interest. Looking at someone with breast cancer isn't entertaining but you can make it interesting. You can go for the extremes of drama and have people getting into dire straits and have real tragedy. You can pile on the suffering, which also seems to pile on the ratings, but I don't want to really be involved in educational TV.

The decision to revisit breast cancer in *Brookside* offers a useful illustration of the circumstances in which external influence can be brought to bear on a drama production. The story was initiated explicitly by the senior press officer for the charity Breast Cancer Care, a high-profile British cancer charity which has generated extensive publicity due to the patronage of Cherie Booth, wife of prime minister Tony Blair. This organisation focuses on the needs of breast cancer survivors and their families as opposed to conducting scientific research into the disease. The senior press officer approached the programme producer in February 1995 (one year prior to transmission) to suggest that it would be realistic and timely to reintroduce 'Patricia' with another breast cancer 'scare'. Although it has become increasingly common for production teams to collaborate with source organisations, programmes regularly resist attempts to lobby for specific issue story lines. This is therefore a rare example of an issue storyline being generated explicitly by a source organisation and acknowledged as such. It was also no coincidence that the storyline was scheduled for early October. October is 'Breast Cancer Awareness month', a world-wide initiative in which media coverage is targeted. This certainly gave the storyline an added social currency and of course meant that the charity generated 'add-on' publicity for their awareness strategy.[2]

The *EastEnders* breast cancer story was devised at the suggestion of a script writer in a regular story conference session; however, the programme also took expert advice on storyline visuals from a variety of sources. There were few anticipated problems with running a breast cancer storyline. As a member of the production team explains:

> A lot of illnesses do, it sounds awful, but do translate quite readily into quite strong dramatic material, and everybody in the audience will have or know someone who has had that experience of going to the doctor, waiting for the results and dealing with being in hospital. It is an incredibly difficult situation [but] the whole experience, whether you've been through it or not, everyone can identify with.

The topic of breast cancer was raised as a potential storyline by one of the script writers and had, according to production staff, 'been knocking about for a long time'. Decisions regarding storyline timing, casting and characterisation and indeed interweaving the storyline with other ongoing storylines are crucial to how the story will play for audiences. As a story editor explained it:

> *EastEnders* is perceived as being an issue-led show but it isn't, it's character- and story-led, so we don't just bolt on issues willy nilly. If you haven't got the character to fulfil that storyline then it won't work. You've got to be careful to make sure that the illness actually impacts on the family dynamics and the character development.

Casting and Characterisation

Casting the role is crucial to the way in which audiences engage with a character. Central to this is the way in which the soap community is constructed with 'insiders' and 'outsiders'. A key element of the production process is therefore whether to run an 'issue' story with an existing character or to introduce a new one to audiences. It can be argued that soap operas take risks introducing new characters to the programme. Indeed soap producers frequently described how audiences dislike cast changes and for up to one year will commonly refer to 'that new family'. Equally, it might be proposed that new characters are introduced to *minimise* risks. Unlike established characters, they can be dispensed with if they prove too disruptive to the soap narrative. Writing principally about the difficulties of introducing gay characters to US soaps, Joy V. Fuqua argues that:

> Conventionally, the *issue du jour* is introduced to the soap opera community . . . through the arrival of a new and oftentimes marginal or peripheral character. Soap operas deploy tentative storylines through the introduction of these marginal characters so that if the narratives prove too problematic, the new character(s) can be written off or redirected. (Fuqua 1995: 200)

Certainly, all production personnel I interviewed acknowledged that 'change' within soap must be carefully managed to counteract the problems which new characters present for audiences. As one *EastEnders* source describes it:

> It takes about nine months to a year for that audience to actually accept [new characters] as part of that family. To run a storyline with them doesn't have the same impact at all. To run a storyline with any of our regular characters that we've established over the years, there's an empathy and sympathy for them and therefore the audience goes with them and feels part of them. That's when you get maximum value out of a story.

In keeping with the *EastEnders* production ethos of 'organic' storylines, they chose to run their breast cancer story with Peggy Mitchell. This decision conformed to soap tradition in reserving a strong role for a middle-aged matriarch, and this character, played by actress Barbara Windsor, was firmly established within the programme. Peggy is pub landlady of the Queen Vic, around which most of the programme narrative is set. Loyal audiences would be familiar with Peggy's character biography – her husband had a lingering death from cancer, with the consequence that she fears hospitals and is fiercely protective of two sons, the central characters, Phil and Grant Mitchell.

The production team believed that Peggy should take on the breast cancer story for several reasons. She had, according to one of the production team, the 'right mentality' for this particular story theme, which was about 'a woman who discovers a lump and then refuses to accept there's anything wrong'. An added factor was that in choosing Peggy the programme could avoid appearing too 'issue-driven', and a strong breast cancer storyline could be used as a device to expand and develop her characterisation. Soap opera audiences are frequently used to anticipating 'issue' storylines from clues in the character's behaviour. The causes of breast cancer are not easily attributable to particular risky behaviour, which made the disease more attractive in soap opera storyline terms. As an *EastEnders* production team member explains:

> If you take a character who smokes and they get lung cancer that would seem too issue-driven. The great thing about a character like Peggy is [her breast cancer was] quite unexpected. At the time there were lots of other issues in her life. She was a character who [audiences] had only really seen pulling pints behind the bar. Suddenly she was in a new environment in a hospital and had a huge medical crisis to go through, so that allowed the character to grow and expand in many ways.

The timing was also 'right' in terms of the overall programme narrative and the Mitchell family in particular. As a production team member outlines here:

> [Peggy's] breast cancer also just fitted in at the time when we were doing lots of other stories that were happening around the Vic. There was a big story happening for Grant and Tiffany at the time. They'd come back and got married off screen so that was a new family dynamic. Tiffany was Grant's new wife. Phil was going through a period of remission with alcoholism so there was all that going on in her life. There was also fairly major moments going on with Peggy and George. She thought George wouldn't love her any more after she'd had the operation. We were able to then use the illness to take them on a new journey.

In the view of the production team, the breast cancer storyline acted as a catalyst and provided a useful device, creating new dynamics and tensions amongst existing characters and developing family relationships. As the same team member continues, 'We're always very careful that we don't just take the illness and treat it as an issue, but make sure it is always part of a much larger dynamic of characters and story situations.'

The fictional biographies of Peggy and her extended family meant therefore that breast cancer could operate as a story device to develop her relationships. The characterisation of Peggy, as built over previous storylines, also meant that the production team could develop a realistic storyline around a central theme of 'denial'. Issues of realism also played a role here in casting and developing the storyline. As an older woman, Peggy was, epidemiologically speaking, at 'high risk' from the disease. In fact, Peggy's character provides one of the rare media portrayals of an older female with breast cancer. News media representations of women with breast cancer are particularly skewed towards younger women with the disease (a study of breast cancer survivors in the news media revealed that 94 per cent of newspaper profiles of non-celebrity women with breast cancer were aged *under* 50 years old). Such stories, featuring women in their twenties or thirties, were seen as 'more tragic' and indeed 'more sexy' in media terms (Kitzinger and Henderson 2000). In this respect, soap opera provides older women with valued matriarchal roles, and viewer empathy can allow older women's experiences to be represented. For source organizations, the emotional dilemma of 'how' and 'when' Peggy would reveal her diagnosis to her family was considered to be a vital component of the story:

> [The team] decided it was going to be [Peggy] and very rightly so. Bang on the right age, you know, perfect dramatic licence in terms of her sons that she was going to have to share this terrible news with, and how would she share it? Every female would have that problem. How would you tell your children? And they followed that with her. She was exactly the right person.

As discussed earlier, *Brookside* also chose to explore breast cancer with an existing character, Patricia Farnham. Although Patricia was no longer a permanent character in the programme, she had been very popular with audiences, and the production team assumed and hoped that these audiences had remained with the programme during her absence. This programme, perhaps more overtly than other British soap operas, has had a commitment to representing characters at different points on the spectrum of social class. Patricia and her husband Max Farnham were introduced originally as a 'yuppie' liberal couple who could play off the more traditional 'working-class' values of other characters. Patricia had a successful career and, according to the producer, the actor had proved extremely popular with women viewers, who enjoyed her realistic portrayal of a modern woman struggling to juggle work and family life, sometimes unsuccessfully. The breast cancer storyline was discussed originally in one of the biannual long-term strategy meetings, and script writers explained that a number of factors influenced their decision to choose Patricia to carry it. The fact that she was relatively young, in her thirties, and that breast cancer was assumed to be perceived as a disease affecting only older women meant that viewers would be surprised and possibly more deeply affected by this new plot twist. The reasoning behind this is discussed as follows:

> We decided to pick a young, attractive woman who people wouldn't have the slightest inkling that breast cancer would come along for her – a successful career female. People's general view on breast cancer is 'Oh, female in her fifties.' If, say Julia Brogan [an elderly character] got breast cancer, people would say 'Oh, won't that be sad.' If you said Patricia's going to get it – the reaction would be 'Patricia!' You already know there is going to be shock value in terms of viewers.

The producer, Mal Young, also saw the story as reflecting the statistical increase in younger women with breast cancer. As has been discussed elsewhere, this was in fact more as a consequence of improved mammography than indicative of an 'epidemic' (Seale 2002: 87). The subject of cancer was a potentially distressing storyline for audiences, but the *EastEnders* production team believed that breast cancer would provide a 'strong' story with which many viewers could identify. However, it remains questionable whether 'everyone' could indeed identify with this storyline, as this view assumes an audience familiar with the issue but largely 'cancer free'. The production priorities of using medical tragedy to develop a character were also apparent in the *Brookside* treatment of the issue. Patricia was characterised as a confident, articulate, middle-class woman whose cancer journey would provide extensive scope for developing her role in the programme – showing her as vulnerable and anxious. The production team also certainly sought to interrupt this fictional character's 'comfortable' life with a shocking diagnosis of cancer, much in the same way as cancer would confront any woman with her mortality. As a script writer describes it:

> Patricia can be nice and settled and middle-class and confident and all the rest of it, but the thought of having breast cancer would terrify anybody. To go through a door with her into theatre is useful for the character, and hopefully the viewers can identify with it.

Taking Audiences Behind Closed Doors?

Soap opera production workers regularly describe the power of the genre to 'take audiences behind closed doors', showing usually private problems such as physical violence or mental breakdown which might not be so easily accessed by other televisual forms (such as news or traditional documentary formats). However, decisions about which scenes will be developed 'on screen' are clearly based on the priorities of drama. Although breast cancer is necessarily a highly medicalised storyline, neither of the programmes under discussion is within the genre of medical drama. The *EastEnders* production team in fact chose not portray any medical procedures in detail. Viewers watched as Peggy was called to hospital for common technical procedures in identifying breast cancer, including mammograms and fine needle aspiration. All of these procedures took place 'behind closed doors', thus excluding audiences. According to production sources the decision was based solely upon dramatic grounds:

> You show whatever is dramatically interesting, so Peggy undressing or having needles go into her wouldn't be dramatically interesting.

The production team did receive some critical feedback from women with personal experience of the disease. A source explained that the format must condense or omit certain scenes to avoid appearing didactic, because 'We weren't making a documentary about what happens when you have breast cancer.' As he continues:

> Inevitably, there are always going to be certain elements that you can't show because you can't show everything. A lot of people who've been through that experience themselves say 'You haven't shown this or that', but we can't be an educational film. If it looks like there are things missing they're simply things we couldn't cover because of time or dramatic function.

The term 'dramatic function' can of course justify the exclusion of realistic but, in television terms, visually dull elements of an issue. Dramatic pace is often at the expense of a more complex realism, and simplification or omissions can be particularly distressing for those who have experience of the problem which is represented.

For one *Brookside* script writer a health and illness story provided an ideal opportunity to draw on wider cultural anxiety about the 'closed' nature of the hospital world. In the following quotation he explains how camera techniques can enhance the dramatic potential of such scenes for audiences:

> When I write things dramatically sometimes I will have a camera focus on the [theatre] door. You can make it seem massive and you see people going in and out, and you're craning your neck to try and peep in. You're almost creating an expectation in the viewers' mind of 'What the hell goes on the other side of there?' It's almost terrifying for a patient what goes on on the other side of a door, but it's useful for the viewer. I think a [hospital] door becomes quite a frightening thing.

There is, however, a powerful potential in the medium to screen 'private moments'. In this context, some of the most potent scenes in the *EastEnders* breast cancer story arise from playing out the process of a woman coming to terms with her cancer diagnosis. In one episode, while Peggy waits at home for her results, we see her break down and lash out at daughter-in-law, Tiffany who is trying nervously to reassure her that everything will be 'OK'. Peggy rejects Tiffany's attempts to pacify her and screams, 'What if I *have* got cancer? That's my death sentence. Are my sons going to have to watch me die?' Scenes such as this are important because they provide rare opportunities to portray the cancer patient 'behaving badly' and to depict ambivalent feelings (such as denial or anger). Cancer patients are commonly characterised in media accounts as beatific, serene figures (Seale 2002). Here was an opportunity to witness a cancer patient, angry and railing against her diagnosis, lashing out unreasonably at her supportive friend, thus allowing audiences a glimpse of some of the challenges commonly faced by those who support friends and relatives through serious illness.

Language

Medical storylines may also raise problems with preparing scripts. For example, with a breast cancer storyline it is important to include just enough medical jargon in scripts to maintain credibility but not enough to alienate lay audiences. The *EastEnders* team achieved this by introducing an 'outsider', namely a breast care nurse, to counsel and advise Peggy. This character was developed principally to translate medical terms into lay language (for audiences) and was believed to fulfil both dramatic and educational functions. In fact prior to undertaking research, the production team were unaware of the existence of breast care nurses, and the team welcomed the introduction of a character who could communicate medical and scientific jargon for Peggy and the audience at home. As the story editor explains:

> I thought 'Great!' because there's someone who can convey the medical jargon in lay terms to Peggy, and that character therefore seems more interesting than the doctor because [doctors] are in and out, they have busy rounds. [Doctors] come in, spout something at you and go. We could build up the character of this nurse and her role in persuading Peggy that an operation would be the best thing for her. It also fulfils the function of being educational in that it actually tells the viewers 'This is the sort of thing that could happen to you if you went into hospital, you would have a nice friendly breast care nurse there helping you through it.' We were being responsible and dramatic and fulfilling a character function as well.

It is simply not the case, however, that all oncology units do have breast care nurses attached. This character undoubtedly presented particularly positive messages concerning patient choice and control over treatment options. Interestingly, it was precisely these elements of the storyline – the breast care nurse and the strong positive messages about treatment options – which attracted some criticism in the press, which dubbed the story 'didactic'.

Members of the production team at *Brookside* circumvented the issue of medical terminology entirely, with scripts which made reference to treatment in passing comments such as 'lots of women get lumps – it could be nothing'. Partly this was due to the central storyline theme of 'new relationships', but it was also due in part to the dramatic requirements of television serials, which, perhaps surprisingly, are considered to work against repetition. As the programme had covered the same topic just two years previously, the danger now was in replaying scenes and using lines that audiences could still remember. As one production team source explains:

> One of the things in a story like that which is a long runner is you don't want to repeat the scenes, although it might be useful in some sense for new viewers. That's where you have to get the distinction right between the drama and a health education video.

An additional, related concern was the problem of including colloquial language in scripts. In other words, how can cancer of the breast be discussed in a realistic yet inoffensive way? Some writers believed that the scripts should reflect gender differences in everyday talk, but felt constrained when faced with writing lines for a male character. As one writer describes it:

> Most men don't call a breast a breast and people can become desensitised with the medical jargon. A lot of men have a great deal of difficulty saying 'breast' so they use euphemisms . . . men don't say things like 'she has a problem with her breast'. They are more likely to say 'she's got a problem with her boobs'. Men have problems saying 'nipple' and I think it's because [the word] is couched in sexuality. Up on screen I don't think the word 'nipple' was used once. If a woman was describing where the lump was in the breast, she would use anatomical reference points, wouldn't she? Because of British reserve, everyday talk could not become everyday on screen, and the people who look through scripts decide which words we can use.

Language is a key area for potential change and reflects wider social and sexual mores. Despite enjoying a public profile as a programme which pushes boundaries, *Brookside* encountered problems with portraying a gay character, Gordon Collins, who featured in early programme episodes. The programme was unable to use the word 'homosexual' in scripts. Over a period of time, however, as the programme developed, the word (which now seems entirely outdated) was used without any problems.

The Role of Suspense and Narrative Pace

Production staff would agree that breast cancer is a serious topic requiring sensitive handling, but the ways in which the issue was packaged for audiences become classic soap opera territory. The potential difficulties of playing a storyline concerned with serious illness thus become largely subsumed in the soap 'tricks' which make unpalatable storylines pleasurable for audiences and drive the plot forward. The suspense and drama of the story were created by the technique of 'shared secrets'. This is exemplified in *EastEnders* characters Peggy and Tiffany, who develop elaborate 'cover stories' to ensure that Peggy's hospital appointments remain secret. Thus in at least eight different scenarios Peggy and Tiffany are forced to invent shopping trips or dental appointments to conceal hospital consultations. Tension is built for audiences not simply in terms of Peggy's cancer (is her lump benign or malignant? will she live or die?) but crucially in terms of her relationships (will Grant discover where she is really going? will George suspect the truth about their relationship split?). Such devices add pathos to key scenes in Peggy's treatment path. Audiences know that she is terrified and about to discover her biopsy results, but must watch as she is casually castigated by her son Grant for pestering Tiffany to accompany her to 'the dentist'.

The hospital scenes are also played for narrative pace. In one episode where Peggy waits for results of her breast lump biopsy, tension builds slowly as the camera returns on at least three occasions to show her still waiting, alone outside the consultation room. Just as she is finally called in to the consulting room, daughter-in-law Tiffany arrives to lend support. As the doctor begins to tell Peggy the news the camera again cuts away, cheating audiences of the diagnostic moment. It is only when Peggy re-emerges that she herself reveals her fate, uttering the words 'I've got cancer.' The episode then cuts immediately to the signature tune in a classic cliff-hanger.

Similar narrative tension is set up in the *Brookside* story, with suspense resting not simply on whether Patricia's cancer has returned but on whether her ex-husband Max will discover her secret. Audiences' prior knowledge is drawn upon as Max and Susannah make increasingly insensitive remarks about Patricia 'playing games'. Patricia makes similarly loaded references to 'the rest of my life', says 'you'll never see me again', and refers to 'my future'. These phrases now have added resonance for audiences who share her secret and who know that Max and Susannah are excluded from this knowledge. However, narrative pace is not always viewed positively, and the conclusion to this breast cancer storyline did generate some tensions between writers and production hierarchy. In particular, some writers were critical of the decision to leave the conclusion unresolved. In the final episode of the week-long story, Patricia receives the results of her biopsy but rushes out of the hospital without revealing her results to Max – thus denying audiences the pleasure of 'knowing'. One production source explains their dissatisfaction with this decision:

It's very *Brookside* that you leave things open to interpretation. So if you want to bring a character back, you haven't said concretely 'Oh I haven't got [breast cancer]' or 'This is my intended plan.' It's to do with the programme really, but on this occasion it did irk us. It was quite a cruel thing to do really. Partly it did fit with the Pat character – you know, 'You've got your life, Max, and you're not particularly interested in mine. Why should I give you details so that you can sleep cosily at night?' But it just seemed too bitchy.

The Issue 'on Screen'

A medical issue such as breast cancer presents some more practical challenges for soap opera. Production staff who worked on *EastEnders* spoke of the problems that radical, body-altering surgery, such as mastectomy, can present for a character who will potentially remain in the programme long after the issue has been resolved. The problem of continuity was cited as one of the reasons why the team decided that Peggy should have a 'less visible' lumpectomy rather than mastectomy (although the story was revisited and she does in fact have a mastectomy). A member of the production team who was involved in the story explained that 'We have to think about costume and what it's going to look like afterwards and what we're lumbering ourselves with. I know that sounds like an awful thing to say, but you have to think about that for a long-term character.' The production worker also recalled continuity problems with a character in another programme who had a foot amputation: 'They forgot about it once and walked around normally. They had terrible continuity problems.' Finally, however, the decision that she should have a lumpectomy at this particular stage was vindicated by research findings and viewed positively by source organisations for communicating the fact that 'a mastectomy is not necessary in all breast cancer cases'.

The *Brookside* team did experience continuity problems in portraying a character who had undergone a mastectomy and the after-effects of chemotherapy. Patricia's wardrobe had to reflect realistically that of a woman self-conscious about her body image, and scenes were edited and reshot to cater for this:

> We had to do a reshoot because Patricia was on screen in a low cut tee shirt and you could see her cleavage. Well, she has only got one breast, so that is a visual thing that has to have a great deal of care taken.

The portrayal of a cancer patient can also be constrained by the willingness and abilities of the actors involved. A common area of concern for women who undergo cancer treatment is the potentially devastating loss of their hair. Indeed there was reportedly strong lobbying for actors in both productions to portray this occasional side effect of chemotherapy, but as one writer revealed, 'then you're talking about contracts and what the actress will do'.[3]

Advice from Outside Agencies

The *EastEnders* production team have on several occasions established collaborations with lobbying/ campaigning groups. The production has had a long involvement with the Terrence Higgins Trust, with whom they liaised over character Mark Fowler, who has become an iconic figure in British television soap opera for his portrayal of an HIV-positive character. As a clearly denoted 'heterosexual' character, Mark could function as a counterpoint to the prevailing myths about HIV and AIDS, challenging victim blame (HIV as affecting only injecting drug users or gay men).[4] The organisation made an agreement with the programme, first, that the character should remain in the storyline for a long period of time and, second, that if the character was to leave it should not be presented as related directly to his illness (Miller et al. 1998). For many years, Mark Fowler symbolised 'living with HIV' in the programme (disclosing his HIV-positive status to a girlfriend in 1990, before it became common knowledge in the fictional community in 1996). The character left the programme in 2003 and we, the viewers, were informed of his death 'off screen' in 2004. The production team reportedly did not wish to depict a death from AIDS-related illness in case it caused undue distress to viewers in a similar position (although this has not been a problem with other health and illness storylines). This story does, however, reflect the contested nature of such collaborations. The Terrence Higgins Trust did not wish to see such a character become ill too swiftly, but the way in which Mark lived a life fairly unhindered by his diagnosis remained a point of criticism for others. Interestingly, Mark acted as a conduit through which bigotry and prejudice could be addressed. Indeed it is worth noting here that Peggy was precisely one of those characters whose reaction to Mark's HIV-positive status revealed deeply held prejudices. The breast cancer story functioned as a way of redeeming her character, and in a Christmas storyline Peggy asks Mark to forgive her lack of understanding.

The extent to which research is undertaken and indeed used to inform a storyline may differ substantially depending on the script writer or particular issue. *EastEnders* engaged breast cancer experts from a number of different cancer organisations and breast cancer charities to advise on story developments and read their scripts. A breast care nurse commented on technical terms. As a spokesperson for one of the charities explains:

> They came to us among others and they did a lot with the Royal Marsden Hospital. [*EastEnders*] wrote the scripts, we commented on what we thought was important, but for medical detail our breast cancer nurse looked through [the script] and advised and said 'Look, there's no way.' I remember some of the [problems] with wardrobe. We went through all the detail of 'Would they have a stethoscope?', what kind of literature they would have in the waiting room, and so our literature was there. It was great our poster was up in the background when the consultant was talking to her. They were obviously trying to make it as real as possible.

It is of course undeniable that these source organisations lack power and ultimate influence over a storyline development. Indeed while source organisations acknowledge the wide reach of soap opera, many of those I spoke with remarked upon the ambiguous nature of any collaboration. As one senior clinician who advised upon both *Brookside* and *EastEnders* breast cancer scripts described it:

> What you wouldn't want is your name to be on the by-line because [soaps] then do with the story what they want. I will give the factual information but I freely acknowledge that this is not a documentary. While we would want to see our name under a *Horizon* programme, in no way would we want to be named alongside a soap storyline, because they will twist the story if it suits them, and that's fine.

Breast cancer, with its powerful association as a 'women's disease', is perhaps most conveniently grafted into the everyday world of the television soap opera with its focus on female experience. The central themes here of denial, concerns about femininity and mutilation of the body, and the ensuing ripples throughout the family dynamics provide significant and rich dramatic potential. In both cases discussed here, the story was given a theme over and above 'breast cancer', with one story concerning 'new relationships' and another addressing the theme of 'denial'. The familiar devices of shared secrets and prior knowledge were used in both cases to engender audience sympathies; thus both stories are interwoven with unjust accusations from other characters who do not have the vital information that audiences have – these women are at serious risk of a potentially fatal disease.

In the next chapter I discuss how production decisions were made concerning storylines with a theme of mental distress, before reflecting upon some of the commonalities and differences between programmes and topics.

Notes

1 *Brookside* revisited breast cancer in episodes which were broadcast over the period of just one week; however, *EastEnders* developed Peggy's breast cancer story over several months.

2 The organisation was not named specifically within the fictional storyline, but the association was worthwhile in terms of 'spinoff' publicity. Thus the PR officer who had suggested this story was invited to take part in a Radio 4 special session discussing controversial issues in TV fiction.

3 The loss of hair following chemotherapy is a concern for women with a breast cancer diagnosis. This was remarked upon by some of the cancer support organisations. As one source explained, 'On our help line when women ring up the big thing is losing hair. It's a terrible thing and that's what they really worry about. It would have been a good thing to be able to touch on it and I think for [Peggy] to have been mortified by that would have been much more powerful than any long-drawn-out radiotherapy. Barbara Windsor [the actor] is so well coiffured and manicured. She may have said "I'm not having any of that" – as an actress [she could] just refuse to do it.'

4 A study by British children's charity Barnardo's revealed that for seven out of ten children, soap opera provides the main source of information about HIV/AIDS. At the time of the research it is likely that Mark Fowler featured in episodes discussing his HIV status (Barnardo's 1993).

CHAPTER 5

Casting the Outsiders: Mental Distress

Introduction

On 19 April 2000 British audiences saw series 6 of the prime-time US medical drama *ER* conclude in typically dramatic fashion with the double stabbing of two popular characters by a disturbed patient. Lucy Knight, a young medical student, does not survive. John Carter, a resident and firmly established favourite with audiences, is left badly injured. Less than a month later a report entitled 'The Psychokiller Strikes Again' appeared in the *British Medical Journal* (Condren and Byrne 2000). The authors condemned the programme unreservedly for misrepresenting the incidence of violent psychiatric patients. Condren and Byrne had watched the other twenty-two episodes of the series and identified twenty-eight patients as, in their view, representing characters with 'psychiatric problems'. A large proportion were depicted as violent (a man smashes his car because of 'demons', a child kills another child, a woman stalks a doctor). Their view was conclusive: the dominant theme presented was one of 'threat'. As they describe it:

> The series, in making such a strong association between psychiatric illness and violence, is following established trends in television news, drama and the tabloid press. It is adding to the process of stigmatisation by the media. (Condren and Byrne 2000)

The executive producer of *ER*, Neal Baer, was swift to respond on a number of counts (Baer 2000). First, he disputed that the patient responsible for the attack on the two medics had indeed launched an 'unprovoked' attack. He highlighted the way the team had slowly built the portrayal of the patient descending into paranoia (for example, begging the medics to stop during a routine lumbar puncture). He disagreed with the retrospective analysis of other episodes, and instead cited numerous instances where medical staff are portrayed as quite clearly helping those in mental distress (a patient who has suffered from psychosis is supported in keeping her baby, a child who injures himself is discovered to be suffering severe side effects from medication). In conclusion he refers to the *ongoing* nature of prime-time drama – John Carter, the victim of the knife attack, becomes dependent on fentanyl and needs the support of colleagues to survive and save his career (Baer 2000: 157). Baer lists a number of weighty institutional collaborations over programme content, including psychiatrists from the National Institutes of Health, UCLA, and Harvard, and ends with the following words:

> In the future, we hope that researchers take a less selective view of the show to bolster their simplistic claims. We welcome debate and responsible dialogue about the depiction of psychiatric patients, and we certainly will strive in the future to be more compassionate in our portrayals, particularly because viewers do form opinions about psychiatric illnesses, at least in part, by what they see on television. We ask in return that researchers like Condren and Byrne present a fairer analysis of the stories. After all, we share the same goal: to portray psychiatric disorders honestly, informatively, and with empathy. (Baer 2000: 157)

This exchange illustrates some useful points and throws into focus the conflict in values which exists between programme makers and those who lobby from a public health perspective. Television fiction is under significant scrutiny, but retrospective analyses of episodes often miss the contextual cues that are understood by audiences and production staff alike. Viewers thus bring all of their previous knowledge to a programme. This episode is likely to be received in a particular historical context: not just across one series but across several *years*. In other words, audiences will have watched characters such as John Carter prior to the 'stabbing' episode and will continue watching long after researchers have finished with their study. These are important points and allude rightly to the nature of serial drama. This does not mean that mapping the contours of a social problem or health issue through basic content analysis is unimportant, but simply that it is necessarily a limited method by which we can tap into production motivations or impact on audiences.

What this example highlights is a serious concern with negative media coverage of mental distress. This has proved surprisingly resistant to change. Mental distress, particularly acute conditions such as schizophrenia, is commonly linked to violence in media accounts. This is significantly consistent, across format (from television news to entertainment) and geography (UK, USA and European media).[1] Characters with mental illnesses depicted in entertainment media are frequently defined solely in terms of their illness (Sieff 2003: 262). Camera angles as well as lighting and music are believed to contribute to signifying the 'dangerousness' of mentally ill characters in television drama (Wilson et al. 1999). Mental illness and public prejudice have a trajectory which predates modern media and is deeply ingrained culturally (Signorielli 1993), but the consistent and frequent portrayal in the media of those in distress as dangerous and volatile does little to support initiatives which seek to present users of services as active citizens.[2]

There are a large number of content analyses of different media output and mental health (Sieff 2003), but as I have pointed out earlier, we know very little about how and why these specific images are produced and what factors influence decision making at the point of production. Most studies conducted in the field of media and mental distress conclude by pleading for greater understanding (and accuracy) on the part of media personnel, but arguably this seems unlikely to change without better understanding how such items are produced.

In this chapter I examine media values which influence how mental distress is represented in television drama. I am less concerned here with correlations between fiction and accuracy than with wider questions of how and why fictional characters with mental health problems are introduced to programme narratives and their role. In analysing common patterns of coverage across diverse media formats, it is sometimes easy to overlook differences and specificities of genre. As Harper suggests, we should explore 'how madness is used metaphorically, particularly within fictional forms' (Harper 2005: 478).[3] In particular the chapter explores the factors which influenced the production team from *Coronation Street* in constructing a storyline about a young woman, Carmel, who suffers from the condition erotomania.

It is, however, also worth reflecting back to *Brookside*'s characterisation of Trevor (Chapter 3). Although *Brookside* personnel would deny that they were in fact portraying someone who was mentally ill, believing that Trevor's behaviour was open to interpretation, audiences, wider media coverage and indeed other fictional characters in the story 'framed' his character as 'mad'. As we see later, Trevor's portrayal conjured up all the images of a stereotypical psychopath for audiences (Chapter 7). Trevor may have been perceived as 'mentally ill' partly because of the lack of motivations included in the storyline for his behaviour. The *Brookside* production team had purposely left a 'gap' to explain his actions. Thus the producer had resisted Trevor being a drunk on the grounds that he wanted to 'take away his excuses'. The 'gap' was filled for audiences, it would seem, with existing, powerful media images of the mentally ill.

The point here is not to argue that sexual abusers are 'in reality' motivated by mental health problems, but, as we shall see, there are interesting similarities in how the two portrayals of Carmel and Trevor were constructed. It may therefore be possible to identify shared production values across different programmes in relation to specific social issues regardless of programme or production staff members. The chapter closes with reflections on producing social issue storylines in television fiction.

Background to the Stories

In March 1993 *Coronation Street* ran a storyline in which Carmel, who is a young Irish nanny, develops an erotic obsession with one of the central characters. Carmel moves in with Gail and Martin Platt to take care of their children – this family is long established in the programme. Carmel becomes obsessed with Martin and fantasises that she is his wife and the mother of his children. One evening when Gail is away Carmel slips into bed with Martin, who has been drinking. She convinces him, falsely, that they slept together. The story culminates in Carmel's (false) announcement that she is pregnant with Martin's child. In dramatic scenes Gail eventually confronts her. The two women struggle physically and Carmel falls down stairs. She is taken to hospital, where we discover that she is not in fact pregnant. Carmel's grandfather arrives to explain that this is a recurring pattern – she has been obsessed with married men in the past.

Generating the Story

Soap opera storylines are of course frequently suggested during the regular story conference where the producer, story editor and script writers quite simply sit around a table and discuss potential future plots. The Carmel story was suggested in one such meeting, and a *Coronation Street* writer describes the routine process:

> There are about fourteen script writers on the programme, and what happens is we have a story conference every third Monday and basically we just float ideas around the room, and then it is discussed from that point on and plotted through. We are actually four months ahead with story lines.

As I pointed out earlier (Chapter 3), the characterisation of Trevor in *Brookside*'s sexual violence story clearly referenced Hollywood films (*Sleeping with the Enemy* and *Fatal Attraction*). The production team at *Coronation Street* also drew upon specific Hollywood films to develop the character of what they termed the 'psycho nanny'. Indeed the production team members even referenced the same film – *Fatal Attraction* – which gave rise to the term 'bunny boiler'. This is of course a derogatory term used to reference a woman with an unreciprocated erotic obsession. In addition *The Hand that Rocks the Cradle* (Buena Vista, 1992) specifically involves a nanny who has lost her own husband and baby and who seeks revenge on the woman she blames. Both of these films portray a family unit torn apart by a 'disturbed' and potentially violent and vengeful (single) female, and can be seen to form part of a 'wave' of Hollywood films which focus on the threat of female power (Faludi 1992). As we shall see, this intertextuality plays a key role in how audiences respond to characterisations.

The concept of a woman obsessed instantly gripped the imagination of the production team. The storyline crucially conformed to the classic soap opera ingredients of high suspense and drama. It terrified audiences who watched a 'disturbed' and manipulative woman threaten the security of a regular (white, heterosexual) family. As the producer describes it here, the character was a 'catalyst':

> Carmel the nanny from hell, and stories like that are very strong – where you get someone new, like Carmel, who introduces a catalyst into a happy family and suddenly it all sort of festers and turns bad. I mean, there's a really good story. I like those better than in the old days – a train crashes into a viaduct.

Here we can see how this new character is clearly assigned a function in the text: to destroy the equilibrium, in this case of a 'happy family'.[4]

Casting and Characterisation

As I explained earlier, the *Brookside* production team prioritised 'suspense' in casting the role of Trevor. The production team at *Coronation Street* had remarkably similar concerns, and deliberately selected an actor who was described by one as source as having 'the face of an angel', in order to conceal, in their words, the 'underlying terror'. There are clear echoes here of the tag lines used to promote *The Hand that Rocks the Cradle* ('Behind a beautiful face, beneath a dangerous smile, lies a revenge that can't be stopped'). Fresh-faced actor Catherine Cusack was cast to appear 'normal' to audiences and disguise her 'true character'. Indeed a new actor was introduced primarily to 'keep audiences guessing', for, as the producer explains, 'If we introduced a character we might say "[She's] got to have a secret", "What is [her] secret?" ' A new character without prior history in the programme could therefore generate and maintain audience suspense. As a script writer confirms:

> It was very important in the casting to believe that [Carmel] was this home-loving girl, because if you did cast somebody slightly dodgy then it immediately gave it [the story twist] away.

It is instructive that priorities of viewer suspense played a central role in decision making over two characters described by audience members as symbolising someone who was 'mad' (Philo 1996a). As with the child abuser Trevor, these roles involved manipulative outsiders. Incidentally, Carmel and Trevor were both cast as Irish, which further underlines their 'otherness' within the community.

The Issue 'on Screen': Language and Imagery

Developing scripts in which pejorative language associated with stigma was used to denote mental distress did not appear to be a problem. Indeed, the question of 'language' was not raised as a potential problem in relation to Carmel or Trevor. Both were constructed as unpredictable and manipulative, and were clearly referred to as having mental health problems by other characters in the community. Thus Trevor was described frequently as 'a nutter' and Carmel was referred to as 'possessed' and in need of 'a damn good psychiatrist'. Members of the production teams deny that it was their intention to fuel existing prejudice about acute mental distress. Indeed, as I have pointed out earlier, the *Brookside* team did not even view Trevor's character as necessarily 'mentally ill', preferring to blame audience responses on the associated media coverage, which dubbed him 'psycho Trevor'. As the producer explains:

> We never said Trevor was mentally ill. It was the media itself putting on words like 'psycho Trevor'. We'd set out to say we don't know what caused [his behaviour]. It might be mental illness. We don't know.

No problems were anticipated with any particular scene or imagery in the Carmel storyline. This is in marked contrast to the dilemmas which production staff recalled when producing storylines on other topics. However, it may also reflect the perceptions of the production team and their approach to the story theme. The *Brookside* team were more concerned with building audience fear and hate towards Trevor to legitimise Mandy's actions than developing his character, and quite clearly did not consider themselves to be contributing to a portrayal of someone in mental distress. This may be understandable, as the central storyline involved commitments to other areas (such as domestic violence, sexual abuse). However, Carmel was from the outset constructed as someone with a mental health condition (albeit a rare one), and it is all the more surprising that the production team did not even consider themselves as having a professional commitment to a mental health story. In other words, Carmel was considered to provide a 'good strong story line' which would transfix audiences rather than providing an account of a young woman in distress. Audiences were, however, left in doubt as to how Carmel should be perceived. In one scene, Gail finally confides her suspicions about the nanny, saying 'Her eyes were cold, it was like she was possessed. She means to take Martin away from me. You didn't see her eyes. She says she will stop at nothing and I believe her.'

The Role of Suspense and Narrative Pace

The familiar dramatic technique of 'shared secrets' was used throughout the Carmel story. Indeed the producer termed this technique the 'panto syndrome'. Thus the story was carefully constructed to allow viewers more information than the protagonists. Audiences knew that Carmel was not to be trusted but other characters did not. As the producer outlines it:

> It's almost like 'He's behind you!' That syndrome where the audience is saying 'You fool!' Where you [the viewer] know that the author lets you into information where you see both characters' lives but they're not privy to that information.

This knowledge adds significantly to the pleasures afforded the soap audience, who can then speculate on future story twists, enjoying the dramatic tension even if their predictions are proved to be wrong (Buckingham 1987: 67–9). Producers use such techniques to draw audiences in to the unfolding narrative. Some argue that in so doing producers oversimplify complex issues and envisage audiences as fundamentally childlike. As Seale describes it, 'scapegoats, stereotypes, heroes, fools, victims, and villains are lined up in a pantomime-like collage of fragments to create an emotional drama' (Seale 2002: 35). Production team members have a powerful belief in the necessity of narrative pace and consider this a firm audience requirement. In the words of one experienced drama writer, 'we must keep telling stories or risk losing momentum' – and more importantly, of course, audiences. As I pointed out earlier, this momentum is vital not only within the context of one specific episode but in terms of ensuring audience interest from one episode to the next, and thus is particularly important for drama *serial*. A television serial will concentrate and condense storylines, balancing what might be considered to be realistic time scales with audiences' viewing pleasures. The producer of *Brookside* justified this as follows:

You have to remember that the audience are rather fickle and switch in and out of soaps. They also like pace or the audience starts to think 'Oh, is this still going on?' So even though the audience say they like reality, they sometimes don't.

This rapid turnover of storylines has been considered to have a very negative impact on those who experience periods of distress and who see fictional characters move swiftly from illness to health (Philo 1996a). However, one script writer justified the priorities of the genre by arguing that stories are simply 'concentrated in a way that's not absolutely true to get the maximum drama out of them, and to get the debate seriously going about what happens in real life'. Indeed narrative pace and the ways in which stories are developed dramatically are viewed as 'fixed' priorities for the genre. The producer of *Brookside* denied that Trevor was constructed as a stereotypical psychopath simply to draw in audiences, and yet at the same time he comments that a 'good' storyline is not worthwhile unless there are audiences willing to watch it;

We only do this so that people can watch! That's the point. There's no point in doing this and thinking 'Oh we've lost, no one's watching it', so we knew we had to make them watch it.

Audiences were gripped by the tense build-up to killing Trevor. The scene offered a compelling mix of intense pleasure and horror. One writer involved in this particular episode described his shock at the response this scene generated from his own (young) daughter:

I've always brought her up to be this mild-mannered, placid person, and she's sitting there watching it as the murder [scene] is going out, and she was sitting there on the couch and she was getting, her cheeks were going red so I knew she was anxious. She was watching, her eyes were glued to the screen, and when [Trevor] started thumping Beth she stood up in the room and was like 'Kill him!' I [thought] I've wasted years of 'Let's be Ghandi-like.' She was saying 'Kill him, Kill him!' I thought, I better have a word with you later.

Indeed, audiences experienced similar feelings of intense hatred and violence towards Carmel. When asked how they would have dealt with the situation if they had been in Gail's position, the response was unequivocal. About two-thirds of the respondents who took part in a research study of media and mental distress responded that they would have acted with aggression or violence towards her (Philo 1996b). Responses ranged in tone from 'slapped her' to 'assaulted her' and even 'killed her'. One respondent who was a psychiatric nurse said he would have 'involved psychiatry/police', but the overwhelming response was a desire to harm this woman physically. The formation of such responses is complex, as Philo points out, but it does seem to suggest that media representations of this type can interrelate very powerfully with direct experience to produce extraordinary affective responses (Philo 1996a: 90–4).

Advice from Outside Agencies

Socially realistic issue storylines generally do provoke particular challenges for production teams. The issue must be at least perceived as having been handled with some degree of 'responsibility' and 'sensitivity' in order to maintain public credibility and bear the scrutiny of campaigning groups. Productions typically employ full-time research staff, yet the level of research undertaken and the extent to which it might be used to inform storylines differ substantially between programmes and indeed with the working practices of the script writers involved. It is interesting that *Coronation Street* did not feel obliged to take any special advice on Carmel's condition. In fact, this character was 'fleshed out' simply on the basis of a single article published in the American magazine *Vanity Fair* (September 1991). As one team member describes it:

> We used that article and that would really explain to you about the whole psychology of Carmel. It is a brilliant article based on a couple of case studies in America. There were loads of court cases about it and a really long trial. The actual story did come about before we heard about the article so that's not really what triggered it off, but as part of the research when we read that it really helped to bring the storyline together. In the conferences as well *all the writers were discussing it*. (emphasis added)

The condition of erotomania is extremely rare, but obsession and stalking are recurrent popular storylines in television fiction. In this instance Carmel becomes erotically fixated on her employer, Martin, who works as a nurse, but more typically the object of obsession is of high status and not known personally to the sufferer. The executive producer proposed that the rarity of a condition portrayed is simply not a problem – 'If it has happened, we can do it.' Sometimes the commitment to a 'strong story' can override other concerns, but it is wrong to assume that mental distress cannot be dealt with sensitively in these formats.

In the past the BBC attracted praise for their sensitive portrayal of Joe Wicks, a young *EastEnders* character suffering from schizophrenia. Indeed the mental health campaign organisation MIND presented the programme with an award for the positive way in which this character was developed. Significantly, the story editor had worked previously on BBC medical drama *Casualty*, and was keen to develop a storyline which could move away from the necessarily medicalised focus of this genre to explore the implications of schizophrenia within a family. The television soap opera with its continuing storyline and emphasis on family life offered precisely this opportunity. As he explains:

> When I did the research I was shocked to discover that schizophrenia affects one in 100 people, and yet nobody ever talks about it . . . *EastEnders* was able to look at the effect that schizophrenia has on a family and on individual relationships. I wanted to humanise it and look at the emotional impact it has on people. (Schizophrenia Home Page 1997)

The characterisation was based on advice from a professional advisor to the National Schizophrenia Fellowship, Dr Adrianne Revely, who later described her experiences with the *EastEnders* team in the *British Medical Journal*. Revely highlights the dilemma for those who consult on storylines and the significant responsibilities such a role entails, not least to their professional colleagues:

> Advising *EastEnders* on their schizophrenia story should be highlighted in red ink on my curriculum vitae. Everyone has been impressed . . . I must really know my stuff if *EastEnders* used me as a source. Of course the downside is that every jarring nuance of the story and every inaccuracy is laid at my door, and there have been plenty of inaccuracies . . . The basic story – Joe's initial diagnosis of psychotic depression and then the diagnosis of schizophrenia – remains true to life. I have begged for the storyline to include modern treatment with a limbic-selective antipsychotic, good response, return to normal life, followed by scenes in which Joe experiences stigma. Stigma is a key issue that we want to be aired, and of course, the very fact that there is an *EastEnders* story at all is destigmatising. Schizophrenia is the last great stigma. (Revely 1997: 1560)

The point I wish to make here is that the substantive topic which forms the basis of a storyline is important; so too is how the topic is positioned culturally. However, an additional factor is the story theme. It would simply be wrong to assume that the *Coronation Street* team developed Carmel in such a way deliberately to fuel prejudice and misconceptions about those with mental health problems. However, here mental illness was used to structure a story on the theme of obsession and undoubtedly intersected with existing public views about those who are mentally ill (as violent, duplicitous). By contrast, the *EastEnders* story of Joe Wicks was from the outset perceived as 'doing mental illness', and was developed accordingly with care and sensitivity. Quite clearly, the consultant who represented the views of the National Schizophrenia Fellowship to the programme was impressed by the commitment of the production team to the issue and saw it as a positive challenge to public misconceptions. In other words, I am not arguing that television soap opera or other forms of serial drama will inevitably portray mental distress negatively. However, it seems clear that characters such as Carmel and Trevor, *regardless of the productions' intentions*, became part of a wider cultural repertoire of media images in which the mentally ill are demonised. The appropriation of conventions used in iconic Hollywood films can operate as important cultural signifiers for audiences and contribute to this process.

Production team members have diverse responsibilities, to audiences, to the programme, to their professional culture. Sometimes there is significant resistance to the levels of criticism that they face, not least from academics. One experienced script writer concluded our interview with the following words:

> In the end we are drama. We're not a sociological documentary or a guide book for sociologists, and although we try not to go terribly wrong we sometimes ignore the truth in favour of a good story, and have to do so because, well, you know, you just have to do so. If we always stuck to the absolute facts we'd have no drama.

Although, as I have noted, the 'truth' and 'absolute facts' are themselves frequently contested, it is important that source organisations understand the conflicting priorities which exist and which can sometimes undermine or obstruct a commitment to a specific issue. Source organisations may assume that responsibility is always directed towards the issue, because for them it is an obvious priority. However, as we have seen, there are other responsibilities which must be balanced by the production team members and which have consequences for how storylines are developed.

Reflections on Producing Social Issues in TV Fiction

Diverse factors influence how a social issue is developed within television fiction. Their significance depends not only on the substantive topic under discussion but also on the production philosophies of team members and the overall programme ethos.

It is illuminating to reflect upon the process by which the different storylines were generated (Chapters 3, 4 and 5). Certainly the timing of the incest/sexual violence storylines may be most explicitly linked to commercial imperatives. Both programmes used issue storylines (coincidentally both involved the same territory – sexual violence) to signal a new direction to audiences. Indeed the incentive for developing both of these storylines came from senior management (of the programme and of the broadcasting organisation). Although commercial imperatives are important for all programmes, it is interesting that certain issues which might be expected to alienate audiences were used effectively to increase their ratings. We have also seen that social issues are introduced into soap opera storylines for other reasons as well (to raise the profile of a character, to resonate with audiences) and by different routes (from script writers, from outside organisations lobbying the programme).

The decision-making process which concerns casting the role is absolutely crucial to how a storyline will play for audiences. The 'look' and familiarity (or unfamiliarity) of an actor selected to take on a serious issue storyline is to a large extent a powerful device to help structure audience response. The decision to run a storyline with an existing member of the cast or to introduce a new character to develop it also tells us something of the cultural significance of an issue. In this sense, casting the breast cancer survivor from within the community (with well-loved, strong female characters) was a decision based on the team's detailed knowledge of their audience. Viewers were thus invited to engage and identify with a serious illness storyline in ways that simply would not be possible with a new cast member. By contrast, the unpredictable and violent Carmel and Trevor were clearly marked out as 'outsiders' in the soap community, not only unknown but with a different ethnic identity to underline their 'difference'. Both characters were brought in especially for these roles and simply left the production when the story was resolved. Whether or not such casting is coincidental, it both resonates with certain stereotypes about Irish immigrants to Britain and signals their status to viewers as outwith the 'British' community portrayed in the programmes. The character of Mandy proved difficult to integrate despite the efforts of programme makers. The main concern here was to generate audience empathy for her position. Viewer letters and responses from audiences (Chapter 7) suggest that she was not successful in attracting the sympathy of viewers, far less their empathy. She was not only a new character without established loyalty, but also a mother who takes back the man who she knows has sexually abused her daughter. In so doing Mandy allows Trevor to abuse their daughter Rachel. She is thus held responsible by audiences for her inability to act.

Other factors have been identified as important, among them not simply whether a character is unknown as opposed to 'established', but also the 'look' of an actor. Again, this was a significant factor in casting Carmel, with the 'face of an angel', and Trevor, known to British audiences from previous roles as a 'likeable guy' whom audiences might trust. Other considerations such as 'looking young' play a role in casting the troubled sexually abused teenager. Audiences must of course respond to the characterisation as realistic, but this must be balanced by ethical considerations which govern casting a genuinely young woman to play difficult scenes.

The extent to which language and imagery present problems depends on the substantive topic. The linguistic terms which may be used to refer to sexual violence or to physical or mental illness are to an extent culturally dictated. However, there is little doubt that it is precisely this area in which soap opera can shift social mores. The level of care taken over medical terminology in breast cancer scripts reflects the commitment to the issue. This can again be contrasted with the approach taken to mental distress. The use of pejorative language which littered scripts referring to Carmel and Trevor might reflect everyday talk, but is unlikely to be seen or permitted with other, more socially approved illnesses. The sexual content of storylines provides the production team with clear challenges in terms of legal restraints and audience sensibilities, involving senior management and regulatory boards, but also undoubtedly involving judicious self-censorship on the part of the producers.

The heavily regulated pre-watershed broadcast environment is an important constraint on story development. Senior management certainly played the most visible role in policing the sexual violence stories (scenes were specifically revised in line with regulations, reshot if necessary and certainly edited and revised). The breast cancer storylines presented more practical problems of wardrobe, and production staff revealed an extraordinary commitment to realism (although some aspects which might be viewed as important to source organisations, such as hair loss, are not always possible). Mental illness as it was developed in the Carmel story may not command the same level of social respect as physical illness such as cancer, and indeed is highly stigmatised. In developing the erotically obsessed character Carmel, the production team considered themselves free from the constraints of a heavy 'issue' story. The team simply did not consider themselves to be 'doing' a mental illness story. In addition, if audience ratings are prioritised other concerns can be overridden.

These concerns are also related to the extent to which production teams involve outside source organisations. Indeed the levels of research undertaken or outside advice sought may also signify the socio-cultural positioning of a substantive topic. Here again we might reflect on the absence of liaison between production team and mental health organisations in comparison with other storylines. This suggests that some socially approved illnesses may be handled in particularly sensitive ways. The portrayal of mental distress in TV fiction (portraying a rare condition or developing the character's behaviour in an exaggerated way) has been frequently raised as a problem by campaign groups. As we have seen in the cases discussed earlier, there are concerns which lie beyond simply 'doing research'. The emphasis upon background research differs substantially between programmes and is often regarded as the remit solely of documentaries or 'hard' news programming. It is also at odds with the professional culture of the writers, many of whom have worked in other areas of drama, and with their self-perceptions as creative artists who should be able to describe the human condition without resorting to facts and statistics.

Serial drama is driven by suspense and narrative pace, and this is no less the case with more controversial or socially sensitive issues. All of the storylines discussed here were paced by cliff-hangers, suspense and narrative tension. The cancer storylines were given momentum by the shared secrecy which surrounded the women's diagnoses and their persistent attempts to deceive those closest to them (as well as switching between scenes of Peggy receiving her diagnosis and other, more mundane stories). The sexual violence storylines were similarly given added pace by dramatic disclosures and powerful imagery. Camera close-ups and cut-away shots heightened this tension and were utilised to draw in audiences who might otherwise choose not to watch this type of material.

Although production personnel are careful that the narrative twists used on an issue such as breast cancer do not compromise the overall commitment to a sensitive handling, their priorities were markedly different when dealing with mental distress. The characters of Carmel and Trevor provide classic examples of popular stereotypes of behaviour associated with the unpredictable psychopath – concealing their true nature behind a charming front. These are images which are clearly borrowed from Hollywood tradition. Indeed both were explicitly based on popular films. Camera techniques were used to engender fear in viewers (Carmel's face was frequently lit from beneath, and the camera lingered on Trevor's face, allowing audiences to witness his knowing looks). The panto syndrome, in which viewers know more than characters, is a well-tested convention, and although it is apparent in all of the storylines under discussion, it was maximised in the characterisations of Carmel and Trevor in particular ways and with specific purpose. Both characters were constructed to conceal their true nature from the wider soap community, thus increasing the drama for audiences when their 'real selves' were finally revealed. These characterisations provide powerful illustrations of how the conventions of soap opera may work against positive and more challenging portrayals of acute mental illness.

The storylines which have been discussed here all come within the area of serious social issues, but there is considerable ambivalence about developing research-based storylines. This touches on dilemmas concerning the roles of education and entertainment, research and responsibility. Producers and script writers may be keen to take on a socially important topic for altruistic or commercial reasons. Production personnel frequently celebrated the power of TV fiction to engage with audiences, yet when faced with any critical response to storylines, regard themselves as being free from the responsibilities of factual media formats ('if it has happened we can do it'). The cancer survivors were depicted with extraordinary care and attention to detail. Partly this may be due to the cultural positioning of the topic (its social integration and those it affects, or at least is publicly known to affect). Breast cancer storylines are more likely to attract the attention of high-status medical organisations or well-established scientific research organisations. Perhaps groups which campaign concerning mental distress are considered to be less socially significant, or perhaps they simply lack the resources or social capital to make their voice heard.

In an increasingly commercial climate, the pressures on these producers to maintain programme positioning, audiences and advertisers are intense. Indeed the extent to which the 'organic' soap storyline philosophy can be applied is surely questionable, if indeed it was ever genuinely possible. It is, however, certain that members of the production team are keen nonetheless to maintain their personal integrity and programme credibility with audiences. The perceived ethos and reputation of a programme are crucial to audience acceptance of a public issue storyline. While a programme can attempt to challenge public opinion on social issues, audiences' perceptions of programme identity are crucial. Both *Emmerdale* and *Coronation Street* have attracted extensive negative publicity over decisions to portray 'gritty' storylines (for example on lesbianism and domestic violence). In part criticism was directed towards the subject matter, but both programmes were undeniably judged harshly for changing their original, 'soft' human-interest remit to pursue storylines which would attract press headlines and also, implicitly, audiences.

Production team members do bring all of their personal experiences, ideologies, prejudices and misconceptions to a storyline. However, the team is managed tightly. In the negotiating process some voices are more powerful than others. In any struggle over content or direction it is senior management who will have the final say. Conflicts may arise when writers believe that their personal integrity is threatened, and staff turnover can be triggered by a new direction for a programme, which is typically announced by the arrival of new senior management.

In identifying the different ways in which diverse issues are mediated by the soap opera production process, we can see that fictional television is certainly not free from all constraints. Indeed soap opera may be under even more pressure, given that these storylines are a commercially produced product. The genre allows audiences literally to go 'behind closed doors' and witness difficult moments (illness, physical violence), but there are many socially important but 'visually dull' dimensions to social issues, and these are sometimes deemed expendable. Ultimately, the production vision of 'what audiences want' and the elements which are considered to constitute a 'strong storyline' provide the most powerful constraints on programme making. I return to some of these lines of debate in conclusion (Chapter 8).

The following chapter reflects on the importance of genre and substantive topic, and discusses the experiences of television personnel involved in developing storylines concerning mental distress in medical drama and in reporting on mental distress for documentary television series.

Notes

1 Media coverage is considered to play a significant role in fuelling public prejudice and contributing to stigmatisation (Wahl 1995; Philo 1996a, 1996b;). Acute conditions such as schizophrenia have attracted particularly negative coverage. In one study, when the general public were asked about appropriate treatment for schizophrenia as many as 95 per cent agreed with enforced treatment – evidence that perceptions of danger perpetuated by media reporting have a role to play in creating cultural acceptance of coerced treatment (Wahl 2003b: 1596). Persistent stereotypes are considered to have an impact on policy decisions: John Hinckley Jr., who attempted to assassinate President Ronald Reagan in 1981; Christopher Clunis, who killed a stranger at a London tube station in 1992; and Andrew Goldstein, dubbed 'the subway psycho' for pushing Kendra Webdale onto the subway tracks in New York City in 1999, have become icons of public fear, and their names are symbolic of the failings of the legal and mental health care systems (Wahl 2003b; Hallam 2002). The murder of Swedish foreign minister Anna Lindh in 2003 by a stranger led the Swedish news media to assume swiftly that the perpetrator was mentally ill, 'controlled by voices' and thus inevitably violent (Rasmussen and Hoijer 2005). Images of the mentally ill in other media formats such as children's cartoons and films have been identified as mainly negative (unattractive, violent and criminal) (Wahl 2003a).

2 On the term 'users of services', see Chapter 6, n. 1.

3 Films such as *Shine* (Fine Line Features, 1996) or *A Beautiful Mind* (Universal Pictures, 2001) which present more positive, 'celebratory' images of mental illness have also attracted criticism, in that they are considered to 'present madness as a narrative complication that is relatively easily overcome, resulting in a triumphant emergence into truth and enlightenment' (Harper 2005: 475).

4 On the function of narrative, see Propp 1968; Todorov 1977.

CHAPTER 6

Social Issues, Production and Genre

Introduction

In earlier chapters I have discussed the different forces and processes operating with or upon fictional television in terms of how diverse social issue
storylines are produced. In this chapter I wish to extend this further and
reflect upon the importance of genre. In other words, how are social issues
'packaged' in other television formats? What are the production priorities
in formats such as documentary or single drama series? Are there shared
concerns at the point of production which cut across genre? In this chapter
I thus take one of the substantive issues discussed earlier, mental distress
(Chapter 5), and reflect on how media personnel working in other areas of
television discuss the production process. This highlights how certain
genres may open up different possibilities. Production priorities of narrative pace, audience ratings and constraints from senior management are
considered, and different issues involved in producing factual television,
such as 'casting' users of services[1] in programmes, are discussed.

Mental Distress in Documentary

Production personnel who are involved in making fictional television are
keen to draw a distinction between themselves and factual news media. As
I have noted, a common phrase running through interviews with television
drama production team members was 'We're not a documentary.' This
implies, first, that television fiction should be excused from the need for
factual basis and, secondly, that as a format 'documentary' is inarguably
more concerned with 'truth' and 'facts'. Now clearly truths and facts
are contested and there is no single message which every charity, organisation or affected person would necessarily agree should be promoted in
the media. At the same time, the format of traditional documentary may

initially appear to be a more appropriate space for positive images of mental health. Mentally ill people can appear on screen telling their stories in their own words. However, the production process is more complex than it may appear. First I identify some problems which we might say are fairly specific to the documentary form, and then examine how the constraints of access, medical power, broadcast hierarchy, and assumptions about what constitutes 'good television' influence representation of mental distress.

Medical Power, 'Casting' and Control

Groups who campaign for more accurate representations in the area of mental health consider 'access to the media' as being vital. Users of services have begun to put themselves forward to speak on television and present their views. Indeed the inclusion of survivor voices is considered to be a crucial part of challenging the stigma which surrounds mental health issues. As part of a wider study of mental health and the media (Philo, 1996a), I discussed this with a number of documentary producers working both independently and for organisations such as the BBC. A key factor is the question of how best to access people with mental health problems. One BBC producer outlined the problems she encountered in making a series of films with the patients of one community health team. In her view, although the filming process involved a series of compromises and negotiations, it was still ultimately easier for the production team to record the experiences of people in psychiatric care than other groups of people in distress. Issues of privacy can be minimised by filming within a hospital environment rather than in people's home. Thus in choosing to portray this particular group, programme makers might overcome potential access problems, but the resulting representation is very limited in the range of conditions and treatments which are included. As a producer acknowledges:

> The most controlled way to see someone who was mentally ill was in hospital. We could just be there. We weren't invading their privacy. We could just be there in the ward and we were there for weeks and months. [The patients] would see us around and we became part of this very weird hospital environment, but it completely skewed the sorts of people and the ways we portrayed both mental illness and the way it was treated.

Producers must balance the needs of three groups: the production crew, the medical profession and the patients. Each group has competing priorities, needs and concerns which may actively work against the aims of the others. Key issues here are access and control. Before a production team can even approach someone in psychiatric care, they must first secure the agreement of the medical staff. Sometimes this is considered to disempower those in mental distress:

> The most insidious [problem] is that mental health professionals protect to an unwarranted degree the privacy of their patients. They do that in the very honest belief that if the general public knew that this person had a mental health problem they would be treated less well, they would be shunned and they would be discriminated against. An awful lot of people flatly said 'No, I wouldn't feel happy allowing you anywhere near them.' There is such a medical hierarchy here that the medics by far have the greatest say, and a lot of them felt for the very best of motives [that the patients should not take part], but that took away from the individuals' right to decide what they wanted to do. The question wasn't even put to them.

Medical staff may even use the fear of future stigmatisation to dissuade patients from identifying themselves in a television film. One producer who interviewed mental health patients institutionalised for many years described how medical staff will discourage patients from 'remembering what they have been taught to forget'. As this television producer explains:

> The medical profession have said [to the patients] 'I wouldn't be interviewed if I were you', 'It will get worse when you go out', 'You're going to be stigmatised when you go outside.' That's a very common one, or 'I wouldn't give an interview if I were you because you don't want to remember what happened to you, do you? That's all past now, you're all right now.'

However, all of the producers I spoke with believed, perhaps unsurprisingly, that these medical concerns were unfounded. In their view, positive audience reaction to the material entirely vindicated their decision to film such interviews. As an independent producer commented:

> If you let someone who has been in an institution take the risk and say 'why I was put into x institution' I know from the audience response, from people who ring the [organisation] or who write to me afterwards, that it is sympathetic to that person's point of view. It is less sympathetic to the medical system that put them there. So the stigma is transferred to the medical profession rather than the individual.

Another important factor is the degree of control which medical staff can have over the hospital environment and the patients. This can extend to the finished product, as staff rather than television professionals can decide 'who is seen' and 'when'. One producer saw this as having a profound effect on the series:

> In the mental health arena [the medical profession] are so used to control.
> They control the patients, they control the hospital environments, and
> having a television crew there who aren't subject to your control – they are
> outside of it – is very threatening. So it wasn't always easy to talk to people
> just when you wanted to, and if there hadn't been that degree of second-level
> control going on we would have made a completely different set of programmes.

Once permission is granted by the medical professionals there is the question of gaining patients' consent. Some producers had experiences of filming very distressed people within psychiatric wards, and there were clear ethical considerations. Particularly problematic was the fact that patients who were disturbed might not fully understand the implications of giving their consent. Medical professionals were acutely aware of their responsibilities as carers to protect the interests of their patients. This was an issue fraught with difficulties and severely jeopardised the level of 'control' which the production team retained over the completed programme:

> When people are extremely ill they are not able to make the decisions they
> would make when they are not ill, so it was very important that [the medical
> profession] had a way of controlling that. But that put huge constraints on
> us as programme makers because the one thing that's very difficult is to give
> up editorial control, because then it becomes a different piece. The only way
> we could get access to patients at all was to agree that they had the right to
> veto once they were well enough to do so.

This veto moved power from the production crew to the medical staff who make decisions over patient participation. The veto also provided an obstacle to the content of the film, which had, in the producer's view, intended to show 'very ill patients, as much as possible'.

The issue of gaining informed consent is more complex than simply securing a signature on a legal document. Patients may experience blackouts or simply not comprehend the full implications of giving permission. Patients may have literacy problems or be unable to understand the legal wording on forms. Techniques designed by producers to communicate the experience of being filmed included showing programme participants their interview on a television monitor. One producer, however saw the concept of 'informed consent' as ultimately impossible. As she says:

I would always go to great lengths to explain to someone what we're going to do, [but] I think there is a limit to how successful this business of asking permission is. What are you asking their permission to do? To cut their half hour interview to ten minutes? I think it's respecting their absolute right to say 'No, I don't want to be filmed', and in that sense it serves a function, but it doesn't get across the nature of the media.

This raises important issues in relation to mental health survivors on television. It seems likely that questions of ethics will become more heavily debated in connection with the rise in numbers of non-professional actors in contemporary broadcasting. Clearly, it is almost impossible to predict quite how people will find their lives altered by their appearance on television and to prepare them for this. A recent study which explored the experiences of reality television participants found that many people appeared to underestimate seriously the cost to their personal lives (Hibberd et al. 2000).

Self-Selecting Patients

Another factor raised by producers was that patients are 'self-selecting', which meant that the range of mental health problems was not represented. One producer believed that by this process of self-selection, the patients themselves contributed to the unbalanced picture which exists. In her view, if someone has been diagnosed as 'chronic schizophrenic' or 'psychotic' then there is little to lose by identifying themselves on television:

> Patients were very self-selective and I think this affects the image that comes across about mental health in documentary. There are only certain sorts of people who feel able to stand up and say 'I have a mental illness and this is what it means for me and here I am.' The image of mental illness is very weighted towards the very extreme end of mental illness, [because] people who are seriously ill have very little to lose. We got a couple of personality disorders, some people with manic depression, and they would say 'yes' to begin with, but they had too much to lose by it and were too afraid of what their friends, neighbours, colleagues would say. The people who did it were almost professionally mentally ill people. The balance was definitely skewed.

The implication here is of course that these are people who will never become well, who are therefore, we might say, 'liberated' from the responsibilities of living in the community where a public appearance on such programmes could contribute negatively to their stigma. This perception neatly transfers responsibility from the producers themselves to the mentally ill patients. The overall framing of such documentaries lies with the production company, and these 'professionally mentally ill' people provide the programme makers with what they consider to be 'good television'.

The Role of Senior Management

A crucial factor which influences media accounts across factual and fictional television is the level of control exerted by the broadcast hierarchy. Production team members are all subject to degrees of control 'from above' or, as one script writer from a medical drama termed it, from 'the people upstairs'. Levels of autonomy differ between programmes, but even independent producers are subject to hierarchical pressures. As one commented:

> Making a documentary is not a democratic process. Even if you're an independent [producer], the money is put up by someone and at the end of the day they have the final decision. They are usually the broadcaster and I think you should never forget that.

These 'final' decisions can focus upon perceived audience needs, and producers may face pressures over content, title or even the accompanying press release. There is often an uneasy relationship between documentary producers and their senior management, who have budgetary and editorial control (Elliot 1992). As Kilborn (2003) points out, changes in broadcasting in the early 1990s, with the appearance of new cable and satellite distribution systems and thematic channels, increased the volatility of the documentary market, with the result that 'most factual/documentary film makers have been forced into some kind of compromise as they become progressively more dependent on their television paymasters. This affects both the subjects they choose and the manner in which they are able to tell their stories' (Kilborn 2003: 32–3). A producer who made a factual film about a psychiatric institution describes her negative experience of organisational hierarchy:

> I think that hierarchically there are pressures to do with content. I did make one documentary where someone very senior said 'It's not shocking enough. It's just not shocking enough.' It was at a viewing and they felt I hadn't made, to put it crudely, as much as I could have done of the material. So against my will it was made more shocking, and one of the senior bosses said 'Look, the switchboard should be jammed after this programme, it should be absolutely jammed', and I found that very difficult. He wasn't necessarily being negative. He might have been saying 'We want outrage because this is an outrageous situation and this is why we made the documentary', but on the other hand I felt the absolute pressure to make it more shocking was questionable.

Decisions concerning the title of a programme are crucial because a 'sexy' title can attract media previews. These in turn are believed to attract audiences. Pressure can thus be brought to bear in relation to how a programme is titled quite simply in order to increase the audience 'hype'. As one source explains:

> That seems of significance because the broadcasters want a title that will catch the eye of newspaper journalists and previewers. So I have had two experiences where I didn't agree at all [with the titles]. I had tried very hard to make these documentaries low key because that material was so awful and people's stories were so tragic, but on the other hand I know that calling it a hyped-up title does increase the hype – you probably get more previews.

The content of press releases to accompany future programmes is also problematic. One documentary producer had written a press release described as 'a bit boring but accurate'. However, the press department of the broadcasting institution rewrote the press release to increase public attention. The producer concluded by saying:

> Whether in the end more people watched the programme or not I don't know, but the pressure to get ratings, to get people to watch these documentaries, is very definitely there.

The titling of documentary series has been the subject of some discussion in the British context. We have witnessed a move towards extreme, headline-grabbing titles, exemplified by the Channel 4 documentary series *Bodyshock*. This season of films included 'The Boy who gave Birth to his Twin' and 'The Riddle of the Elephant Man'. The content of these programmes was often dealt with sensitively, but the titles ensured considerable pre-transmission publicity.[2]

Making 'Good' Television: The Nature of the Beast

Television requires gripping visuals, and decisions about what to show or omit play a key role in the overall framing of social issues for audiences. This was a central concern for producers and a point of potential conflict with medical staff. Producers, under constant pressure to find or indeed to create 'televisual' moments, can find their efforts blocked by medical professionals who may simply veto access to patients in distress. According to media personnel there are two inherent problems. First, the medical profession lacks respect for the television industry, and second, they are considered simply to misunderstand 'the nature of television'. As an example of this, a producer recounted clashing with medics over scenes which were considered to be particularly intrusive on patient privacy. In this producer's view, the medical profession fail to comprehend the medium of television and the needs of audiences. As she concludes:

> You are making television and you're making something which has to attract people to watch it, otherwise you've failed in everything you have tried to do, and *it's the nature of the beast.* It has to hold people. It has to be something you switch on and you become absorbed in and the only way to do that is to use particular techniques, you have cliff-hangers. (emphasis added)

Each of the producers interviewed was working within what we might broadly term 'serious documentary' formats. It was, however, common for factual television producers to speak of 'casting' documentaries and to comment implicitly on the use of narrative devices more commonly associated with television fiction. This perceived need for dramatic visual moments influences not only the ways in which mentally ill people are represented when they are ill, but also, crucially, how they are represented when they are well. For documentary producers, the need for audience-pleasing pace and structure can affect decisions about the content of their films. As a BBC producer explains, this can be at the expense of a more balanced picture of mental illness. Here she recounts her experiences of filming in a psychiatric institution:

> There are two stages I think where what you need as a programme maker conflicts with basically what is there – one is in the filming of it and another is in the editing. You are looking for some drama. You know you need a dramatic moment and you know you need it relatively soon and you know you need a resolution. There were times where we were absolutely frantic to get a section because we knew it was an aspect that was going to be covered. *Regardless of how frequently sections happen in the real world*, we knew it was going to work for television. (emphasis added)

The required narrative pace is often of course at odds with the reality of mental illness, where people may recover only to relapse later. In the view of some television personnel, their own perceptions of audience needs must be prioritised. One documentary producer recognised the potential for presenting misleading images of mental illness and even 'exploiting' interviewees, but simply comments that 'There is no point in making boring telly about boring people.' As she explains:

> In the editing, what you need to make telly work is a story. No television programme or the sorts of documentaries we were making would have held

without a story, perhaps without narrative development. Now that doesn't reflect reality. There are an awful lot of times where people were being fairly interestingly ill, then getting better, then more ill again, so what we did in the editing was to generate narrative.

As earlier sections have demonstrated, the documentary producer is under significant pressure to produce 'stories'. As Elliot describes it:

These producer-directors lack the events and statements of news; they lack the contests of the sports producer; they lack the scripts and actors of drama. The documentary-maker has to make it happen, to create an art object out of a factual, free-floating reality. (Elliot 1992: 32)

However, as we have seen, the methods used to create 'reality' may contribute to a distorted picture of those in mental distress.

Portraying Mental Health?

One of the key complaints from mental health campaigning groups is that frequently portrayals of people in mental distress, albeit well-intentioned, can fall into the 'cup of tea' syndrome. Portraying someone making a cup of tea operates as a cultural shorthand for symbolising 'normality', for 'being well'. The criticism is that this image hardly serves to change the impression of users of services as passive, helpless victims. The makers of television, with their dependency on dramatic visual moments, will happily feature people in crisis, but when these people recover from their illness, production teams struggle to make 'good television' out of normality. One producer argued that unless you are making a 'training piece for television' it is exceptionally difficult to represent mental health visually:

For us it was much more interesting when someone had a crisis, because it was *much more television* than the fifth or sixth therapy session where they are talking to their worker. It just doesn't make television, and the being ill process is kind of interesting for nearly all the time that someone's ill. When they start to get better it's only interesting in bits. You don't want to film it all, and it was very difficult, because a lot of people thought that we lost interest in them when we had to start tailing off the filming. (emphasis added)

This comes perilously close to voyeurism in relation to the mentally ill. It also raises important ethical questions about the effect of featuring people in a way which makes them feel that television was interested in them only when they were behaving 'oddly'. Being 'well' does not apparently command the same attention. As the same producer concludes:

Being well is dead boring because mostly people are much more interesting when they're ill. They just are. We tried to find seminal events, but largely we would end up with them in their homes or them in the park. It's a real problem, actually. There's no way we're ever going to be able to show people well because it's not good television. I mean it is good training, but it's not telly. Often it is a limitation that television is a medium that we most frequently use to allow people to meet people who are mentally ill, because television is a very specific medium. We don't have a mass medium which doesn't depend on being involving, like having a story or some kind of structure.

In the end, budgetary constraints may also be a key factor here. There clearly are very many positive and dynamic images of mental health which could be featured other than simply 'walking around a park'. This is to present a stereotypical and limited representation of a diverse group of people. Organisations of users of services have been formed specifically to challenge 'passive' and 'victim'-focused images of mental illness.

Taking Words out of People's Mouths

Producers themselves may be personally committed to presenting more positive or sympathetic images of mental illness, but organisational pressures can overrule this concern. For example, one producer believed very strongly that patients should speak for themselves to balance the negative visual content of her film series. Pressure 'from above', however, dictated that the patient stories were given by 'voice-over'. This producer pointed out that it is only fairly recently that it has been viewed as 'politically correct' for the medium of television to give a voice to disempowered individuals, and acknowledges the 'survivor/victim' dilemma as highly problematic:

It is a massive problem in this area. For example, when I was making one of these films, visually some of the people looked absolutely terrible and had been absolutely wiped out by their experience of incarceration. I knew that they hadn't been wiped out by it and I would have preferred to have given them more time to speak in their words, but then I was put under pressure to put their stories in the commentary. I felt that would give the impression that these people couldn't speak for themselves.

There are clear factors which influence decision making over how interviewees' stories are presented in the documentary format. Most simply, it is far quicker to paraphrase someone else's story to 'fit' with the overall programme agenda – you can make them say more or less exactly what you want them to say. Another significant concern is that the story should be made easily comprehensible for audiences. As a producer described it:

> I was told more than once that either the person speaking wasn't making sense or that the audience wouldn't be able to understand. If this was the case of course you could deal with it in subtitles – this allows the person to speak for themselves, but it still takes more time than a voice-over written by someone else.

This particular producer overcame such problems by using a combination of methods. Her films did use voice-over to paraphrase the person's story, but intercut this with footage of individuals telling their own stories.

Production values play a key role in decision making here. For example, by using voice-over the film avoids being labelled as 'worthy' or being perceived as 'access television', in which the production company does not have complete editorial control. The 'house style' of both the production company making the series and the broadcast channel will also dictate the extent to which people speak for themselves. Thus perceptions of how the audience 'wants its information' and 'what it is capable of grasping' are used to justify the paraphrasing of speech. An added concern is that for the production company, the use of commentary facilitates a constant 'authority' voice for viewers. As this producer explains further:

> The more voice-over you have in proportion to the interviewees, the easier it is to transmit your own authority, easier too to remind the audience 'we did this', 'revealed that', put your own stamp on the film.

Problems about access and representation in media are not confined to the field of mental health but extend to other disempowered or minority groups. However, if public perceptions of people who have experienced mental distress are to change positively, it seems crucial that these individuals are allowed the space and time to speak for themselves. David Crepaz-Keay, deputy director of Mental Health Media, has discussed the problem of what he terms the 'missing voice' in mental health representations. Survivor organisations frequently lack the resources of the large-scale mental health 'official' organisations and often find it difficult to identify survivors willing to act as media sources at short notice. As Crepaz-Keay comments:

> It's more difficult to get a quick survivor response. It is easy to talk to the Royal College of Psychiatrists', Sane's or Minds's press office who can have someone on *Newsnight* within a few hours' notice. While other people continue to speak

on our behalf, the perception of people as patient continues. Just because it's hard work, doesn't mean you shouldn't. (Prasad 2002)

The BBC has agreed that wherever possible the service user's voice should be included and that journalists will receive training on reporting disability issues. Clearly there are spaces where survivors may gain access to media. New, more radical factual formats such as *Video Diaries* mark a deliberate attempt by the BBC to allow those disenfranchised in the wider media to present their views (Cross 2004). Recently there has been an explosion in the use of new technology, with associated opportunities for diverse underrepresented groups to make their own representations. It remains to be seen whether or not this will have an impact on wider public understandings concerning this area.

Media Impact on Users of Services

The presence of a television production crew in a psychiatric institution highlights additional issues of duty of care and ethics, and concerns about the impact of the television camera on behaviour have been widely discussed in terms of reality television. The producers I interviewed were highly aware of this impact, particularly with respect to some people who were severely disturbed. One producer recalled her experience of filming four days each week within a hospital:

> We were doing things that fed into their illness. Like one chap had delusions that he was paranoid, and he completely felt that the hospital was out to get him, and he was frightened to death, and he thought he had hired this film crew to record every instance in order to keep the hospital on their toes. In some cases there were people who thought there were cameras in every room. There was one chap who thought that cameras were following him, and the doctor said 'But they are!'

Often a producer is faced with a conflict between contributing to someone's distress and making a film which has maximum visual impact. Decision making here rests entirely upon the personal integrity of the producer. One producer explains why the subject of mental illness may present a dilemma for 'media people' in particular:

> It's really hard for people who [work in] media and what you're looking for is the intensity and drama because that's what makes good television. It's incredibly hard not to get seduced by that. I actually think it's far too easy to wind someone up, someone who has delusions or psychosis, and you're

creating something in their head. Of course for you it's great TV, and there were a couple of occasions where I think we came too close to that.

Again, economic restraints play a major role in such decisions. One producer outlined how the production budget determines flexibility over such issues. A producer is unlikely to have the luxury of losing valuable footage, given that the majority of documentary films on mental illness must be completed within two or three weeks. Even if a patient is obviously 'acting up' for the cameras, the piece will become part of the final product if the team are working to a tight schedule:

> If I had been making that film over a limited period of time, I would have had to carry on [with the interview], or at least I would have felt I had to carry on because you can't waste filming days. They are far too expensive.

On some occasions this producer did allow film to be transmitted which included someone who was obviously performing for the camera. The decision was taken to screen such scenes, in her view, to illustrate the effect of the filming process on individuals:

> One thing I don't really think we disinterred was the effect we were having on [the patients]. Occasionally it comes through. In one scene one of the women is having a very manic high, and you know it is just for the cameras, but that was the sort of thing we wanted to keep in to say there is a level of this going on.

We cannot of course judge how such scenes are received by audiences and whether indeed these moments are perceived simply as performances to camera. Contemporary audiences are perhaps more aware of the artifice of television production and possibly less willing to accept unproblematically that they are being presented with authentic material.

Mental Distress in the Single Series and Medical Drama

There are, however, spaces where more positive representations of mental illness can occur. It is important to examine the production values which underpin these portrayals. The BBC hospital drama series *Casualty* (BBC1, 1986–) has consistently drawn praise for producing fairly challenging storylines on mental illness.[3] Indeed in a systematic study of images of mental health in media, this programme emerged as one of the very few to critique the way in which mental illness is culturally constructed (Philo 1996a). To understand why this may be the case, it is crucial to examine the way in which *Casualty* storylines are worked through from ideas stage to final draft.

This programme places a high value on background research. This is not simply in terms of reading newspaper cuttings or medical journals but also includes practical experience, when writers visit hospital departments to observe patients and discuss cases with medical staff. A script editor for the programme explains this prioritising of personal research:

> What is absolutely fundamental is that the writer really researches the story. At the end of the day *Casualty* is a research drama. It has to have that credibility about it. We would always encourage new writers to go to a casualty department anywhere in the country.

Script writers are not only encouraged to identify their own contacts in the medical or social services profession, much as specialist news journalists do, but are also supported by regular medical advisers on the programme. An experienced script writer describes her first experience of becoming involved: 'I got my first commission [for *Casualty*] and then went off and researched it in my local hospitals, Guys, Greenwich. I just spent a night and observed, watched cases, talked to the nurses.' The programme also paid a consultancy fee to allow her to discuss a future abortion storyline with a gynaecologist.

At an organisational level, *Casualty* has regular medical advisers who are embedded within the production. Thus from the earliest stage a storyline will be checked for inaccuracies. As a script editor outlines here:

> We have three medical advisers, so they are on hand, and obviously at the [initial] stage it is very important that the medical advisers give the stories the thumbs up. Often we would have cases where a medical adviser would say 'This would never happen', so obviously we chuck the story out. Every single stage goes to a medical adviser for checks on dialogue. Once we've had all the medical notes back and the producer's notes and the script editor's notes, we then have a meeting with the writer and they go away and rewrite again. Even when a script has been finalised there are usually changes. A doctor might say 'Well, actually he wouldn't say or do that.'

An additional factor which may influence the quality of scripts on other programmes is the relative looseness of deadlines. One script writer considered this as a crucial factor which is often overlooked. She believes that the pressure of deadlines is less immediate for *Casualty* writers and that this can have an influence on the product:

The beauty of *Casualty* is the amount of freedom you have, which you have on [police series] *The Bill* also, but they're putting out so much more that they have to be tighter with it. [On *Casualty*] there's quite a lot more time, so you are able to rush around and find out about your subject much more.

Challenging Representations

More balanced images of mental illness do not simply emerge from the input of the medical profession or official campaigning organisations. It is valuable to consider cases where mental health activists or users of services have been involved in creating programmes concerned with mental distress.[3] The writer Donna Franceschild created the six-part drama series *Takin' Over the Asylum* (BBC2, 1995), which won a BAFTA award for best serial. She received a Royal Television Society award for best writer and the Mental Health in the Media award in the same year. She is often asked to comment on media and mental health issues, and her commitment to this area is evident in this series, which offered a radically different approach to mental distress. The programme was praised by mental health service users for depicting psychiatric patients as not just articulate but also witty and humorous, critiquing and subverting our expectations of the mentally ill. This type of treatment is fairly rare; the more common theme is that of the mentally distressed as the object of ridicule or parody in television programmes (Philo 1996a). The programme was originally titled *Making Waves*, but pre-broadcast research with audiences found that potential viewers preferred *Takin' Over the Asylum*. This provides a more explanatory title, alerting viewers to the programme setting and alluding to the subject matter. It clearly references the phrase 'the lunatics have taken over the asylum', which has moved into public currency and is commonly used to illustrate 'a world of policy making gone mad' (Cross 2004: 214).

Despite critical acclaim, the programme failed to attract large audiences. The decision to alter the title was not made by the writer but between the programme producer and the controller for BBC2. The producer explains here that it was the subject rather than the title which was responsible for low viewing figures:

> The real problem for me was that such a wonderful show was watched by such a small proportion of the television viewing audience, [and] I'll take full responsibility for [changing the title], because I was the producer. Certainly when we researched the different titles, the one that we ended up with was the one that got the most positive response from the likely television viewing audience. I think there was what would appear to be at first sight a difficult subject matter and a real problem of convincing a large audience that they should conquer it.

The programme had a deliberate agenda to challenge public misconceptions of the subject. The writer was acutely aware of the problems in this field. She also took special advice from campaigning groups on mental health. As the programme producer recalls:

> Although that area is regularly visited in television drama, that particular approach is not and the sheer involvement of [the writer] is very unusual. [The writer] worked closely with mental health organisations, especially SAMH, Scottish Association for Mental Health, and that was an important thing.

An additional factor which should be emphasised is support for a writer from within the broadcasting hierarchy. In this case there was significant support for the writer to challenge existing perceptions of mental illness. As he outlines:

> I think the serial did an extraordinary amount for people who watched it in changing perceptions. There are very few things that got the same reaction from people [with mental health problems] and who derived a complicated comfort from the programme. Donna had such a strong line to the mental health organisations that I for myself trusted what she was doing. She was committed to them in a basic way.

The commitment of those involved in the production and the support from within the broadcast hierarchy combined to ensure that the programme succeeded in challenging negative attitudes to psychiatric patients. This support may be rare, but it does exist. An independent producer who has for many years been concerned with changing the media image of mental illness considers hierarchical support as fundamental. With her two most recent films she was given this support. This meant that in terms of content she had relative autonomy to present the kind of 'low key' image that she wanted and was not 'under any pressure at all to dramatise or up the hype in terms of the material'. As she explains:

> I think there are interested people in the hierarchy in television who think that to have been institutionalised for sixty years is a quiet and terrible drama in its own right. To have a woman sit in front of a camera is as dramatic as anything that you can cobble together.

On Performance and Mental Distress

Each year the British media greets the latest series of reality game show *Big Brother* (Channel 4) with an almost equal mixture of delight and opprobrium. Pages of newspapers and magazines are filled with articles criticising the latest contestants for symbolising 'dumbed down' Britain, while the tabloid press rake up the contestants' past misdemeanours, estranged family members and ex-lovers. In the seventh series of the programme (2006), the British public were fascinated by pre-broadcast publicity alerting viewers to the news that one of the contestants suffers from Tourette's syndrome. Significant debate focused on the appropriateness of his inclusion in this type of programme (Porter 2006). However, within just a few days attention shifted entirely when another participant, a young Scottish Asian man, left the programme after declaring his plans to self-harm. This contestant, Shahbaz Choudhary, was featured on the front page of the *Sun* newspaper under his words, which declared, 'I'm a dead man walking. I came to die on this programme. I'm going to prove it' (Cox 2006). The programme experienced a significant media backlash and led to a number of features which questioned the principles and ethics of the production staff. Ironically the protest was led by the *Sun*, which has been accused repeatedly of the worst excesses of discriminatory reporting in relation to mental health.[4] With unfortunate timing the celebrity gossip magazine *Heat* introduced the new contestants with the striking strap line 'Unleash the mentalists' (23 May 2006). In the following days the ethical code of the programme was endlessly debated by website forum users and mental health charities alike (Brook 2006). Organisations including the Samaritans, the Mental Health Foundation and SANE expressed their condemnation of the programme for including such fragile characters. A spate of complaints was sent to the regulatory board, Ofcom, after the visibly shaken Choudhary appeared in front of a live audience on the spinoff programme *Big Brother's Little Brother*. Here he took full responsibility for his behaviour, admitted that it was 'car-crash television', and concluded that he was unsure whether he would survive in the outside world. Later Choudhary gave interviews to various journalists in which he admitted to having lied about his mental health history to programme psychologists.[5]

Dr Andrew McCulloch, chief executive of the Mental Health Foundation, wrote an open letter to Channel 4 director of television programming Kevin Lygo and condemned the programme's treatment of mental health issues, saying:

> This kind of programming can make individuals who are distressed a laughing stock and this will only seek to feed the discrimination that already impacts heavily on people suffering from mental illness. It is disappointing that Channel 4 seems to have little regard for vulnerable contestants in the Big Brother house. I should be interested to know what screening and welfare measures are in place to protect contestants. (Brook 2006)

Yet the Channel 4 head of factual entertainment and the producer of Brighter Pictures, a subsidiary of Endemol, brushed off the furore on the grounds that this was simply the latest round of criticism for a programme which is criticised each year. A key part of their defence rested on the assertion that audiences do not, contrary to what we might believe, see *everything* on the programme:

> The amount of support Shahbaz got in the diary room, in the confidential part of the diary room with the psychologist and the producers that we don't show, was huge. There's a layer of support before they go in, [it] is there in a strong way while there, and [it] is equally strong when they come out. We can't express that onscreen because it's private. (Gibson 2006)

We are told repeatedly that one of the distinguishing features of reality television is its concern with making the private public. In all its variant forms the genre inevitably raises ethical issues in terms of representation (Hill 2005). John Corner (2002) writes of a post-documentary age in which more serious documentary must be located within new forms of production and consumption. For Corner, programmes such as *Big Brother* offer what he terms:

> A predefined stage precisely for personality to be competitively displayed (the intimate face-to-camera testimony of the video room being one privileged moment) and for its 'ordinary' participants to enter the celebrity system of popular culture with minimum transitional difficulty (we know them as performers already), if only for a brief period. (Corner 2002: 264)

This episode is worth noting because it raises a number of salient points in relation to mental health and factual programming. Reality TV has been considered to offer innovative ways of engaging audiences with media texts. In the case discussed above, online forum users argued over the authenticity of scenes involving Choudhary and his threat of suicide. Was this simply an extreme version of the 'performance' enacted by all housemates? Had his fellow housemates who ostracised him (stealing his clothes and his food, leaving the room when he entered) become bullies? Were they simply dealing reasonably with a publicity-hungry contestant? Some fans speculated on whether Channel 4 would intervene. Others suggested that it was not the contestants who were being exploited. As one angry *Big Brother* forum user, 'Dave_the', writes:

> If anything, Shahbaz has exploited CH4, the BB housemates and the viewers. He said he deliberately lied about his mental health to get onto the

programme and kill himself. He had no thought of what that would do to the people going into the BB house with him . . . Shahbaz is a selfish, driven nutter, he knows exactly what he is doing, he lied and manipulated his way into the BB house. (Dave_the 2006)

For some commentators the apparent extraordinary lack of concern expressed by the hierarchy at Channel 4 is easily explained. *Big Brother* is delivering the youth audiences that every advertiser desires and as a consequence has become immune from criticism within the channel. A few years ago Brian Winston pointed out that such popular factual entertainment represents 'the price of survival' for more serious programming (Winston 2000). As one critic explained, *Big Brother* has become 'the untouchable bedrock on which everything from extra episodes of *Dispatches* to critically acclaimed single dramas such as *The Road to Guantanamo* are built' (Gibson 2006). As many have argued, the nature of reality television means that it can open up new possibilities for audience-production relations (see van Zoonen 2004), but equally programmes such as this can become a new and different arena for the stigmatisation of the vulnerable.

Conclusion

This chapter has identified a series of factors which may influence how the discrete topic of mental distress is represented in a range of 'non-news' television programming. The production process is a genre issue and more complex than might be assumed. The format of 'serious documentary' may at first appear a more appropriate space than fictional genres in which to portray mental distress, but television producers face significant demands of pace and narrative and work in an equally intense environment with their own organisational and economic constraints. In this climate, underlying assumptions about audience needs and what constitutes 'good television' (the 'nature of the beast') with dramatic moments can outweigh other concerns, and can result in distorted and misleading images of mental distress, even to the point where mental health patients are provoked to behave badly. Writers and producers are not autonomous – independent producers must take advice from those further up the broadcast hierarchy to ensure an ongoing relationship. Support from within this hierarchy can ensure that more challenging portrayals of mental health are produced. Equally, as has been illustrated, organisational power structures can override the personal commitment of writers and producers to this area. These debates are likely to move to the fore as reality television formats compete for audiences and as channels become economically reliant on those formats' success.

Notes

1 There are debates concerning how those who have been through the psychiatric system would wish to be referenced. The term 'service user' has been criticised for its implication that those who 'consume' psychiatric services have the rights of other 'consumers' and have sought such services willingly (Plumb 2003).

2 An extreme example of this is documentary/sitcom hybrid *The Missing Chink* (Channel 4, January 2004). This series of short sketches aimed to challenge the lack of representation of the Chinese community in British television, yet was condemned for its 'blatantly racist title'. Complaints were lodged with Ofcom and Channel 4 (who said the title was an 'ironic comment'). A viewer who entirely supported the aims of the programme commented that 'I don't see why Channel 4 should get away with perpetuating this kind of racism when there would be a massive outcry if the title was dealing with another ethnic minority and using an obviously pejorative term' (*Guardian*, 21 January 2004).

3 *Casualty* has provided Saturday evening viewers with a radical depiction of hospital life for twenty years. Although the programme is somewhat pedestrian in pace as compared with programmes such as *ER*, it attracted considerable criticism. Conservative politicians were furious at its emphasis on the lack of government funding for the NHS. The programme portrayed accident and emergency staff as turning to alcohol, popping pills or smoking heavily to cope with the severe pressures of the NHS conditions. The programme agenda was described as, 'Combining the values of a soap, a punchy political concern, documentary reportage and the thrilling elements of fast-action disaster movies' (Kingsley 1993: 12).

4 A striking example of this was the furore generated by the *Sun*'s reporting of celebrity ex-boxer Frank Bruno. The front-page story 'Bonkers Bruno Locked Up' (23 September 2003) generated public outrage and was condemned by mental health organisations as 'ignorant reporting'. Readers threatened to boycott the paper, and it swiftly organised an appeal in Bruno's name for funds to support a mental health charity. Marjorie Wallace, chief executive of SANE, has discussed how *Sun* editor Rebekah Wade and her predecessor David Yelland struggled to replace the words 'nut' or 'mad' in preferably three letters. Wallace simply suggested 'ill'. The paper clearly misjudged their readership, but it is uncertain whether this is 'evidence' of changing public opinion concerning mental illness or simply an expression of public empathy for a popular public figure. Bruno is remembered by the British public as the lovable underdog who challenged American boxer Mike Tyson.

5 The involvement of medical professionals in such programmes is frequently offered as evidence that participants are not exploited. We are rarely privy to how this works in practice. Endemol UK (responsible for *Big Brother*) also made *Shattered* (2004, Channel 4). This involved contestants competing for a cash prize by depriving themselves of sleep and subjecting themselves to tests

including electric shocks. One doctor who was part of the ethics panel said the programme makers ignored their recommended ban on electric shocks, but 'unlike a hospital ethics committee, this one had no power of veto'. She continues, 'We had to examine how far producers could be allowed to torture their participants in the name of entertainment' (Lyall 2004). The programme makers rebutted claims that they had exploited participants and said that audiences were too sophisticated to assume that sleep deprivation was safe. Those who accept invitations to participate in such panels may be entirely unaware of their lack of influence over the eventual product. This seems to highlight the potential professional gap between medical and television professionals.

Part IV Social Issues and Television Audiences

CHAPTER 7

Public Understandings, Sexual Violence and Safe Spaces

Introduction

In earlier chapters I have identified the diverse production factors which influence how different social issues are 'packaged' and 'framed' within and across different television formats (soap opera, drama and documentary series). In this chapter the focus shifts from the television production process to address how audiences 'make sense of' social issue storylines. I discuss a reception study of sexual violence in the television soap opera *Brookside*.[1] The chapter therefore builds on Chapter 2, which explores the philosophies and ethos of the production team members, and also develops Chapter 3, which examines the production background to this story of sexual and physical violence. I have already highlighted how the production team discussed their 'imagined' audience and the ways in which the audience was implicit in decisions made over story development (casting, characterisation and narrative pace). This chapter is designed to provide insights into the relationship between the production team and their audience.

There were three main stages in the group sessions. This is a technique which has been applied to other studies of media and public belief and has been developed at the Glasgow University Media Group (Philo 1990, 1996b; Miller et al. 1998; Miller 1994). Participants first completed a brief questionnaire covering basic demographic characteristics and television viewing habits and were asked the question 'Should the issue of child sexual abuse be portrayed in soap opera?' They were then split into smaller groups and given a set of photographs to work with (of the scene in *Brookside* where Trevor rapes Rachel; see figures 7.1–7.4 below). Participants were asked to write dialogue for the scene, and then returned to the group to discuss their responses to the topic of child sexual abuse in television fiction and specific characterisations and themes in the *Brookside* story.

The first section of this chapter involves mapping audience reactions and responses to the topic of child sexual abuse in television soap opera. The second explores reactions and responses to specific characterisations including the abuser and the 'victims'. The final section explores how a story of this type may have an influence on public understandings concerning the issue, such as the complex and ambiguous emotions experienced by an abused child. My overall aim here is to explore possible links or disconnections between how messages are constructed for the imagined audience by programme makers and how they are received by audiences. At the same time it is also possible to examine the role of these programmes in everyday life.

I have discussed the contours of the Jordache storyline in *Brookside* in earlier chapters (Chapters 1 and 3). Here I simply wish to note that the participants were not selected as *Brookside* 'fans' and they were not given any information about the story or plot so far. This allowed me to explore the impact of the programme and also the considerable publicity generated by the story. Participants were a mix of male and female, of different ages (range from 13 to 66 years) and different social backgrounds (see Appendix for details, including codes used in sources of interview quotations below). Some had identifiable experience of sexual abuse and domestic violence ('special interest' groups of teenage survivors, social workers, women's aid workers). Others had no identifiable experience prior to the sessions ('general population' groups). As numerous studies have identified, the television soap opera is surrounded by gossip and 'talk'. Conducting focus group discussions allows the preservation of some of the elements of social culture in which such television storylines are discussed, and the sessions were structured to help diffuse a potentially difficult topic (see Barbour and Kitzinger 1999; Carter and Henderson 2005).

Sexual Violence in Television Soap Opera: Audience Responses

Participants were first asked to respond to the question 'Should the issue of child sexual abuse be portrayed in soap opera?' The aim of this was not simply to conduct a poll of their opinions but rather to examine how people perceived the issue, how they related to abuse in their own lives, and how media representations may affect them. It was also important to gauge their individual responses prior to any group discussion of the topic as a whole. Posing the question allowed the group to become focused on the topic. The responses were overwhelmingly positive. Most people answered the question (56). Of these, 70 per cent (39) believed that the topic was appropriate for television soap opera. Just 5 per cent (3) stated that it was not appropriate for the soap opera medium and 25 per cent (14) responded that they were 'unsure'.

Key Factors in Audiences' Acceptance of Child Sexual Abuse in TV Soap Opera

Reflecting 'the Everyday'
It was striking that all of those who had direct experience of sexual abuse (identified either as survivors or as working in the field of sexual violence) responded positively to the issue being raised in television soap opera.[2] Their positive responses were motivated by three distinct concerns: first, fictional storylines might help to increase public awareness of the issue; second, these storylines might reduce isolation for those currently in an abusive situation; and third, portraying sexual violence would fulfil the remit of television soap opera as reflecting 'real life'. The following quotations illustrate these points:

> I think it is important as it will show that this really does happen. (male, 16, YC, regularly watches *Brookside*, no personal experience of sexual abuse)[3]

> Sexual abuse is a real-life issue that should be dealt with in order to prevent preconceptions and misinformation circulating among the public. (female, 18, PSS, sometimes watches *Brookside*, personal experience of child sexual abuse)

> To let children know that it is wrong because usually the abuser will tell them it is natural or normal. (female, 17, SSS, regularly watches *Brookside*, no experience of sexual abuse)

> It breaks the silence and lets women and children know that they're not alone. (female, 32, WO, regularly watches *Brookside*, experience of working with sexual abuse survivors)

> It is so prevalent a crime that silence should be broken by mainstream media. (female, 46, WO, never watches *Brookside*, experience of working with sexual abuse survivors)

To integrate a story of child sexual abuse into the 'everyday' was, in itself, considered to be an important achievement. In reflecting the contours of everyday life, the soap opera can highlight the lived reality of sexual abuse. As the following quotation from one young woman encapsulates it:

> The thing is that the soap makes [child sexual abuse] part of everyday life, which it is, so [*Brookside*] have got three stories going on at once, someone

starting up the pizza place or whatever. (female, 18, regularly watches *Brookside*, PSS, no experience of sexual abuse)

Television soap opera may challenge hitherto 'hidden' problems in potentially very powerful ways. This format enables the depiction of 'everyday life', and the interweaving of different storylines (for example, switching from a mundane domestic storyline about starting a new business to one involving sexual violence) in the same episode may capture the attention of audiences in a powerful way. John Tulloch has reflected on this in relation to his research on Australian soap opera *A Country Practice*, and has highlighted the ways in which production personnel sometimes 'balance' such stories. As he writes:

> Some writers worry that the multiple strands detract from their (often very heartfelt) health or other risk messages. Others argue that soap opera's tendency to have 'balancing stories' – where one narrative strand, in some indirect way, parallels or throws light on another – will re-inforce health and social messages. (Tulloch 2000: 77)

The Importance of Reputation

Research participants who believed that child sexual abuse should be included in fictional drama considered that *Brookside* was, among other fictional programmes, particularly appropriate. The programme was consistently referred to as 'hard-hitting' and clearly had a reputation for handling 'gritty' storylines. Comments were made frequently such as 'I think *Brookside* usually gets it right' (female, US). These responses suggest that the sexual violence storyline was viewed within the wider context of programme reputation and other storylines which dealt with 'difficult' social problems. In particular, regular viewers recalled an earlier 'date-rape' story. One school student outlines here why this programme has a distinctive reputation:

> In other soap operas they'll have a storyline like someone will die and the whole community will be devastated for like, a week. Then they'll all go back to their normal lives. They'll hardly mention that character and it's really unrealistic. With *Brookside* you see the continuing effects of the father's abuse, the younger child starts to rebel and go against her parents and the older one turns away from men. That makes it a lot more convincing because it shows how longstanding the effects are. (female, PSS)

Most participants expressed the belief that fictional portrayals could contribute to a social climate in which victims could disclose abuse without fear or shame.

> The soaps do a really good job. I mean, twenty years ago when [child sexual abuse] was never covered in any soaps, children were growing up, really worried, being abused, never telling anybody. Now the soaps have brought out these subjects and maybe children will see it on TV and say 'well, it's happening to her, it's happening to me', and tell somebody. (FMW)

The storyline was perceived as particularly helpful to abused children. A social worker who dealt regularly with child sexual abuse cases commented that actually 'seeing' the abuse scenario could help children gain not only the courage but the 'language' needed to disclose:

> [Abused] children need to have language and [*Brookside*] gives children the words to use. I'm not saying they would copy, but they would get an idea of what to do, who to talk to, because kids are manipulated and brainwashed and bribed. (female, SW)

The positive portrayal of survivors was considered to challenge the self-blame experienced by some survivors. One young woman (from a general population group, but who revealed in confidence later that she had been sexually abused)[4] describes this as follows:

> Widespread knowledge like [*Brookside*] would reduce the feelings of guilt that the child would feel and, you know, 'I'm not a freak, I didn't bring that on myself.' (female, FMW)

Participants who worked with sexual abuse survivors expressed some caution. Many described previous negative experiences of liaising with journalists and programme makers in connection with their work. For this group, media attention could generate positive results 'only if [soap operas] *dispel* myths as opposed to perpetuating them' (emphasis added) (female, WO). These professionals had directly experienced the impact of television representations of sexual violence, as one participant explains:

> Producers should remember their responsibility because there [are] always calls to women's organisations after something has been on [television]. It heightens awareness, or helps women name something that's happened to them. Often it does pass on information, but if there's absolutely nothing to pass on then it's quite dangerous and can *increase* isolation. I think that often programme makers aren't aware of the power of the media and how it influences people's lives. (female, WO)

This is an interesting point. Clearly in interview industry professionals speak frequently about the power of the medium. However, the views expressed above do not assume that the power of television coverage is always inevitably positive.

Key Factors in Audiences' Rejection of Child Sexual Abuse in TV Soap Opera

Simply Entertainment

In spite of the above positive comments, there were a minority of research participants who thought sexual abuse storylines were not appropriate material for soaps. All three participants who held this view were older (aged between 53 and 66 years old) and had never watched the programme. None of the group members indicated that they had personal experience of sexual abuse, although in subsequent discussion one woman mentioned in passing that she had been 'accosted' by a stranger in the local park when she was a child. The women considered that soap opera should avoid such a topic because it could compromise audience viewing pleasures and they viewed the genre as one which provided 'entertainment'. A woman who had enjoyed 'larger than life' soap operas such as the American prime-time series *Dallas*, and who deliberately avoided British 'gritty' soaps, comments as follows:

> It's probably hiding my head in the sand but I like to be entertained. I know it's going on outside and I know I can read about it when I pick up any newspaper or magazine, but when I'm in my living room I really want to be entertained. I don't want something that I find horrible. (female, RP)

Other members of the same group made similar comments: 'I watch TV for enjoyment. Abuse, sexual or otherwise, I would not enjoy (female, 53, RP, never watches *Brookside*, no experience of sexual abuse) and 'Soaps should be mainly light entertainment' (female, 66, RP, never watches *Brookside*, no experience of sexual abuse).

These participants were from an older generation than the other research participants. It is possible that the views of younger people reflect an important generational difference (in how they use soap operas, their expectations of the genre and their views of appropriate methods by which to inform the public about social issues in general).

Key Factors in Audiences' Uncertainty Concerning Child Sexual Abuse in TV Soap Opera

Research participants who expressed uncertainty about the inclusion of sexual violence in television soap opera did not share any characteristics in particular, though none had any obvious contact with the issue through personal or professional experience. These participants did view increased public awareness of sexual violence as important, but believed that it might not be possible for such programmes to balance the competing demands of 'entertainment' and 'responsibility':

Entertainment and Responsibility

Soaps are supposed to reflect real life. However, as regards turning child sexual abuse into something 'entertaining' I'm not really sure. (female, 25, FLT, regularly watches *Brookside*, no experience of sexual abuse)

It depends on how it's portrayed. (female, 29, OW, sometimes watches *Brookside*, no experience of sexual abuse)

The public should be made aware, but would it be interesting to watch? (male, 17, SSS, rarely watches *Brookside*, no personal experience of child sexual abuse)

The issue should be dealt with, as it is serious enough that it should concern everyone. On the other hand, I think that the issue may be too personal to deal with on TV. (male, 18, PSS, never watches *Brookside*, no personal experience of child sexual abuse)

Perceptions of Negative Impact on Family Life

Other reservations focused on concern about false allegations or about loss of innocence, reservations which were also expressed by some of those who opposed fictional portrayals altogether. Some research participants were concerned that fictional representations could lead to false allegations (this opinion was not held by anyone who revealed personal experience of abuse or who worked in the field). For some, the genre of soap opera reflected 'real life' too closely:

Do you not think it just puts something into [a child's] mind that wasn't there? Some children's imagination will run away with them and they'll make things up in their own mind to give the police a hard time to sort out truth from fiction. I think probably from television they get that sort of thing. It's different reading it in a book, but when they're confronted with a soap situation, that's just like our everyday life. (female, RP)

The source of the woman's response above was her daughter, a police-woman who worked with the child protection unit (and disliked this aspect of her job intensely). There are often significant tensions between police and social workers in response to child abuse cases, and clearly her view reflects this. The notion that children were vulnerable to television influence was a recurring theme across several 'general population' groups:

Children have got really active imaginations and you could be giving your wee sister a bath or something and you don't know what they're going to say. (female, PSS)

There was also concern about the impact of portrayals on younger children in threatening to undermine their 'innocence'. Participants who believed that this story could raise awareness and help counter the isolation of survivors were, in some cases, quite unprepared to contemplate the idea of their own children or siblings watching the Jordache story. One young woman who had praised the storyline said:

My little brother's only seven and my Mum watches Brookside. He hasn't actually asked about anything yet and I don't know how my Mum would handle it. I mean, he's only seven. She'd probably just say 'That's a bad man.' He's completely innocent. It's like taking his innocence away from him. (female, FMW)

The concept of childhood innocence echoed powerfully across the general population groups. As one teenager attending private school observed wistfully:

It's nice to have a childhood that's not marred by all that kind of stuff at the beginning because for the rest of your life you've got to deal with that. (female, PSS)

People also expressed concern that 'normal' children could be harmed by fictional accounts. For example, the following exchange between school students makes this distinction:

PSS1: If someone at that age was being abused then it would help if they did see [Brookside] because it would make them more able to understand that other people were going through it as well, and that it wasn't just them and it wasn't their fault, and it could help them.
PSS2: But most children aren't [being abused].
PSS1: I agree. It could harm the majority of children who were having a totally normal childhood. (PSS)

In 'general population' groups people also talked about the difficulties which such portrayals presented for parents:

Brookside is depending on parents telling their children [about sexual abuse] because if they didn't then there could be a lot of fear among children. They're actually pushing parents to tell children things that they might not otherwise do. (FMW)

Some younger participants also expressed concern about the negative impact of such information on their own childhood.

> When I was small my Mum used to go out on night shift and I used to crawl into my Dad's bed and sleep with him. If I'd been told about sexual abuse then I'd have been scared to go in bed with my father. (FMW)

Such attitudes were common and suggest that while people agree 'in theory' that any child is at risk of abuse, there is still significant resistance to giving information about the issue. The recurring theme within those research groups without experience of sexual abuse was that information on sexual abuse may result in fear and corrupt childhood innocence.[5] The ideology of childhood, it seems, may act as a powerful barrier to giving children information. Such attitudes also reveal the way in which the 'innocence' of the non-abused child is contrasted with the 'corruption' of the abused child. If in reinforcing the 'innocence' of the non-abused child the abused child is conversely positioned as 'damaged', this may contribute to the very negative impact on the self-image of abuse survivors.

The novelty of public discussion of this issue is also likely to contribute to these responses. Indeed it would be interesting to explore contemporary audiences' ideas about the same material as such topics have moved further into the public domain. In this case, however, the persistent representation of child abuse and what to do about it were considered in terms of the possible 'corrupting' effects on 'normal' childhood.

The Nature of Representation

Debates about the manner in which television soap opera should develop storylines based on child sexual abuse focused on three central dilemmas: 'realism' versus 'idealism'; explicit representation (in particular how acts of sexual abuse should be portrayed); and programme makers and their need to maintain responsibility alongside delivering audiences.

Research participants were uncertain when asked if television soap opera should portray the negative consequences of disclosing abuse or instead promote an idealised version of what should happen after a child discloses. One teenage boy explains:

> Well, it might be a good thing see for people who have been sexually abused, and then if they're watching telly, right, and the person gets caught and everything's all right, it might make them tell. (male, YC)

Personal experience was again a key factor in people's attitudes to the range of experiences which should be represented. One woman recounted that a friend had been placed in social services care by her mother. She placed her daughter in care to avoid terminating a relationship with an abusive boyfriend. This personal experience had a profound impact on the participant's views about the ways in which television soap opera should portray sexual abuse.

> I'd like to think that happens once so many billion times, in which case [the programme] wouldn't deal with it. For television the general is what you want to go for rather than the specific. We all know what people are like, you know, if [audiences] see one thing they label everything as being exactly the same. (female, US)

There was an identifiable distinction between those participants in 'general population' groups and those with personal or professional experience of sexual abuse. Social workers admitted that young people might be dissuaded from disclosing if there were negative repercussions shown in fictional portrayals of the issue. Despite this, the respondents ultimately believed that 'realism' should be the determining criterion. This is an important point and should be of key concern certainly for programme makers. If indeed there is any suggestion that representations of the issue might lead to reluctance to seek help, then this is a repercussion which should be taken very seriously. Decisions made about running a story with these consequences should not be taken lightly.

All participants (including the teenage survivors of sexual abuse) were adamant that 'acts' of abuse would be inappropriate to be screened. The graphic depiction of abuse was considered to be entirely inappropriate. The phrase 'the power of suggestion' was repeatedly used across the sessions. The power of suggestion was believed to be a significant feature of television soap opera and other forms of television drama: 'If you're a good producer or director then you can show it by other means' (female, US). *Brookside* was considered to provide a responsible portrayal of acts of sexual violence:

> You can get the point across really easily by not showing [the abuse]. They did that quite well in *Brookside*. You just went 'Oh shit' every time [Trevor] started walking up those stairs. (female, OW)

A young woman who had been sexually abused expressed a similar view. She too had found that the abuse of Rachel had been conveyed with care in the programme:

It would just be too horrible but something like [*Brookside*] was OK. (female, TS)

There was, however, some concern that the power of suggestion might also result in ambiguity for audiences. If abuse was simply alluded to then it might cause misunderstandings. Younger children in particular might be unable to make sense of these scenes:

If you just saw father and daughter cuddling, then wouldn't children think that [abuse] could just start with a cuddle? (female, FMW)

As I discussed earlier, the format of television soap opera is frequently criticised on the grounds that such programmes feature sensational stories simply to increase viewer ratings. Indeed many participants assumed (correctly) that *Brookside* had increased audiences as a result of tackling domestic and sexual violence. People are aware of the commercial imperatives which underpin such programmes, and audiences may take salacious pleasure in viewing 'hyped-up' scenes. As one woman commented:

Brookside probably had really high figures that week [of the abuse]. People aren't watching it for the knowledge but for the specific scene. (female, FMW)

The commercial concerns and aesthetic codes which drive these stories have been discussed earlier from the perspectives of the production team members, and are familiar to audiences. As one participant explains, 'At the end of the day a soap's got to have high [viewing] figures and got to have cliff-hangers' (male, FME). In the next section I discuss some of the responses to specific characterisation in the Jordache story.

Responses to Narrative Themes and Characterisation

Acceptance of the 'Jekyll and Hyde' Abuser

The character of Trevor Jordache generated great hostility within audience groups. As I noted earlier (Chapter 3) Trevor was framed as unpredictable, manipulative and violent. His extreme behaviour – overtly charming with neighbours while simultaneously abusive 'behind closed doors' – made a striking impact on participants.[6] The combination of wife beater and child sex abuser/paedophile encapsulated the notion of the archetypal 'psychopath' for those participants who had no direct experience of these issues. The term 'psycho' was reiterated throughout these audience groups. Indeed many participants referred to the way in which

Trevor had the 'look of an abuser', which signified to audiences that 'we all knew he was bad' (female, US).

> [Trevor] walked in the room and he had that look about him, you know? And you knew there was something not quite right about him before he even did anything. I could never understand why everybody else on the Close didn't pick up on it. He was really set up as Mr Psycho, wasn't he? You know, he did so many bad things – I mean, he did everything, didn't he? (female, US)

The character was compared with other fictional villains. For one man Trevor symbolised the television soap opera equivalent of the central character in the popular film *Silence of the Lambs* (Rank/Orion, 1990): 'Trevor was just like Hannibal Lecter' (male, FLT).

Trevor was described by people without experience of abuse as an 'over the top' character (on the grounds that 'he did everything', abused his daughters and hit his wife). In contrast, those who had specific direct knowledge about sexual/physical abuse instead praised the character for representing 'the links between physical and sexual abuse' (female, WO). However, there was not necessarily a desire to witness a more 'realistic' portrayal of an abuser among those who saw him as unrealistic and over the top. There was clear ambivalence here. Some participants recounted stories of known abusers in their neighbourhood (local teachers or neighbours) and expressed a firm belief that abusers can be 'anyone'. The same people, however, rejected the idea of a more realistic character (a familiar soap character being cast as an abuser in the programme). Such attitudes reveal deep fears and reflect the anxiety which surrounds sexual abuse. As one young woman explained:

> [Abusers] are usually the nicest people, you would never bloody know, that's what's wrong. If [*Brookside*] were really to deal with issues then you would have people wandering around not being able to trust anybody. (female, US)

Audiences were undoubtedly drawn in to the scenes in which Trevor engineers his return to the family. Several participants referred explicitly to the way in which production techniques were employed to frame his character for audiences. Their responses contrast the 'obvious' and 'safe' dramatic representation of the 'panto villain' in the television soap opera with the 'unsafe', terrifying abuser who looks normal but could be a neighbour or colleague:

> That's the problem with something like this. I mean, you knew your man Trevor was a psycho, but in real life it's always normal people. You just look at him. The camera looks into his eyes and then 'Oh no!' (female, OW)

We saw like the look in his eye after they've left the room and stuff. If it's real life you don't see the look. So we're getting all this information that [the characters] aren't. It's quite difficult to put yourself in their position because they don't see [Trevor] round the corner and him walking down the street going 'Ah hah! Back in! Ah hah!' (Female, US)

This suggests that people are willing 'in theory' to accept messages that abusers are not necessarily strangers, could be anyone and cannot be identified by how they look. However, those without experience of abuse are not willing or perhaps not ready to be presented with a fictional abuser who is framed as 'the man next door'.

Through Trevor's introduction to the programme as a new and short-term character, audiences were able to dismiss him as 'evil' or 'mad' and take horrified pleasure in his manipulation of the family. If the production team had cast the abuser from the existing pool of actors, then this would have been far less easy to do. This point is made by a student in one of the research sessions:

If you had found out that Max [a regular, likeable character] was abusing his little boy it might have been more valid – well, not more valid but more worrying than Trevor. (female, FME)

The obvious next stage of developing sexual abuse storylines in soap opera would appear to be the casting of a 'known' character in this role. As I discussed earlier (Chapter 3), there is still reluctance on the part of programme makers to do this. The discussion above suggests that producers are correct in assessing 'what audiences want', but complex themes such as 'cycle of abuse' or intergenerational abuse are difficult to challenge without moving away from the 'panto baddie'. Constructing Trevor as 'villain' played on public knowledge of television codes in which the 'baddie' is clearly defined for audiences. As one participant explains:

Before you knew he was going to do anything you suspected. Beth talked about how she had been abused, and you know how you can tell who baddies are in TV programmes before you had seen him do anything? (FME)

The scenes which were recalled as particularly significant (such as when Mandy first allows Trevor back into the family home) suggest that audience pleasure was maximised when audience members were in the exclusive position of receiving more information than the key players. This supports the analysis by the production team members (Chapter 3).

Audiences discovered that Trevor had not in fact changed through the 'look in his eyes', achieved by the actor shots to camera directed 'to them' as viewers. As audiences watched Mandy struggle to decide whether or not to trust Trevor and allow him back into her life, the dramatic tension was enhanced for audiences by the prior knowledge that she should not.

Participants 'knew' that Trevor was 'bad' but few knew why. His motivations for perpetrating the abuse were unclear in the text. There were clues given in the narrative about the motivations of other characters, but no similar explanation for his abusive behaviour. This gap resulted in overwhelming responses to him as 'evil', 'a baddie' or simply a 'psycho', but participants found it very difficult to expand on this. Alternative explanations drew on existing popular theories such as that of the 'cycle of violence':

> I don't know, it could have been that he was abused when he was a child, because quite often that's the case. People who're abused are more likely to abuse when they're older. (male, PSS)

Some perceived Trevor as a psychologically disturbed individual. Thus his behaviour was the result of his individual pathology, rather than abuse of power:

> If he's not been put off by prison then that shows that it's something inside him, that's the way he is or he would stop himself. If it's not something psychological then he wouldn't do it again, but that showed that that's just him, that's the way he gets his kicks. (female, FMW)

> It was almost as though he was psychologically disturbed, and he beat his wife and he was a child molester. (female, US)

Many participants in the general population groups were entirely unsure about why Trevor had abused his daughters. The simple idea of recidivism was common and here participants revealed their close knowledge of the details ('Trevor did it before. He did it to the oldest girl [Beth] at just about the same age, fourteen' (female, OW)).

These are responses which echo the dearth of debate about the motivations of abusers in factual media. Debates rarely extend beyond the 'cycle of abuse', or the problem is framed as symptomatic of other social problems such as alcoholism. Constructing men who abuse as paedophiles operates to obscure discussions about power (Kelly 1996). Participants in general population groups did occasionally refer to his abuse as 'something about power?' (female, FME), but in contrast those who worked with survivors of abuse or who had been abused themselves always linked his actions to abuses of power. These participants did not consider that linking sexual and physical abuse was exaggerated. Instead this was considered to be completely realistic:

> I thought [the combination of physical and sexual abuse] was very good because the whole thing was about control. The man was very in control. (female, SW with TS group)

Rejection of the 'Collusive' Mother

Mandy Jordache presented audiences with a significant dilemma. Although no one expressed the view that she was deserving of the abuse, it was remarkable that few of the 'general population' audience participants considered her to be sympathetic or someone with whom they could identify. A mother who allowed her abusive husband to return to the family and failed to protect both daughters from abuse alienated a significant number of participants who had little knowledge of either domestic violence or sexual abuse. In contrast social workers and representatives from women's organisations praised Mandy's portrayal. She was considered to provide a rare and accurate portrayal of a woman who survives abuse but is isolated in a safe house with the problems of caring for her daughters alone. As one participant describes below, this character symbolised the continued pressures experienced by women who leave an abusive partner:

> [The programme conveys] the pressure on this woman, how difficult it was looking after the children on her own, being in a different area, just living in fear. In a way Mandy took him back and there was less fear because *she knew where he was*. (female, WO)

In many respects Mandy presented the most complex dilemma for audiences. Trevor provoked unproblematic feelings of hostility and fear, Beth and Rachel elicited unreserved feelings of sympathy, but Mandy was typically described as 'weak' or 'irritating'. Participants speculated about her lack of action: 'Why didn't she just call the police?' She frustrated and exasperated those in general population groups and was described as 'such a wet' (female, FME). In the group session with young women who had been sexually abused, the passive behaviour of this character was understood to be the result of experiencing long-term abuse. As one participant explained, 'Trevor's hurt her and now she's hurt and it's affected her' (female, TS). For those without this knowledge, Mandy's lack of action was incomprehensible, although, as one participant, explained it was not 'indifference, she doesn't act on what she knows' (female, FMW).

For some, this characterisation reduced the credibility of the overall storyline. The following exchange occurred within the research session with school students and reflects the gap in understanding of Mandy's behaviour.

> PSS1: To say that you could be sexually abused with your mother just down-stairs and her not know is a bit far fetched. I mean, [mothers] say they don't know but they normally do.
> [Author]: Why do you think that? Do you remember reading it or seeing it anywhere?
> PSS1: Well it's your mother, you know, she knows everything about you. (male, PSS)

Mandy was not only perceived as being responsible for the abuse of her children but also criticised for remaining with an abusive partner. The extent of Trevor's physical violence (in several scenes Mandy was shown being punched, kicked and beaten) was also considered by some participants as unrealistic (for those without any identifiable experience of domestic violence). These participants thought that 'no woman would remain with such a man'. As a university student explained:

> I don't know anyone who's been abused, but I'm not sure it's like that. I get the impression that there's women who put up with it for years and years, but it's not always a daily ritual, and because sometimes it happens rarely they say 'Oh that's not really him.' Whereas if you're living with someone like Trevor who did that to you every single day, you could hardly come up with the argument 'That's not the Trevor that I love', could you? (female, US)

The problem of 'mother-blaming' is well documented in literature about abuse (Hooper 1992) and was also familiar to members of the women's agencies group:

> Other people that I'd spoken to about [the programme] at the time were saying 'Oh for goodness sake, what did she take him back for?' You know that exasperation. If you're not working in this area and you haven't experienced it there's not that tolerance. (female, WO)

The character also reportedly generated anger amongst those who saw her as representing their own mothers who had 'failed' them. A Women's Aid worker recounted how she had spoken with a woman who had been sexually abused and had what she describes as 'this distorted anger towards their mother':

This woman was really struggling with this anger and came in after [*Brookside*] were portraying about the 'collusive' mother taking him back. She said to me, 'But it means nothing, just look at *Brookside*, that's what all mothers do.' And it was really hard, it was really distressing for that woman, and I'm sure for lots of women in that position, because it confirmed for her that all women will take [the abuser] back. (female, WO)

For those respondents whose own family experience was not abusive, the portrayal of Mandy was alien to strongly held beliefs about 'motherhood'. Audience participants who knew women in the same position found her portrayal realistic, whereas other groups expressed irritation and frustration at the abused wife and mother. This is a problem for agencies which attempt to challenge 'mother-blame' in cases of incest and 'victim-blame' where women live with domestic violence. Different feminist campaigns have tried to challenge negative public attitudes towards women who live with abusive partners (Kitzinger and Hunt 1993).

Understandings about Surviving Sexual Abuse: Anger and Denial

Beth Jordache appeared to make a powerful impact upon research participants. Participants across the groups praised her characterisation and repeatedly commented upon Beth's 'strength' and 'anger'. As one young woman said:

Beth was quite strong and she seemed to turn it into anger. I think she understood more about what was going on. Perhaps more than Rachel did. [Beth] had been through it before so she was quite determined that it wasn't going to happen again and quite protective of her sister. (female, FMW)

Those research participants who worked in the field of sexual violence welcomed this positive character and saw her as a role model with whom young survivors of abuse could identify. Beth challenged negative attitudes towards victims of abuse. Indeed, the pervasive nature of negative assumptions about abuse survivors was reflected in sessions with 'general population' groups in which comments were made that 'victims' would be 'scarred for life' or inevitably progress to becoming abusers themselves. A school student who had not watched the Jordache story believed that:

[Sexual abuse] would have such a big effect on your life psychologically that even if you made a conscious effort you don't know what you might do. (male, PSS)

Beth challenged such attitudes towards victims of abuse and, as one project worker from a women's support organisation describes it:

> I think Beth has shown amazing strengths in trying to protect herself, her sister and her mother, and at times appearing stronger even than her mother and taking control of things. (female, WO)

Audience reactions suggest that this character played a key role in conveying positive messages about survivors of abuse both to those who had experienced sexual abuse and to those who had no prior knowledge of the topic. The stigmatisation of sexual abuse survivors is potentially very difficult to challenge. One young woman who had watched the storyline (but had no other identifiable experience of sexual abuse) reflected that Beth's ability to come to terms with her abuse was unrepresentative. The strong characterisation of the abuse 'victim' did not, in her view, 'fit' with preconceived ideas about being 'scarred for life'. As she commented:

> [Beth] seemed to deal with [the abuse] quite well. She seemed to be really level headed about it, you know, saying to her sister 'It happened to me.' I don't think her character is affected by it as much as a real person would be. She seems to have got on so well. (female, FME)

Group participants also debated Beth's lesbian identity. Research participants quite clearly linked this new plot twist to the sexual abuse she had suffered and considered this to be a direct consequence of her father's abuse. As the school student quoted earlier explains, 'you see the continuing effects of the father's abuse . . . the older one turns away from men' (PSS). Other participants made similar comments: 'She might not even be a lesbian. It might just be because she's off men' (FME). Some participants saw the story as contributing to negative perceptions of gay men and women: 'People will think only people who have been abused when they're younger are gay' (FME). Those who worked with young women who have been sexually abused expressed concern for the message this conveyed to young survivors:

> Beth's very anti men just now. It appears she is in love with her friend Margaret but the fact that they've chosen the abused girl is disappointing. (WO)

> I think my fear was it might concern folk who'd been sexually abused that they would be off men and become lesbian. (SW with TS group)

For the young sexual abuse survivors, there was surprise that Beth would embark on a sexual relationship with anyone:

If that happened to her, she'd be like, yuck [shudders]. She'd be scared to do it with anybody altogether. (TS).

The portrayal of Rachel was more complex. This character conveyed the message that abuse victims often have mixed or confused feelings towards their abusers, such as denial, guilt, love and loyalty. This is a very important message, and it is a measure of the impact of the programme that participants understood that despite her abuse, 'Rachel still loves her Dad.' The characterisation of Rachel was commented upon within the session involving young survivors of abuse, and her challenging behaviour was perceived as reflecting their own. These teenage girls described Rachel fondly as 'cheeky' and 'a wee brat'. One said 'Give her an inch and she takes a mile.' Their social worker considered Rachel's 'difficult' behaviour to be typical and looked around the group of young women as she said '[Rachel's] now staying out and rebelling and having problems at school, does that ring a bell?' (SW with TS group). One participant who knew close friends who had been sexually abused drew on this knowledge to frame Rachel's denial:

Beth was grown up and of a different age. Younger ones don't know that [abuse is wrong]. They're usually told 'I really love you, that's why I'm doing this to you', 'Don't tell anybody, it's our secret', 'If you do tell on me I'll get into a lot of trouble', so there's a whole lot of guilt. That young girl's feelings are quite typical, you know. (female, US)

Rachel's 'state of denial' did, however, cause some confusion for infrequent viewers. Some people in general population groups doubted that she had indeed been sexually abused, because 'It's difficult to see how Rachel could have escaped the feelings of resentment and hatred for her father that the mother and Beth had' (female, US). Television soap opera viewing is not a seamless activity and infrequent viewers may miss vital information which contextualises character motivation and actions (Liebes and Katz 1990). However, in this instance it is interesting that, as discussed earlier (Chapter 3), a source revealed that the production team had simply 'forgotten' about Rachel and her abuse. It would appear that this absence managed *at the same time* to communicate with some success the confusion which is commonly experienced by the sexually abused child.

The sexual abuse survivor tends to be underrepresented in the media partly because of legal restrictions which influence how news media may feature children. Responses to these fictional characterisations suggest that this is a key area in which the form of television soap opera may be progressive. Indeed the strong and positive characterisation of Beth has been raised spontaneously in other studies about media coverage of child sexual abuse. It is worth reflecting upon the words of one young woman who was sexually abused by her stepfather:

> Victims [of sexual abuse] on TV, they're like a big shadow, all blacked out. That makes me feel terrible. I thought 'I'm going to grow up and I'm going to be scared of everything'. But Beth she's so strong, she's got a grip of everything. Before that everything I saw seemed to say that if you were abused you'd be strange, different, keep yourself in a wee corner. Watching Beth has really helped me. (Kitzinger 1999: 3)

Responses to Killing Trevor: Guilty Pleasures

It is rare that fictional accounts of child sexual abuse portray the killing of an abuser.[7] Participants expressed guilty pleasure particularly for the episodes which climaxed in Trevor's death. This development gripped viewers. As one woman commented, 'It sounds terrible but it was a story that you actually sat down to watch' (female, FME). Participants expressed tremendous pleasure in viewing the build-up to this and the techniques used to build tension. The following comments reflect the sheer audience pleasure:

> I was frightened when I was watching it. See when [Trevor] jumped up and he wasn't dead, I was like that, jumping in my seat and all that. See when [Mandy] did stab him I was just waiting for him to jump up again. (male, YC)

> I found [Trevor] evil. The way he treated his family and the way he kept coming back to life, they just couldn't get rid of him. (female, FME).

> I remember when they buried the body in the garden I kept being frightened to look out the window [laughs] in the middle of suburbia! [Female, OW).

Clearly, the framing of Trevor's character was crucial to audience acceptance of this act. Participants in both general population and special knowledge groups expressed delight at Mandy's actions:

> I would have done the exact same thing if I'd been in [Mandy's] shoes. (female, YC)

> The compelling thing was what was going to be the payback for this man and his behaviour, so I equally was delighted when they killed him. (psychologist with TS group)

The story appeared, at least for some research participants, to have conveyed that Mandy had simply no alternative course of action:

It showed that legal justice isn't any form of effective justice. (female, FME)

Despite the pleasure which viewers gained from watching the abused wife finally take action, this culmination of a previously well-handled storyline was described by some participants as having 'undone the good work' which had been achieved by earlier episodes.

I think it's a shame that they did that because it seems so far fetched, and everything else they did was quite true to life. (female, FMW)

I mean, *Brookside* had a good storyline going and they completely ruined it by doing what they did. (female, OW)

By killing him and burying him in the back garden for me it just wrote off all the good parts. (WO)

The session with teenage survivors, however, revealed that for at least one young girl, the much-hyped murder scene had in fact provided an incentive to watch the programme:

I was reading about it and I read that [Mandy] was going to murder him with her daughter, and I started watching. (female, TS)

For these research participants, the killing of an abuser in a prime-time television soap opera fulfilled 'revenge fantasies'. None of the teenage girls expressed the slightest doubt that Mandy and Beth had 'done the right thing', as the following exchange illustrates:

TS1: I would've done the same as well.
TS2: If you ask me [men who abuse] shouldn't have a chance to live.
TS3: They done bad and as soon as they get out they do it over and over again.
TS2: [Soaps] should either have [abusers] going to jail for life, not getting back out or getting murdered or something.
TS3: Or molested.
TS2: Yeah, something like that happening.

However, in groups which did not share this experience of sexual abuse, the killing of Trevor was assumed to have only negative effects on those people in a similar position. As one young person said:

Figure 7.1 Trevor goes upstairs: Channel 4, *Brookside*, 30 April 1993

I can see why they did it but if people are in that situation then obviously they can't do what [Beth and Mandy] did. [*Brookside*] didn't show a way out of it, show [Trevor] getting better or anything, and he'd gone into prison and come out just the same. (female, FMW)

The Script-Writing Exercise: Understandings of Complex Emotions

There were some clear differences between the audience groups in how they responded to the different characterisations of members of the Jordache family and certain elements of the storyline development. As we have seen, prior experience or knowledge of sexual violence was a key factor in how research participants understood and identified with the characters. In this section, I begin to explore the influence of the television soap opera storyline on research participants, and focus not on what audiences bring to their viewing experience (in terms of pre-existing knowledge, gender or social class) but on what they might 'take away' from it.

The potential for television soap opera to communicate complex emotions was revealed in the results of the 'script writing exercise' used during the group sessions. Participants were given a set of photographs (figures 7.1–7.4) taken from the key scene in which Trevor sexually abuses his

Figure 7.2 Trevor stands outside Rachel's room: Channel 4, *Brookside*,
30 April 1993

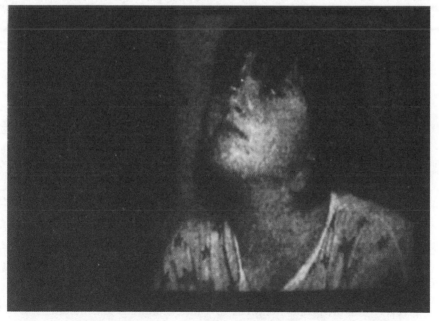

Figure 7.3 Rachel listens to her father: Channel 4, *Brookside*, 30 April 1993

Figure 7.4 Beth runs upstairs: Channel 4, *Brookside*, 30 April 1993

daughter Rachel. Working in small groups, participants were asked to produce dialogue to match the photographs.

It is instructive to compare the actual dialogue which appeared in the episode and the scripts which were produced by research participants. As noted earlier, the scene in which Trevor rapes Rachel was considered to be a 'turning point' in the Jordache story. The participants were given no information about the plot and had to work purely from the photographs.[8] Some were extremely accurate in their reproduction of the dialogue and in reproducing key themes from the story. This is a summary of the scene:

(TREVOR VICIOUSLY BEATS MANDY THEN CLIMBS THE STAIRS TO RACHEL'S BEDROOM. HE HESITATES THEN ENTERS THE ROOM AS RACHEL LOOKS UP SLEEPILY.)
Trevor: Rachel. It's okay.
Rachel: Is Mum okay?
Trevor: She's fine, she's asleep. I'm cold, are you going to warm me up, eh? Just give me a cuddle like you used to. You lie down, there's a good girl. I used to lie awake in prison wishing you could give me a cuddle.
Rachel: Did you?
Trevor: Hundreds and hundreds of times, hundreds and hundreds of times.

(BETH RETURNS HOME TO DISCOVER MANDY LYING INJURED. SHE RUSHES UPSTAIRS AND CHECKS EACH BEDROOM BEFORE SLOWLY OPENING RACHEL'S DOOR. AS SHE SEES TREVOR AND RACHEL TOGETHER IN BED A LOOK OF HORROR CROSSES HER FACE.)
CUT TO SIGNATURE TUNE AND CLOSING CREDITS.

(Brookside, 30 April 1993)

THE FOLLOWING MORNING RACHEL IS WITHDRAWN.
Mandy: (TO RACHEL) He won't do anything more to you. I'm sorry I wasn't there to stop him.
Rachel: He didn't do anything, he's my Dad.
Beth: Rachel, listen, I know what happened because he did the same to me before he went to prison, but what you've got to understand is none of it's your fault.
Rachel: I didn't want him to be like that. I trusted him. He said he needed a cuddle.
Mandy: Now don't you worry. Mummy won't let him touch you again. Ever.

(Brookside, 3 May 1993)

On 10 June 1994, thirteen months later, a group of private school students produced this version of the scene:

Trevor: Hello, darling. (WHISPERED, CONFIDENTIAL TONES, SECRETIVE) I'm really cold tonight. . .Why don't you give your daddy a cuddle?
(MOVES CLOSER, LIFTS EDGE OF DUVET)
(RACHEL APPREHENSIVE, SLIGHTLY AFRAID ALTHOUGH NAIVE, TRUSTFUL AND ACCEPTING. DOESN'T REALISE FULL IMPLICATIONS OF EVENT)
PANIC RISES WITHIN BETH, MUTTERS
Beth: Please don't let him be in there with her.
(APPROACHES TENTATIVELY WITH FEAR OF DISCERNING HER FATHER IN BEDROOM).
(GUILT IN MOTHER): Mandy: How could I have let this happen to them?
Beth: He can't hurt her again. We're here now. You'll be OK.
Rachel: (CONFUSED, HURT THAT FATHER HAS BETRAYED HER, DISBELIEF) Why did this happen to me? Is it my fault? Will I ever feel the same again?

On 15 March 1994, eleven months after the programme, a group of state school students produced this version of the scene:

AS TREVOR MAKES HIS WAY UP THE STAIRS HE HAS ONLY ONE THING ON HIS MIND. THE RESULT WILL BE STEALING

HIS DAUGHTER'S CHILDHOOD. WE COULD IMAGINE WHAT
HIS THOUGHTS WOULD SAY. MAYBE HE HAS A CONSCIENCE
AS HE STOPS OUTSIDE RACHEL'S ROOM.
RACHEL IS SURPRISED TO SEE HER DAD.
Rachel: Dad, what are you doing here?
Trevor: It's all right. I'm lonely and a wee bit cold, give your dad a cuddle.
Beth: Oh my God, I hate him, please no, I'll kill him.
RACHEL IS CONFUSED AND THINKS HOW COULD MY MUM
LET HIM DO THIS TO ME?
Beth: He did it to me too. Don't worry, we'll never let him do it again.
MANDY DOESN'T KNOW WHAT TO SAY. SHE FEELS HELPLESS
AND FEELS SHE LET IT HAPPEN AND MAYBE SHE COULD
HAVE STOPPED HIM.

There are striking similarities between these scripts produced by audience participants and the original dialogue. The scripts closely replicate
key phrases used by Trevor to gain access to Rachel's bed ('I'm really cold
tonight . . . Why don't you give your daddy a cuddle?'; 'I'm lonely and a
wee bit cold, give your dad a cuddle'). The scripts also address the possible effects of abuse on Rachel ('Will I ever feel the same again?', 'The result
will be stealing his daughter's childhood'). They reproduce Beth's fear and
feelings of protectiveness towards her sister ('Please don't let him be in
there with her', 'Oh my God, I hate him, please no, I'll kill him'). The
scripts address Mandy as a collusive mother ('Mandy doesn't know what
to say. She feels helpless and feels she let it happen and maybe she could
have stopped him', '(Guilt in mother) Mandy: How could I have let this
happen to them?'). The scripts replicate the actual dialogue next morning
when Beth and Mandy try to reassure Rachel ('He can't hurt her again.
We're here now. You'll be OK', 'He did it to me too. Don't worry, we'll
never let him do it again').

The similarities between the viewer reproductions of such themes and
the actual broadcast dialogue are all the more striking when you examine
the scripts produced by those who had no knowledge of the story. The following script was created by a group of retired women who had no prior
knowledge of the actual storyline and had never watched the programme.
It was created just five months after the scene was transmitted (6 October
1993).

FATHER MAKING WAY UP TO BEDROOM. REACHES BEDROOM
DOOR. DAUGHTER LOOKING SCARED.
Younger daughter: Please don't touch me. I don't like it.
Older daughter: What are you doing in there, Daddy?

Younger daughter: Go on, tell Mum what has been happening.
Mother: I don't believe it.
Father when confronted says, 'This is nonsense, I wouldn't do anything like
    that.'

This script is markedly different from the other two scripts above. The difficulties of a child preventing abuse were not addressed in any respect. The role of the mother is not problematised. The abuser is confronted by the women instantly and flatly denies the abuse. This account of abuse lacks the complexity and emotion of the other scripts. It is simplistic in its framing of the child's ability to prevent abuse and her subsequent insistence that her mother should be told. There is no space given here to 'denial' or complex, mixed emotions experienced by the child towards her abusive father or unsupportive mother. Scripts based upon prior knowledge of *Brookside* described Rachel as having a mix of emotions (confused, hurt, naive and trustful). In other words, there are different, competing emotional feelings. The script produced above simply refers to the child as 'scared'.

This exercise shows that those participants who had watched the unfolding *Brookside* story retained key phrases and were able to reproduce dialogue with remarkable ease. In addition to closely reproducing the actual scene and specific lines of the script these participants, also demonstrated an understanding of the complex, hidden family dynamics. The relationship between abuser and victim, mother and daughters, and older and younger sister were all explored. It seems extraordinary that viewers of the programme were able to do this given that there was a gap of about one year between watching the original episode and being asked to produce a script.

Some Reflections

The discussion above suggests that television soap opera may have an important influence on public understandings. It appears that in this case *Brookside* was successful in communicating important, often complex, messages about the issue for audiences with no other experience of abuse. Indeed this was the first time that some of the general population group participants had watched a television programme about the topic, which suggests that at the very least serial drama can bring particular issues to different audiences. Key moments in the story, particularly the rape scene, took audiences literally 'behind closed doors' to the moment of abuse. This made a profound and lasting impact upon those who had watched the scene. Participants were able to recall imagery and reproduce dialogue from the scene almost verbatim many months after the episodes were originally transmitted.

The potential of the genre of television soap opera to portray the complexity of coming to terms with abuse over time may be particularly important. Certainly, for those who had themselves been sexually abused, the characterisation of Beth and Rachel as visible survivors rather than 'hidden victims' provided crucial figures with whom it was possible to identify.

The story provided an important opportunity to tackle pervasive myths about abuse and was, in this respect, welcomed by those with personal or professional experience in the field. However, there were some important differences between some groups, depending on their own experiences. This highlights potential gaps between the intention of producers and responses by audiences. Mandy's perceived failure to protect her daughters from abuse and herself from physical violence was viewed as 'collusion'. This would suggest that the programme was successful in confronting some myths around 'victim-blame', but not others. The lack of empathy and indeed frustration expressed towards Mandy by general population groups reflects the power of negative assumptions about women who remain with abusive partners.

But those who rejected Mandy as a sympathetic character did not do so on the grounds of having 'misunderstood' or 'misread' the intended message. These participants understood that Mandy had been constructed (by the production team) as deserving of audience empathy; however, they rejected this message on the grounds of logic and personal experience as well as a powerful ideology of motherhood ('I'm sure it's not like that', 'your mother . . . knows everything about you').

There were other key differences in terms of specific themes and responses to characters. Participants with no special knowledge of the issue perceived Trevor as representing a 'mentally ill' deviant. Those with experience of the issue saw his abusive behaviour as motivated by the desire for power and the wish to control his family. The combined physical and sexual abuse was perceived as unrealistic and exaggerated by those without prior knowledge of these issues. By contrast, those who had experience of working with abusers and abuse survivors (social workers, Women's Aid workers) considered that the story made important and realistic links between physical and sexual violence. Strongly held beliefs about abusers as being simply 'evil' or 'mad' were reinforced for general population groups by Trevor's unpredictable and volatile characterisation, although these dimensions of his character added considerably to storyline tension and narrative pace.

The Jordache story arguably increased knowledge and understandings about the language, reality and effects of abuse. However, as I noted earlier, the general population groups largely rejected the idea of identifying or empathising with Mandy. This appeared to be on the grounds that 'a mother would always know' if her child was in danger, that they themselves would take swift action against an abuser and that abusers are identifiable. This apparent failure to communicate some of the more complex and problematic aspects of the mother's position or to raise debates around 'why men abuse' reflects the dearth of debates in the wider media. However, the *Brookside* text may be an important factor. Trevor was introduced as an external and short-term character and had no prior history in the programme. If the abuse had been perpetrated by a regular, established character, then it is possible that participants might have engaged more fully with debates concerning the motivations for abuse and how it may be prevented. As it was, the character was easily sidelined as mentally disturbed. Indeed through the character's construction as a 'monster', research participants were spared the potentially threatening figure of the abuser as 'the ordinary man'. Participants with no special knowledge of the issue accepted in theory that abusers 'can be anyone', yet in practice rejected the idea of a more complex fictional portrayal of an abuser. The source of this belief rested on fears about personal safety: in other words, whom could you trust?[9]

Participants also seemed willing to accept in theory that 'any child' can be at risk from abuse, yet in practice resisted the idea that children whom they knew might be. Indeed it is difficult to see how positive messages can circulate when there are such strong feelings that a 'normal' childhood could be damaged by just knowing about sexual abuse. Television fiction was considered by some to increase the likelihood that children would make false allegations, though those who had experience of working with children who have been abused challenged this view as simply incorrect.

Thus, despite significant support for the idea that television fiction should portray child sexual abuse, there are at the same time considerable anxieties and ambiguities in terms of prevention and education. The very same participants who praised the programme still rejected the idea of their own children or those they knew watching the story. In other words, these representations were perceived as contributing to a more positive social climate for those who had already been abused, but not for 'innocent' children. The fear of corruption of innocence or of the malicious, false allegations of the naive child were entirely absent in those groups where members had some specific knowledge and understanding of the issue from direct experience. Such concerns connect with deeply felt fears about the existence and nature of sexual abuse, and also arguably reflect the public anxiety which surrounds the inclusion of new and unfamiliar topics in the television soap opera. In this respect we can assume that responses may change as the topic moves increasingly into the domain of popular culture.

So what does this tell us about the relationship between production team and audiences? Certainly it would seem to support the view that producers, script-writers and other programme personnel do 'know' their audience (see Chapter 3). There were clear and identifiable links between the decisions which were made by members of the production team concerning characterisation and story development and how audiences responded. The camera techniques used to frame Trevor were successful in building suspense and narrative tension. Beth was a strong and confident role model for younger people and particularly important for young survivors. Though the consequences of Rachel's abuse were not dealt with immediately, due to human error, this delay in fact appeared to communicate important messages about the 'denial' of the abused child who still loves her father and wants him to remain with the family.

Examining the production context of a storyline in addition to exploring how audiences respond can help to generate valuable insights into the communication process. It has been possible to explore how the production team conceive of their audience and the extent to which audiences interpret storylines in the ways in which production teams intend.

Notes

1   The focus groups in this study involved sixty-nine participants in twelve sessions and took place in the West of Scotland (see Appendix). These sessions were tape-recorded and fully transcribed and then analysed manually (involving a coding framework in which numerical codes were applied across each group to highlight variations in response). Participants completed an exercise using photographs taken from a storyline rather than actually watching a television programme. This was to guard against generating an artificial affective response to the material and also to preserve ethical commitments, particularly towards those who might themselves have experienced abuse. Some of this was discussed in an industry report I produced for Channel 4 television and which was submitted on behalf of the channel to the National Commission of Inquiry into Child Abuse at the request of Michael Grade (Henderson 1996).

2   The groups were structured to include those who had an identifiable 'special knowledge' of the issue (young women who were survivors of sexual abuse; professionals who worked in the area, such as social workers) and 'general population' groups (involving participants who were randomly chosen to reflect different social backgrounds and demographics).

3 Where extracts have been taken from participant responses to individual questionnaires, I have also noted participants' sex, age, group description, *Brookside*-watching frequency, and experience of sexual abuse. Where participants discussed these issues in the group session, I have included details of group ID.

4 It is impossible in practice to 'screen' participants for experiences such as domestic violence or sexual abuse. Some participants in 'general population' groups did reveal, in a confidential questionnaire which was completed at the close of the session, that they had been sexually abused. Sexual abuse and domestic violence are of course still very difficult topics to discuss, and some of the responses from those in 'general population' groups may be influenced by direct experience which was not revealed in the research session. The groups were 'naturally occurring' in that participants knew each other prior to the session, but they were not family groups, as it was considered to be a difficult topic to discuss in this setting (see Philo 1996b:103). Where possible, I have identified when participants in 'general population' groups are speaking from direct experience (knowing someone who was abused or were themselves abused). All of the groups were facilitated by myself and were tape-recorded and fully transcribed. Martin Barker highlights some useful principles of conducting and presenting qualitative research (Barker 2003).

5 It has been noted elsewhere that people frequently believe that others, particularly 'weak' groups such as children, are more influenced by mass media texts than we are ourselves. This is termed a 'third-person effect' (see Höijer 1999: 188).

6 In other studies Trevor was described as typically representing someone suffering from schizophrenia. As one woman explains, 'that man who is the child-abuser and the wife-beater – he looks like schizophrenic – he's like a split personality, like two different people. First he gets like self-pity and he brings flowers and works his way back into the house and you could feel sorry for him, then he's a child-abuser and a wife-beater' (Philo 1996a: 96).

7 The story received further media attention when a young woman was allegedly inspired by the programme to kill her abusive grandfather. Press coverage framed the case as a 'copycat' murder. Just as Beth was motivated by protecting her sister from abuse, so this young woman tried to protect a younger sister from sexual abuse. Typical headlines linked events to the programme: 'Judge's pity for "Brookside Killer": Abused Teenager Took Cue From TV Murder' (*Daily Mail*, 19 July 1995); 'Girl Copied TV To Kill Evil Grandad' (*Daily Mirror*, 19 July 1995); 'Brookside Copycat Girl Kills Grandad' (*Daily Star*, 19 July 1995). A police officer was quoted in these reports and said the woman had been 'clearly influenced' by the programme. He is quoted as follows: 'We found entries in her diary about the plot and newspaper cuttings in her bedroom about victims of child abuse taking their revenge' (*Daily Mail*, 19 July 1995).

8 Figures 7.1–7.4 are photographs used in the script-writing exercise (Channel 4, *Brookside*, 30 April 1993). An additional photograph showing Beth and

Mandy comforting Rachel the next morning was also included (Channel 4, *Brookside*, 3 May 1993).

9 There have been recent attempts by film makers to explore the 'paedophile' in more complex ways and subvert audience expectations (*Hard Candy*, Lions Gate Films, 2006; *The Woodsman*, Newmarket Films, 2004; *Little Children*, New Line Cinema, 2006).

Part V Television Fiction and Public Knowledge

CHAPTER 8

Conclusions

Introduction

John Thornton Caldwell has pointed out that the discipline of cultural studies 'tends to gloss over one of the most important components of tele-visuality – the industry' (Caldwell 1995: 24). In this book I have been mainly concerned with the industry – with articulating the production factors which influence how different substantive topics are selected and subsequently developed within popular television programmes. In the case of sexual violence I have been able to trace this process through to explore audience understandings. Inevitably the cases I have discussed here are culturally specific, 'snapshots' of a dynamic process which reflect mainly UK production contexts. They are also potentially time specific, address-ing television production when those working within the industry were beginning to witness the intensified demands of commercial imperatives, the proliferation of channels and the fragmentation of audiences. In this concluding chapter I wish to extend the debate and briefly address the ide-ological struggle over prime-time entertainment in terms of wider ques-tions concerning cultural forms, public knowledge and citizenship. These are matters of central importance not least in the current climate, where prevailing 'culture wars' means that US media and popular television in particular are under significant scrutiny from those with a conservative agenda.

Production Matters

Few would argue that the television serial has brought a staggering array of issues to diverse audiences. Dorothy Hobson describes it thus: 'domes-tic violence, murder, gay and lesbian sexuality, race, drugs, child abuse, transsexuality, divorce, breast cancer, male impotence, menopause. The list is endless and the effects endlessly positive' (Hobson 2003: 210). I hope to have demonstrated in earlier discussions that a list of issues risks oversimplifying the complex and dynamic nature of the production process. Tensions over programme direction, ideological commitments and perceptions of audiences needs are played out within and around these issues. Furthermore, we cannot simply assume that the effects are necessarily 'endlessly positive'.

In the first section below, I begin by outlining some key findings from the production case studies, before considering how these might link with existing ideas about television fiction and the soap opera as a relatively 'open' television format. Finally, I conclude with some thoughts on directions in media and communications research.

Production Factors

British television fiction has always been considered to be distinct from the American context, where advertisers have far more direct input into the programme (Geraghty 1991: 4). Indeed advertisers are held responsible for having 'profoundly influenced the aesthetics of American television drama' (Gripsrud 1995: 28). Despite this, as we have seen earlier, there is considerable pressure experienced by producers in terms of the positioning of their programme, and implicitly producers do share the concerns of advertisers (audience demographics), a fact which has repercussions for how stories are selected and cast. Despite the current impact of reality programmes in contemporary broadcast schedules, the television soap opera is still a vital format for a broadcasting organisation. Such programmes occupy an important position, represent the key ratings strategy and contribute to the overall image (and economics) of the channel. The format is thus closely monitored, in terms of language and imagery, by internal senior management and external organisations. The soap storyline is subject to self-censorship at the level of the producer, who, as we have seen, is keen not to jeopardise the relationship with senior management. The writers are far less concerned with these priorities. The soap storyline, as has been demonstrated, is the product of many different men and women at different points within the organisation. Soap opera production team members do bring all of their experiences (prejudices, misconceptions, expertise) to bear upon constructing a story for audiences and are sometimes explicitly encouraged to do so, acting as a surrogate audience.

Despite the way story development is framed in the discourse of some soap production workers – that is, as simply highlighting the 'natural' concerns of the characters – television soap production is a (commercially driven) process and storylines do not simply 'mirror' natural concerns. Certain issues may be adopted in order to drive the programme in a particular direction. These 'big stories' are assigned to particular existing characters (because of their 'look', their soap history or their demographic appeal). New characters can be introduced to take on a particular storyline, thus allowing the production team the freedom of 'trying out' a character and also enabling the character, and the issue, to be dispensed with if the story is not well received by audiences (or indeed by senior management).

There is undoubtedly programme diversity, but there are clearly some concerns which are shared by all soap operas regardless of their institutional context or their production ethos. Shared narrative codes and formal structures require pace, notably the use of cliff-hangers (Buckingham 1987). That there is an implicit role played by the 'imagined' audience in these sorts of decisions is not a new observation (see Espinosa 1982; Gans 1957). But addressing the perspectives of those who play a role in story development beyond the programme producer or channel senior management allows us to see the role played by the 'imagined audience' at every level. As David Buckingham writes 'Every decision – from killing off a character to selecting their wardrobe – entails making assumptions about viewers and the potentially diverse ways in which they may respond' (Buckingham 1987: 35). Exploring these assumptions allows us to witness the production process as a dynamic site of struggle and negotiation; a feature that is sometimes neglected in studies of TV fiction production. The script-writers, story editors and consultants who work in television soap opera frequently provide different accounts of the background to story development from the 'official accounts' of senior management, but their perspectives are often overlooked. Examining the role of these less senior production workers provides valuable insights into the 'team process' and can reveal a significant level of commitment to storylines not only from the producers but also from 'those on the ground'.

Diversity

There is value in addressing how this process works across different programmes. The soap genre is not a single entity, and while it has been argued that there is considerable diversity between European, US and British soap opera (Liebes and Livingstone 1998), there is also arguably diversity within a specific cultural context too. It is possible to see in practice how the philosophies and ethos of production teams bring their vision to their work (thus mapping intra-genre diversity). Different programmes do vary importantly in their self-image and agenda. Some actively pursue an 'agenda setting' ethos, whereas others favour 'entertainment'. However, this can be subject to change. The problem of 'inference' on the basis of textual analysis alone becomes significant here when viewers, media critics or indeed academic researchers assume that a production team is 'obviously' engaged in producing social education television, but in practice the same team holds a self-image in which they are simply reflecting back the events of the world.

These key differences in reputation, philosophy and ethos clearly interconnect, influence the production priorities of different soaps, and in turn relate to the nature of representation. Both *Brookside* and *Emmerdale* tackled sexual violence within the family; however, *Brookside* attempted to portray the moment of abuse (a risky departure for a pre-watershed soap) whereas *Emmerdale* tackled the topic retrospectively, thus dispensing with the need to portray the abuse or the abuser. This suggests that both productions 'knew' their audiences and recognised that audiences bring different viewing expectations to a particular programme.

Socio-Cultural Factors

In mapping the wider socio-economic context within which storylines are produced, we can address the often implicit relationship between the values presented in the story, those involved in making the story and those in the wider society. By delineating or unpacking the underlying assumptions about what constitutes a 'good soap story' and 'what audiences want', it is possible to examine the priorities and values of the soap production team and their assumed audience.

Exploring the production context of diverse substantive storyline topics allows us to address wider questions about whether some issues are socially approved and others are not. Breast cancer, mental distress and child sexual abuse have been shown to be positioned very differently, and this had clear consequences for the nature of representation. Breast cancer and child sexual abuse were perceived by production team members as topics deserving of serious commitment, whereas mental distress (in this case erotic obsession and stalking) formed the basis of a gripping plot designed to drive the narrative pace, rather than performing any social education function. This reflects how specific issues are positioned within a specific cultural context. It also arguably reflects inequities of access to media and of credibility awarded to source organisations working in diverse fields. The extent to which outside agencies are permitted to become involved in the production process here becomes an index of their relative power. The support of breast cancer organisations was explicitly sought and research on the perpetrators and survivors of sexual abuse was conducted; by contrast, no research was undertaken into the type of mental distress stories that the team wished to tell. This has identifiable consequences for the specific development of storylines (for example, the editing of sexual violence scenes and the care taken over portrayals of the breast cancer survivor). Montgomery has observed how public health organisations and environmental groups sometimes directly approach the makers of fictional programmes to play a role in educating the American public about issues:

> As long as such appeals are made in modes acceptable to the entertainment industry, they will be tolerated, and may even be encouraged. Such requests will be accommodated to the extent that they are compatible with the needs of entertainment television. (Montgomery 1989: 223)

Here I simply wish to reinforce the point that soap operas do under certain circumstances take on issues at the behest of source organisations (see *Brookside*'s breast cancer story). However, as Montgomery correctly suggests, there is a distinct power imbalance. Story development does not rest with outside agencies but within the production team and organisational hierarchy. To assume that a fictional storyline will necessarily increase public understandings in a positive way is to invest the soap opera with a role and responsibility that may be unfeasible. It is also important to note that audiences may not respond in ways which the programme makers anticipate or which policy makers or source organisations would wish (see, for example, how general population groups rejected identifying with the plight of the 'battered wife'). Put simply, collaborations with soaps must be carefully judged and not assumed to produce a direct line to necessarily 'better' representations. Important opportunities may be found in liaising with particular programmes which have an identity which allows for a mutually beneficial collaboration. More challenging representations are unlikely to be developed without a personal commitment from producers and writers.

There is a curious paradox in that source organisations and lobbying groups are swift to 'blame the media' for inaccurate or insensitive portrayals, yet few organisations would resist the opportunity to collaborate with what they see as a powerful force for public persuasion. Although any study of news making would be considered incomplete if it neglected to address the role of sources, the same fascinating 'tug of war' over the fictional storyline remains largely unexplored. The 'struggles' for definition and how these are resolved are important in that they may reveal a great deal about the relative power wielded by different groups.

Research, Statistics and Soap Sense

A central aim of this book has been to address the discourse which exists concerning the use of outside research for soaps. I hope to have demonstrated that there is no simple correlation between such research and representation. In particular, the writers subscribe to a professionalism culture in which they perceive themselves as artists, a point also noted about writers on American prime-time series *Dynasty* (see Gripsrud 1995). There is no single view within each production about story development and the use of outside research. Explicit inter – production conflicts are always resolved in favour of those with power – in other words, senior management – but script writers fiercely guard what autonomy they do have, and have considerable commitment to their professional integrity and their ability to bring the human experience to screen.

Social issue storylines bring particular responsibilities and scrutiny, yet despite this, as with any story, narrative pace and aesthetic codes were nonetheless used to engage audiences. We have seen in detail how traditional soap devices such as the 'cliff-hanger' were used to different extents and with different purposes (to engender empathy for 'insiders'; to elicit hate for 'outsiders'), and how decisions made over casting and characterisation were premised on previous knowledge of what might work for audiences. Indeed, much as there has been identified a 'news sense', I would argue that soap opera production personnel bring an instinctive 'soap sense' to their work. While this soap sense is not necessarily ever explicitly defined or spoken of, it nonetheless operates as a constant guide to shape production decisions in particular directions. Members of the team understand what works for audiences in specific ways. Industry practitioners and academics may not share the same 'lingo', but industry professionals do theorise about audiences (Caldwell 1995). To this I would add that whereas sociological studies of news production have emphasised that 'the "audience" or the "public" has a kind of phantom existence' (Schudson 1993: 156), those members of production teams working in television drama have audiences perhaps more in mind than other broadcast professionals.[1] This can, as we have seen in previous chapters, both limit and expand the possibilities for representation.

The Importance of Genre

A central theme running through the production interviews with different programme personnel were the distinctions made between the genres of soap and television documentary. However, it is possible to identify commonalities, with documentary makers operating within some of the same constraints as soap opera production teams. The requirements of narrative pace, cliff-hangers and engaging the audience are elements which are not confined to television fiction but are important factors for other television programme makers. There is also no simple correlation between including users of services (as opposed to fictional characters) and framing mental distress in more challenging ways. Issues of privacy, ethics and stigma may work against including certain groups of mental health service users. Central issues such as filming psychiatric patients in hospital because of ease of access immediately exclude groups of users who would possibly present very different accounts of their experiences. The level of control exerted by the medical hierarchy was also noted as an important factor in securing access to patients. The problem of 'self-selecting' patients, people who were seen as 'professionally mentally ill' with little to lose by identifying themselves on screen, was perceived by documentary makers as the patients themselves contributing to media accounts (skewed towards the violent or unpredictable). In this area the role played by the broadcasting hierarchy may be very important. Documentary makers have spoken of the hierarchical pressure to produce dramatic accounts of mental distress. In some respects TV drama producers may have more autonomy over the eventual product than do documentary makers, even those who produce documentary series independently.

In other respects, it was possible to identify the factors which might facilitate more challenging portrayals. Here there are four key factors at the level of production, which may influence the nature of representation in other non-news television formats. First, the relative easing of deadline pressure allows for carrying out more thoughtful independent research; second, the ethos of a programme may facilitate more critical representation that challenges prevailing images; third, the personal experience of production team members can engender commitment to a specific area; and finally, the support of senior broadcasting management can override the constraints of working towards 'the popular' or 'the familiar'.

A Progressive Form?

The repetition, seriality and unresolved narrative structure of soap opera have been cited as reflecting the 'essential' nature of femininity (Modleski 1982), the 'culturally constructed skills of femininity' (Brunsdon 1981) and the organisation of 'women's time' (Hobson 1982). In this respect, studies of romantic serials have been concerned with exploring the formal structures of the genre in relation to questions of women's subordination and wider structures of patriarchy (Lovell 1981).

The studies mentioned above have, broadly, characterised the genre of television soap opera as inherently 'progressive' in its focus on women and the domestic sphere. While the older female viewer is unlikely to be part of the audience sought by advertisers, television soap opera provides a vital role for the older woman, the matriarch, traditionally at the heart of the narrative. This meant that *EastEnders* was able to provide a valuable counterpoint to the images of the young female cancer survivors which dominate media reporting of the topic, and to challenge the existing marginalisation of older women's experiences in mainstream media.

The repetitive nature of soap, with its core of established characters, may also allow a level of identification and empathy which is impossible to replicate in other fictional forms (for example, the single play). This familiarity and repetition of course also allow viewers to bring a distinctive historical context to the airing of a social problem, which would simply not be possible in news and documentary programming. The structure of the television serial facilitates 'coming to terms' with an issue over time and can include important emotional dimensions of ambivalence, confusion, anger and denial.

These possibilities are constrained by a number of factors both internal and external (organisational ethos, regulatory and censorship issues, underpinned by commercial imperatives). The relative 'openness' of television fiction has been identified as a vital space which 'enjoys significant advantages over journalism which make it, *potentially at least*, more flexible in the way it can deal with issues' (emphasis added) (Schlesinger et al. 1983: 77).

Thus groups of people can be brought together in a television drama who would never have shared screen space in news or documentary programmes (for example, 'terrorists' and members of security forces). The fictional format can thus enable discussion of the philosophy and motivations of groups, a discussion which may be absent from other media. However, this is a potential and not a 'given'. Television fiction is subject to, 'the commercial pressures of the rating battle and . . . the constraints and possibilities of the genres and narrative styles they adopt' (Schlesinger et al. 1983: 77).

Certainly television fiction may be progressive in its sheer ability to depict that which is so often absent from our screens: 'the abused and abuser', the 'patient' at the point of medical diagnosis. These are important portrayals which would quite rightly be governed by legal and ethical considerations in any other format. The serial nature of television soap opera also enables the revisiting of issues over time, and thus it is in theory possible for audiences to witness the trajectory of personal trauma over time (unlimited time), but in practice of course this too is a possibility and not a given.

Managing Risk

The lack of risk taking in television soap opera is a theme which reverberates through studies of American television. It has been seen to characterise the production process, in which the overriding concern is to avoid issues that will 'split the audience' (Intintoli 1984). Dorothy Hobson argued in her early study of *Crossroads* that 'Although the solutions to problems may not be seen as progressive, it is often the raising of those problems in fictional forms that is important' (Hobson 1982: 131). Yet even in the cases discussed here, we can see that under certain circumstances audiences are provided with radical resolutions to social problems. The portrayal of an abused wife killing her abuser to protect her children could be considered fairly radical. It provided a rare representation of a powerless woman taking control (the act also fulfilled revenge fantasies for young survivors of sexual abuse). This is not to overstate the ability of the genre to move outside the consensus. Some issues, such as incest or homosexuality, which may explode the family structure have in the past been 'simply ignored' in television soaps (Modleski 1982). These same issues may be beginning to form the basis of regular storylines, but these risks are still managed, incorporated and ultimately neutralised. Broader substantive themes may be governed by wider cultural concerns and reveal socio-cultural anxieties (for example, the necessity that Trevor had abused Beth only once), and potentially these tap into concerns which are beyond the programme. Such decisions may equally, however, operate to heighten the threat of these issues to the soap community and consequently intensify tensions for audiences. In the case of the abusive fictional characters, there was no attempt to integrate them within the soap structure; they were always intended to be 'written off ' (Fuqua 1995). By drawing upon traditional characterisations of the 'villain' and using cues from popular cinema films, a deeply threatening story of sexual violence may be transformed almost into pantomime (see Chapter 3). Furthermore, despite what has traditionally been observed about the soap opera narrative and its engagement with audiences, not all members of the audience need identify with the fictional 'problem'. Instead it would seem that production teams must generate 'affective' engagement. In short, what matters is that audiences 'care'. It is this element which will deliver and sustain audiences for the production.

Researching Television

In comparison with writing about television news media, the 'non-fixed' nature of the soap serial (the ways in which storylines continuously shift and characters change) makes it a difficult format to analyse in simple ways. Christine Geraghty describes writing about soap opera as 'a perilous business. There is no fixed object of study over which the critic can pore, hoping to extract a further nuance' (Geraghty 1991: 7). As discussed above, the lack of narrative closure in television soap opera defines the format, but this has had significant consequences for how such programmes have been studied and conceptualised. As Robert C. Allen writes:

> The absence of a final moment of narrative closure also indefinitely postpones any moment of final ideological or moral closure in the open serial. This probably makes the open serial a poor vehicle for the inculculation of particular values, but it does mean that open serial writers and producers can raise any number of potentially controversial and contentious social issues without having to make any ideological commitment to them. The viewer is not looking for a moral to the story in the same way he or she is in a closed narrative, even a closed serial. This is not to say that open serials are not ideological constructs, but it is ultimately not in their interest (or that of their producers or sponsors) to be seen to take sides on any particular issue or to appear to be overtly didactic. (Allen 1995: 21)

Thus the serial nature of the television soap opera is considered to raise problems for academic researchers who wish to apply models of inquiry such as the concept of 'preferred reading' to the fictional genre (Morley 1981). Yet as the material discussed earlier surely illustrates, producers do sometimes 'take sides' and can, despite their best efforts, appear didactic in handling social issue stories. Indeed, these texts are commonly assumed to be 'open' (Seiter et al. 1989; Gillespie 2005), but it is not impossible to identify the ways in which certain perspectives are promoted. Close examination of language and imagery, addressing how specific characters are positioned in relation to the soap community and how aesthetic codes are drawn upon to frame their viewpoint, can help to establish a 'preferred meaning'. If this is pursued in combination with analysing the dynamics of production, and clarified still further by linking these processes to audience reception, it is possible to build a more complete picture of the nature of storyline messages and their intended and actual *meanings*. To do otherwise is to risk losing our focus on influence entirely (Corner 2000). As Corner observes, 'So much conceptual effort has been centred on audiences' interpretative activity that even the preliminary theorization of influence has become awkward' (Corner 1991: 267).

Rather than considering 'active' audiences as opening up new ways of conceptualising audiences as consumers, the emphasis on audiences' ability to resist media messages has arguably 'closed down' areas of investigation. Researchers working within this field have been accused of embracing the politics of popular culture indiscriminately and diverting attention away from questions about power and inequality in contemporary society (Philo and Miller 2001; Deacon 2003: 218).[2] Indeed Eldridge et al. argue along similar lines that:

> This is an orthodoxy which dismisses questions of media power . . . It is certainly misleading to assume, as some 'new revisionist' authors seem to, that pleasure is inherently revolutionary and 'oppositional' readings can be equated with 'liberation' in the real world. (Eldridge et al. 1997: 156)

The study of audiences and an issue storyline (Chapter 7) demonstrates that it is important to explore not just social class dimensions of reading but also social experiences and knowledge about the world (see Philo 1990). While audiences do actively engage with television fiction and do of course often gain pleasure from their viewing experience, the readings of soap opera storylines are patterned. Different people within the groups may respond differently to storyline messages, but this is not the same as saying that audiences produced different *meanings*, as some have argued (Fiske 1987; Hobson 1982, 2003). These are different responses to the *same* meaning. For example, no member of the groups recorded here 'read' the abuser as being anything other than 'abusive' (and indeed we might ask if this is something we would wish to celebrate if they had). Some research participants who had no prior knowledge of issues in sexual abuse or domestic violence thought that the character's behaviour was exaggerated. Other research participants drew upon their existing knowledge of sexual abuse and saw his characterisation as wholly representative of a man who was motivated by the desire for control. In other words the research participants responded differently to the character; they did not produce different meanings.[3]

The audience responses were also remarkably uniform and followed clear patterns of knowledge, experience and the use of logic to consider possible effects or consequences. These findings would seem to challenge Dorothy Hobson's famous statement that 'there are as many different *Crossroads* as there are viewers. Tonight twelve million, tomorrow thirteen million; with thirteen million possible understandings of the programme' (Hobson 1982: 136). Indeed in *Soap Opera* (2003), Hobson revisits this argument. As she explains:

[Audiences] interpret the text according to what they choose to take from it and this may change according to their own circumstances and experiences. This does not mean that there is no overriding 'meaning' in the text – there is, of course, the meaning inscribed by the creators – but this is their meaning and what every viewer does is broadly read the text for the overall meaning and then distil it into their own particular areas of interest . . . This is not just a negotiated reading or a polysemic understanding, but rather an active choice of what aspect of the programme they wish to take. (Hobson 2003: 166–7)

This seems more than reminiscent of the individualistic 'uses and gratifications model', in that Hobson argues that messages in the television serial are selected in line with existing beliefs (audiences 'interpret the text according to what they choose to take from it'), but she also argues that the soap genre 'is constantly imparting information and educating its audience about a myriad of issues' (Hobson 2003: 210). This latter statement suggests these programmes can play a role in changing, not merely reinforcing, beliefs. Furthermore, audiences are simply not making up different meanings every time a television programme is transmitted, nor are they using these meanings in infinitely different ways. Indeed if there were no shared 'frameworks of understanding' then the format would just not work for audiences. The audience study discussed in Chapter 7 demonstrates the importance of audiences' knowledge or experience of the substantive topic under discussion, developing other research on what audiences bring to their viewing experiences (Schlesinger et al. 1992). However, as we have seen, it is also possible to begin to tap into questions of 'what audiences take away' from their viewing experience (in terms of media influence and exploring meanings and memories). Put simply, it is possible to demonstrate that television fiction has an influence on audiences and can communicate messages about a traditionally taboo topic to people who had no previous experience to draw upon. The potential for television fiction to influence audience understandings is subject to constraints, however. Audiences do not receive information in a cultural or social vacuum. Media messages are mediated by other important factors: by what audiences already know, by other culturally powerful messages already in circulation (for example, the ideology of 'motherhood'). I wish to argue simply that popular television and public knowledge should not be mutually exclusive. It should be possible to integrate the valuable insights from studies of media consumption and production in fruitful ways – as Deacon suggests, 'in ways that permit conceptual distinctions without resorting to moral hierarchies' (Deacon 2003: 219–20).

TV Fiction and Commercial Imperatives

Television fiction has been identified as an important conduit for messages which may challenge prevailing discourses about the world, but there is serious concern that frequently programmes are constructed simply to fulfil the requirements of 'what advertisers think the public likes' (Spigel 2004). Lynn Spigel (2004) analysed how American television returned to 'normality' in the wake of the attacks of 9/11. Television fiction, including a specially written episode of *The West Wing* (NBC, 3 October 2001), played a key role. This programme acted as a 'fictional schoolroom' to educate viewers about those who threaten the USA. In so doing, the episode (which features a group of high school students trapped in the White House after a terrorist bomb threat) 'speaks to viewers as if they were children or, at best, the innocent subjects of historical events beyond their control' (Spigel 2004: 245). This, Spigel concludes, provides us with an example of how 'public service discourse' operates to 'solidify American national unity *against* the "enemy" rather than to encourage any real engagement with Islam, the ethics of US international policy, or the consequences of the then-impending US bomb strikes' (Spigel 2004: 244; emphasis in original).

Television fiction is thus at the heart of contemporary debates concerning advertising and commercialisation, citizenship and consumerism, and niche broadcasting or 'narrowcasting' (Gripsrud 2002; Costera Meijer 2005; Murdock 1999). The concern is that increased commercialisation is having a detrimental impact on quality and diversity in television output, particularly in USA and European broadcast contexts. Costera Meijer (2005) considers that television soap opera (and other forms of non-news television) can offer new and valuable insights into how to be a citizen and involve people in democratic culture. Others see the responsibility as resting firmly with producers to continue to take risks and promote challenging and diverse programming *despite* what advertisers think. After all, it is producers who ultimately control television products, and with this power comes ethical responsibilities. As Gripsrud concludes:

> This ethical responsibility cannot be disclaimed by saying that 'people want what we're making' because people might also (and perhaps *rather*) want a different and better product . . . It is not unthinkable that live executions on TV would attract quite a large, shock-hungry audience. When even the most hard-boiled of commercial TV executives still would not broadcast such stuff, it indicates that they accept at least *some* ethical limitations to what sorts of wishes from audiences they are happy to satisfy. (Gripsrud 2002: 290)

Television fiction, and serial drama in particular, communicates with very large numbers of people and frequently presents messages about the world which relate to important social problems. It is also a site of struggle for different groups in society. Future studies of such formats might reveal useful insights about the state of the broadcasting industry in general, the commercial imperatives faced by programme makers, and the role that economic pressures play in influencing output. However, it would also be possible to explore social and cultural change in the wider society by examining which groups or perspectives are being promoted or are neglected in TV fiction at different points in time and even across diverse cultural settings. In addition, addressing the ways in which the wider media frames these issues, and how 'the public' and those involved with monitoring programme content respond, may reveal important insights into the direction of society. I hope in this book to have illustrated the cultural and societal importance of 'sharing stories'. Graham Murdock (1999) argues that sharing stories is essential if we are to foster the capacities and reciprocities of 'full citizenship'. Drawing on the words of John Mepham (1990), Graham Murdock argues that it is precisely through these stories that we can raise questions which are vital to a healthy democratic society:

> What is possible for me, who can I be, what can my life consist of, how can I bring these things about? What is it like to be someone else, to be particular kinds of other people? How does it come about that people can be like that? We have to make an unending effort to answer questions like this so that we can . . . make imaginatively informed choices and responses to other people . . . These questions and these capacities and skills are basic to having a sense of self, an identity, and to fair dealing with others within a system of social relationships. (John Mepham 1990: 60, quoted in Murdock 1999: 12)

At the very least, it is to be hoped that the material discussed here has demonstrated that the television soap opera, and indeed other forms of television fiction, represent an important public space in which these questions may be raised. *How* such questions are raised, by *whom* and *with what consequences* are surely worthy of serious study for all those with an interest in media power.

Notes

1 News journalists are believed to have little knowledge of or indeed interest in their audiences. Schlesinger found that the audience research which was made

available to BBC journalists was 'sporadic'. Production personnel had vague ideas about their audiences based on personal interactions or assumptions. Schlesinger concludes that 'The gap between producer and consumer does not pose severe problems because it is filled with the conventional wisdom of a professionalism which is largely self-sustaining . . . Ultimately the newsman is his own audience. When he talks of his professionalism he is saying that he knows how to tell his own story' (Schlesinger 1987: 134). Philip Elliot came to a similar conclusion in his study of a documentary series produced for the Independent Television Authority. He found that the opinions of colleagues in the television world can be more important than considerations of the audience 'out there' (Elliot 1972). Contemporary studies of news media production might produce different findings, as news media is arguably becoming more audience led, but recent interviews with science journalists support the view that it is the organisation or channel which seeks audience research, not journalists themselves (Henderson and Kitzinger 2007).

2   Ann Gray and David Morley both disagree with those who criticise 'the popular culture project' as 'depoliticised' and consider this to reveal a (gendered) position on what constitutes a legitimate territory in media studies/cultural studies. This, Gray argues, is to have a very narrow (arguably male) definition of what constitutes politics and to disregard the feminist/sexual politics agenda which informed much of the popular culture project (often conflated with active audience research). As she explains: 'when researchers turned their attention to the ways in which meaning is produced at the moment of reading, to the actual viewing, reading, listening, contexts, and to the eruptions of daily life into an understanding of media reception, they were also interrupting existing models and approaches. These operated within neat, confinable and measurable models of reception and the certainties of analysis of institution, ownership and control of the media as well as media content and message' (Gray 1999: 24). Morley condemns the wave of attacks on this research as 'Soviet-style' and considers it a call to return to 'the eternal verities of sociology or of political economy', which in his view would wrongly displace valuable concern with gender, race and ethnicity issues (see Morley 1999: ch. 10).

3   Celeste Condit in her study of *Cagney and Lacey* discusses similar findings (Condit 1989). Justin Lewis discusses this case study in detail in his excellent account of issues concerning preferred readings/meanings (Lewis 1991). Stuart Hall has since reflected on the encoding/decoding model and explains it was never designed to be a lasting or grand model. As Hall explains, 'the slippage between preferred meaning and preferred reading is what does the damage. Because preferred reading appears to put it on the decoding side, whereas preferred meaning is on the encoding side, not the decoding side. Why is it there? Well, it is there because I don't want a model of a circuit which has no power in it. I don't want a model which is determinist, but I don't want a model without determination. And therefore I don't think

audiences are in the same positions of power with those who signify the world to them. And preferred reading is simply a way of saying if you have control of the apparatus of signifying the world, if you're in control of the media, you own it, you write the texts – to some extent it has a determining shape' (Hall 1994: 261).

Appendix: Focus Group Session Participants

Table 1 Special interest

Group description	ID code	No. of participants	Age range
Social workers	SW	4 female	27–35
Representatives from five different women's organisations	WO	5 female	31–46
Teenage sexual abuse survivors	TS	5 female	13–14

Table 2 General population

Group description	ID code	No. of participants	Age range
Youth club committee members	YC	4 male, 4 female	16–26
State school students	SSS	5 male, 5 female	17
Private school students	PSS	4 male, 4 female	17–18
Flatmates (East End, Glasgow)	FME	2 male, 4 female	19–22
Flatmates (West End, Glasgow)	FMW	3 male, 3 female	20–1
University students	US	3 female	21–6
Foreign language teachers	FLT	3 female, 3 male	25–34
Office workers (secretaries/ cleaners)	OW	5 female	27–45
Retired people	RP	3 female	53–66

References

Ahmed, K. (1998), 'Newest Resident on the Street Moves in on the Faithful with a Big Change in Mind', *Guardian*, 17 January.

Alasuutari, P. (1999), *Rethinking the Media Audience: The New Agenda*, London: Sage.

Allan, S. (1998), '(En)Gendering the Truth Politics of News Discourse', in C. Carter, G. Branston and S. Allan (eds), *News, Gender and Power*, London: Routledge, pp. 121–40.

Allen, R. C. (1995), *To Be Continued: Soap Operas Around the World*, London: Routledge.

Ang, I. (1985), *Watching 'Dallas': Soap Opera and the Melodramatic Imagination*, London: Methuen.

Armstrong, S. (2006), 'Go Figure Black Viewing', *Guardian*, 22 May.

Arnold, S. (2000), 'An Everyday Story of Cancer', *Observer*, 25 June.

Atkinson, R. (2006), 'Big Brother's "Freak Show" has Produced the First Warts-and-All Disabled Person on TV – When Will the Soaps Follow?', *Guardian*, 11 July.

Baer, N. (2000), 'Clanging Critics', *Western Journal of Medicine*, 173: 157–8.

BARB (2006), *Britain's Most Watched TV – the 1980s*, London: British Audience Research Bureau, 3 May, available at www.bfi.org.uk/features/mostwatched/research.html.

Barbour, R.S. and Kitzinger, J. (1999), *Developing Focus Group Research*, London: Sage.

Barker, M. (2003), 'Assessing the "Quality" in Qualitative Research: The Case of Text-Audience Relations', *European Journal of Communication* 18: 315–35.

Barnardo's (1993), *HIV and AIDS: Who's Telling the Children?*, London: Barnardo's.

Baym, N. (2000), *Tune in, Log on: Soap, Fandom and Online Community*, London: Sage.

BBC (2003), 'Soap Plot "Boosted Cancer Checks" ', available at http://news.bbc.co.uk/1/hi/health/2804413.stm.

Bellos, A. (1994), 'Close to the Edge', *Observer*, 13 March.

Bielby, D. D. and C. Lee Harrington (2005), 'Opening America? The Telenovela-ization of U.S. Soap Operas', *Television and New Media* 6: 383–99.

Bindel, J. (2006), 'From Disfunctional Dyke to Designer Doll', *Guardian*, 12 June.

Born, G. (2004), *Uncertain Vision: Birt, Dyke and the Reinvention of the BBC*, London: Secker and Warburg.

Boyle, K. (2005), *Media and Violence*, London: Sage.

Braverman, R. (1994), *Brookside: The Journals of Beth Jordache*, London: Boxtree.

Brook, S. (2006), ' "Unhappy" Shahbaz Leaves Big Brother House', *Guardian*, 24 May.

Brown, M. (2001a), 'Bubbling Over', *Guardian*, 12 February.

Brown, M. (2001b), 'Drama Out of a Soap: Will Emmerdale Benefit from a Popstars-Style Stunt?', *Guardian*, 14 May.

Brown, M. E. (1990), *Communication and Human Values: Television and Women's Culture*, London: Sage.

Brunsdon, C. (1981), 'Crossroads: Notes on Soap Opera', *Screen* 22(4): 32–7.

Brunsdon, C. (1995), 'The Role of Soap Opera in the Development of Feminist Television Scholarship', in R. C. Allen (ed.), *To be Continued: Soap Operas Around the World*, London: Routledge, pp. 49–65.

Brunsdon, C. (2000), *The Feminist, the Housewife and the Soap Opera*, Oxford: Clarendon Press.

Brunsdon, C., J. D'Acci and L. Spigel (eds) (1997), *Feminist Television Criticism: A Reader*, Oxford: Oxford University Press.

BSC (1993), *Complaints Bulletin, Broadcasting Standards Council*, 31 (August).

BSS (1994), *Report of Helpline Run for Channel 4:2–3 October 1994*, Manchester: Broadcasting Support Services.

Buckingham, D. (1987), *Public Secrets: EastEnders and its Audience*, London: BFI.

Burchill, J. (1998), 'Telly Most Horrid', *Guardian Weekend*, 2 May.

Burkeman, O. and S. Goldenberg (2006), 'Why it Takes a Television Series to Draw Attention to a Real-Life Human Drama', *Guardian*, 5 May.

Byrne, C. (2006), ' "Footballers' Wives" shown Red Card After Ratings Slump', *Independent*, 4 May.

Cable, S. and N. Page (2003), *The Soap Pack: A Guide to Getting Your Organisation or Campaign Involved in Soap Operas*, London: Bright. Available at www.bright-place.org.uk.

Caldwell, J. T. (1995), *Televisuality: Style Crisis and Authority in American Television*, New Brunswick, NJ: Rutgers University Press.

Cantor, M. (1971), *The Hollywood TV Producer: His Work and His Audience*, New York: Basic Books.

Carlin, J. (2003), 'The Healing Power of Soaps', *Independent*, 28 November.

Carter, C., G. Branston and S. Allen (eds) (1998), *News, Gender and Power*, London: Routledge.

Carter, S. and L. Henderson (2005), 'Approaches to Qualitative Data Collection in Social Science', in A. Bowling and S. Ebrahim (eds), *Handbook of Health Research Methods*, Milton Keynes: Open University Press, pp. 215–29.

Collins, L. (1995), 'Anna's all Write with the Girls', *Sun*, 28 January.

Condit, C. (1989), 'The Rhetorical Limits of Polysemy', *Critical Studies in Mass Communication* 6(2):103–22.

Condren, R. and P. Byrne (2000), 'The Psychokiller Strikes again', *British Medical Journal* 320: 1282.

Conlan, T. (2002), 'TV Soaps "Are Not Fit For Family Viewing"', *Daily Mail*, 10 May.

Coombes, R. (2003), 'Broadcasters Block Asian Health Soap Opera', *British Medical Journal* 326: 110.

Corless, F. (1995), 'Closedown on Beth: Brookside Write Out TV's Anna Instantly', *Daily Mirror*, 14 June.

Corner, J. (1991), 'Meaning, Genre and Context: The Problematics of "Public Knowledge" in the New Audience Studies', in J. Curran and M. Gurevitch (eds), *Mass Media and Society*, London: Edward Arnold, pp. 267–84.

Corner, J. (2000), '"Influence": The Contested Core of Media Research', in J. Curran and M. Gurevitch (eds), *Mass Media and Society*, London: Edward Arnold, pp. 376–97.

Corner, J. (2001), 'The "Public", the "Popular" and Media Studies', in G. Philo and D. Miller (eds), *Market Killing: What the Free Market Does and what Social Scientists Can Do About It*, Harlow: Longman, pp. 152–7.

Corner, J. (2002), 'Performing the Real: Documentary Diversions', *Television and New Media* 3: 255–69.

Costera Meijer, I. (2005), 'Impact or Content? Ratings vs Quality in Public Broadcasting', *European Journal of Communication* 20: 27–53.

Cox, E. (2006), 'I'll Kill Myself on Telly', *Sun*, 23 May.

Creeber, G. (2004), *Serial Television: Big Drama on the Small Screen*, London: BFI.

Cross, S. (2004), 'Visualizing Madness', *Television and New Media* 5: 197–216.

Culf, A. (1995), 'Brookside Backs Down Over Lesbian Kiss', *Guardian*, 7 January.

Curran, J. (1991), 'Mass Media and Democracy: A Reappraisal', in J. Curran and M. Gurevitch (eds), *Mass Media and Society*, London: Edward Arnold, pp. 82–117.

Dave_the (2006), 'Mental Health Charity and C4', contribution to online discussion, Channel Four Television, Big Brother 6 forum, posted 5 June.

Davies, J. (1997), 'An Awful Dilemma Born of Knowing Too Much', *Mail on Sunday*, 30 November.

Deacon, D. (2003), 'Holism, Communion and Conversion: Integrating Media Consumption and Production Research', *Media, Culture and Society*, 25: 209–31.

Dignan, C. (1998), 'Vicars Study EastEnders to Fill Pews', *Sunday Times*, 24 May.

Dunleavy, T. (2005), 'Coronation Street, Neighbours, Shortland Street: Localness and Universality in the Primetime Soap', *Television and New Media* 6: 370–82.

Dyer, R., C. Geraghty, M. Jordan, T. Lovell, R. Paterson and J. Stewart (eds) (1981), *Coronation Street*, London: BFI.

Eldridge, J., J. Kitzinger and K. Williams (eds) (1997), *The Mass Media and Power in Modern Britain*, Oxford: Oxford University Press.

Elliot, P. (1972), *The Making of a Television Series: A Case Study in the Sociology of Culture*, London: Constable.

Elliot, P. (1992), *Television Producers*, London: Routledge.

Espinosa, P. (1982), 'The Audience in the Text: Ethnographic Observations of a Hollywood Story Conference', *Media, Culture and Society* 4: 77–86.

Faludi, S. (1992), *The Undeclared War Against American Women*, New York: Anchor.

Fenton, N. (2000), 'The Problematics of Postmodernism for Feminist Media Studies', *Media, Culture and Society* 22: 723–41.

Fenton, N., A. Bryman, D. Deacon and P. Birmingham (eds) (1998), *Mediating Social Science*, London: Sage.

Fiske, J. (1987), *Television Culture*, London: Methuen.

Franklin, B. (1997), *Newszak and News Media*, London: Edward Arnold.

Franklin, B. (1999), 'Soft-Soaping the Public? The Government and Media Promotion of Social Policy', in B. Franklin (ed.), *Social Policy, the Media and Misrepresentation*, London: Routledge, pp. 17–38.

Fuqua, J. V. (1995), 'There's a Queer in My Soap! The Homophobia/AIDS Story-Line of One Life to Live', in R. C. Allen (ed.), *To be Continued: Soap Operas Around the World*, London: Routledge, pp. 199–212.

Gans, H. J. (1957), 'The Creator-Audience Relationship in the Mass Media: An Analysis of Movie Making', in B. Rosenberg and D. White (eds), *Mass Culture: The Popular Arts in America*, New York: Free Press, pp. 315–24.

Garnett, T. (1998), 'Recipe for a Dust Up', *Sight and Sound*, 18 January.

Geraghty, C. (1991), *Women and Soap Opera: A Study of Prime Time Soaps*, Cambridge: Polity.

Geraghty, C. (1995), 'Social Issues and Realist Soaps', in R. C. Allen (ed.), *To be Continued: Soap Operas Around the World*, London: Routledge, pp. 66–80.

Geraghty, C. (1996), 'Feminism and Media Consumption', in J. Curran, D. Morley and V. Walkerdine (eds), *Cultural Studies and Communications*, London: Edward Arnold, pp. 306–22.

Gibson, D. (2006), 'Every Year, it's the most Extreme Ever', *Guardian*, 5 June.

Gillespie, M. (ed.) (2005), *Media Audiences*, Milton Keynes: Open University Press.

Gitlin, T. (2000), *Inside Prime Time*, Berkeley: University of California Press.

Gray, A. (1992), *Video Playtime: The Gendering of a Leisure Technology*, London: Routledge.

GUMG (1976), *Bad News*, London: Routledge and Kegan Paul.

GUMG (1980), *More Bad News*, London: Routledge and Kegan Paul.

GUMG (1982), *Really Bad News*, London: Writers and Readers.

GUMG (1985), *War and Peace News*, Milton Keynes: Open University Press.

Gray, A. (1999), 'Audience and Reception Research in Retrospect: The Trouble with Audiences', in P. Alasuutari (ed.), *Rethinking the Media Audience*, London: Sage, pp. 22–37.

Gripsrud, J. (1995), *The Dynasty Years: Hollywood Television and Critical Media Studies*, London: Routledge.

Gripsrud, J. (ed.) (1999), *Television and Common Knowledge*, London: Routledge.

Gripsrud, J. (2002), *Understanding Media Culture*, London: Arnold.

Hall, S. (1980), 'Encoding/Decoding', in S. Hall, D. Hobson, A. Love and P. Willis (eds), *Culture, Media Language*, London: Hutchinson, pp. 128–38.

Hall, S. (1994), 'Reflections upon the Encoding/Decoding Model: An Interview with Stuart Hall', in J. Cruz and J. Lewis (eds), *Viewing, Reading, Listening: Audiences and Cultural Reception*, Oxford: Westview Press, pp. 253–74.

Hallam, A. (2002), 'Media Influences on Mental Health Policy: Long-Term Effects of the Clunis and Silcock Cases', *International Review of Psychiatry* 14: 26–33.

Hardyman, R. and G. Leydon (2003), 'Media Influence on Behaviour', *British Medical Journal* 326: 498.

Harnden, T. (1997), 'EastEnders Image of Dirty Drunken Irish Upsets Envoy', *Daily Telegraph*, 25 September.

Harper, S. (2005), 'Media, Madness and Misrepresentation: Critical Reflections on Anti-Stigma Discourse', *European Journal of Communication* 20: 460–83.

Hastings, G., M. Stead, J. Kitzinger and L. Henderson (1999), *The Role of Media Advocacy in Challenging Health Inequalities*, London: Health Development Agency.

Henderson, L. (1996), *Incest in Brookside: Audience Responses to the Jordache Story*. London: Channel Four Television.

Henderson, L. (1999), 'Producing Serious Soaps', in G. Philo (ed.), *Message Received*, Harlow: Addison Wesley and Longman, pp. 62–81.

Henderson, L. (2000), 'Gen Wird Popular: Inhalte Und Rezeption Der Beitrage Zum Thema Brustkrebsforschung in Der Britischen Medien', in D. Jazbinsek (ed.), *Gesundheits Kommunikation*, Weisbaden: Westdeutscher, pp. 229–45.

Henderson, L. and B. Franklin (2007), 'Sad Not Bad: Images of Social Care Professionals in Popular British TV Drama', *Journal of Social Work* 7: 133–53.

Henderson, L. and J. Kitzinger (1999), 'The Human Drama of Genetics: "Hard" and "Soft" Media Representations of Inherited Breast Cancer', *Sociology of Health and Illness* 21: 560–78.

Henderson, L. and J. Kitzinger (2007), 'Orchestrating a Science "Event": The Case of the Human Genome Project', *New Genetics and Society* 26: 1–19.

Henderson, L., J. Kitzinger and J. Green (2000), 'Representing Infant Feeding: Content Analysis of British Media Portrayals of Bottle Feeding and Breast Feeding', *British Medical Journal* 321: 1196–8.

Hibberd, M., B. Kilborn, B. McNair and P. Schlesinger (2000), *Consenting Adults?*, London: Broadcasting Standards Commission.

Hill, A. (2005), *Reality TV: Audiences and Factual Television*, London: Routledge.

Hill, J. (1986), *Sex, Class and Realism: British Cinema 1956–1963*, London: BFI.

Hilpern, K. (1998), 'A Death in the National Family', *Guardian*, 6 March.

Hobson, D. (1982), *Crossroads: The Drama of a Soap Opera*, London: Methuen.

Hobson, D. (2003), *Soap Opera*, Oxford: Polity.

Hodgson, J. (2003), 'TV Watchdog Warns on Soaps and "Soft" News', *Evening Standard*, 8 April.

Hoggart, R. (1959), *The Uses of Literacy*, London: Penguin.

Höijer, B. (1999), 'To be an Audience', in P. Alasuutari (ed.), *Rethinking the Media Audience*, London: Sage, pp. 179–94.

Holland, P. (1997), *The Television Handbook*, London: Routledge.

Holland, P. (2004), 'The Politics of the Smile: Soft News and the Sexualisation of the Popular Press', in C. Carter and L. Steiner (eds), *Critical Readings: Media and Gender*, Maidenhead: Open University Press, pp. 68–86.

Hooper, C. (1992), *Mothers Surviving Child Sexual Abuse*, London: Routledge.

Howe, A., V. Owen-Smith and J. Richardson (2002), 'The Impact of a Television Soap Opera on the NHS Cervical Screening Programme in the North West of England', *Journal of Public Health Medicine* 24: 299–304.

Howe, A., V. Owen-Smith and J. Richardson (2003), 'Television Programme Makers Have an Ethical Responsibility', *British Medical Journal* 326: 498.

Intintoli, M. J. (1984), *Taking Soaps Seriously: The World of Guiding Light*, New York: Praeger.

ITC (1993), 'Programme Complaints and Interventions', *Quarterly Report*, July.

Kay, J. and H. Bonner (2001), 'Alma; I'm So Angry with Corrie', *Sun*, 18 June.

Kelly, L. (1996), 'Weasel Words: Paedophiles and the Cycle of Abuse', *Trouble and Strife* 33:44–9.

Kilborn, R. (1992), *Television Soaps*, London: Batsford.

Kilborn, R. (1994), 'How Real Can You Get? Recent Developments in "Reality" Television', *European Journal of Communication* 9: 421–39.

Kilborn, R. (2003), *Staging the Real: Factual TV Programming in the Age of Big Brother*, Manchester: Manchester University Press.

Kingsley, H. (1993), *Casualty: The Inside Story*, London: BBC Books.

Kitzinger, J. (1999), 'A Sociology of Media Power: Key Issues in Audience Reception Research', in G. Philo (ed.), *Message Received*, Harlow: Addison Wesley and Longman, pp. 3–20.

Kitzinger, J. (2004), *Framing Abuse: Media Influence and Public Understanding of Sexual Violence Against Children*, London: Pluto Press.

Kitzinger, J. and L. Henderson (2000), *The Role of the Media in Public and Professional Understandings of Breast Cancer*, London: NHS R & D Programme.

Kitzinger, J. and K. Hunt (1993), *Evaluation of the Zero Tolerance Campaign*, Edinburgh: Edinburgh District Council.

Kitzinger, J. and P. Skidmore (1995), *Child Sexual Abuse and the Media*, Glasgow: Summary Report to the ESRC.

Laurance, J. (1997), 'We Know Life can be Cruel but has Brookside Finally Gone Too Far?', *Independent*, 3 July.

Lawrence, J. (1995), 'Will Soap's Prisoner of Conscience Walk Free?', *Independent*, 8 May.

Lawson, M. (2002a), 'No Through Road', *Guardian*, 14 October.

Lawson, M. (2002b), 'Close Encounters', *Guardian*, 14 October.

Lewis, J. (1991), *The Ideological Octopus: An Exploration of Television and its Audience*, London: Routledge.

Liddiment, D. (2005), 'Why Street Cred Matters', *Guardian*, 19 September.

Liebes, T. and E. Katz (1990), *The Export of Meaning: Cross-Cultural Readings of Dallas*, Oxford: Oxford University Press.

Liebes, T. and S. Livingstone (1998), 'European Soap Operas: The Diversification of a Genre', *European Journal of Communication* 13: 147–80.

Livingstone, S. (1988), 'Why People Watch Soap Opera', *European Journal of Communication* 3: 55–80.

Livingstone, S. (1990), *Making Sense of Television: The Psychology of Audience Interpretation*, Oxford: Pergamon Press.

Livingstone, S. (2004), 'The Challenge of Changing Audiences', *European Journal of Communication* 19: 75–86.

Livingstone, S. and P. Lunt (1994), *Talk on Television: Audience Participation and Public Debate*, London: Routledge.

Lovell, T. (1981) 'Ideology and *Coronation Street*', in R. Dyer, C. Geraghty, M. Jordan, T. Lovell, R. Paterson and J. Stewart (eds), *Coronation Street*, London: BFI, pp. 40–53.

Lyall, J. (2004), 'Alarm Call Over Reality Gameshow', *British Medical Journal* 328: 173.

MacDermid, A. (1997), 'Doctors Reject Change after TV "Mercy Killing"', *Herald*, 4 July.

Martín-Barbero, J. (1995), 'Memory and Form in Latin American Soap Opera', in R. C. Allen (ed.), *To be Continued: Soap Operas Around the World*, London: Routledge, pp. 276–84.

McCartney, J. (1997), 'Nobody Thinks this is Real . . . do they?', *Sunday Telegraph*, 30 November.

McLean, G. (2006), 'Suds Lore', *Guardian*, 22 May.

McNair, B. (1998), *The Sociology of Journalism*, London: Arnold.

McNicholas, A. (2004), 'Wrenching the Machine Around: EastEnders, the BBC and Institutional Change', *Media, Culture and Society* 26: 491–512.

McQuail, D. (1994), *Mass Communication Theory: An Introduction*, London: Sage.

Mepham, J. (1990), 'The Ethics of Quality in Television', in G. Mulgan (ed.), *The Question of Quality*, London: BFI, pp. 50–70.

Michael, M. and S. Carter (2001), 'The Facts about Fictions and Vice Versa: Public Understanding of Human Genetics', *Science as Culture* 10: 5–32.

Miller, D. (1994), *Don't Mention the War: Northern Ireland, Propaganda and the Media*, London: Pluto Press.

Miller, D., J. Kitzinger, K. Williams and P. Beharrell (1998), *The Circuit of Mass Communication*, London: Sage.

Millwood Hargrave, A. and L. Gatfield (2002), *Soap Box or Soft Soap? Audience Attitudes to the British Soap Opera*, London: Broadcasting Standards Commission.

Modleski, T. (1982), *Loving with A Vengeance: Mass Produced Fantasies for Women*, New York: Routledge.

Montgomery, K. C. (1989), *Target: Prime Time*, New York: Oxford University Press.

Moreton, C. (2001), 'The Best Stories Never End', *Independent on Sunday*, 4 March.

Morley, D. (1980), *The Nationwide Audience*, London: BFI.

Morley, D. (1981), 'The "Nationwide" Audience: A Critical Postscript', *Screen Education* 22: 32–7.

Morley, D. (1986), *Family Television: Cultural Power and Domestic Leisure*, London: Comedia.

Morley, D. (1999), ' "To Boldly Go": The Third Generation of Reception Studies', in P. Alasuutari (ed.), *Rethinking the Media Audience*, London: Sage, pp. 195–205.

Moyes, J. (1995), ' "Brookside" Death Verdict Triggers Rush for Refuges', *Independent*, 18 May.

Murdock, G. (1999), 'Rights and Representations: Public Discourse and Cultural Citizenship', in J. Gripsrud (ed.), *Television and Common Knowledge*, London: Routledge, pp. 7–16.

Murdock, G. and J. D. Halloran (1979), 'Contexts of Creativity in Television Drama: An Exploratory Study in Britain', in H. Fischer and S. Melnik (eds), *Entertainment: A Cross-Cultural Examination*, New York: Hastings House, pp. 273–85.

Myers, J. (2006), 'Jack Wells and Marc Cherry Express Concerns about Product Placement', 18 May, available at www.mediavillage.com.

Nariman, H. N. (1993), *Soap Operas for Social Change: Toward a Methodology for Entertainment-Education Television*, Westport, CT: Praeger.

O'Donnell, H. (1999), *Good Times, Bad Times: Soap Operas and Society in Western Europe*, London: Leicester University Press.

O'Kelly, L. (1994), 'The Summer of Lesbian Chic has Female Friends Dancing Cheek to Cheek', *Observer*, 5 June.

Peretti, J. (2000), 'What's Your Problem?', *Guardian*, 15 March.

Philo, G. (1990), *Seeing and Believing: The Influence of Television*, London: Routledge.

Philo, G. (ed.) (1996a), *Media and Mental Distress*, London: Longman.

Philo, G. (1996b), 'The Media and Public Belief', in G. Philo (ed.), *Media and Mental Distress*, London: Longman, pp. 82–104.

Philo, G. (ed.) (1999), *Message Received*, Harlow: Addison Wesley Longman.

Philo, G. and M. Berry (2004), *Bad News from Israel*, London: Pluto Press.

Philo, G. and L. Henderson (1999a), 'Audience Responses to Suicide in a Television Drama', in G. Philo (ed.), *Message Received: Glasgow Media Group Research 1993–1998*, Harlow: Addison Wesley Longman, pp. 82–9.

Philo, G. and L. Henderson (1999b), 'Why Go to Casualty? Health Fears and Fictional Television', in G. Philo (ed.), *Message Received: Glasgow Media Group Research 1993–1998*, Harlow: Addison Wesley Longman, pp. 93–105.

Philo, G. and D. Miller (2001), *Market Killing: What the Free Market Does and what Social Scientists Can Do About It*, London: Longman.

Platt, S. (1999), 'Home Truths: Media Representation of Homelessness', in B. Franklin (ed.), *Social Policy, the Media and Misrepresentation*, London: Routledge, pp. 104–17.

Plumb, A. (2003), 'The Challenge of Self-Advocacy', *Feminism and Psychology* 3:169–87.

Pool, H. (2006), 'Squaring the Circle', *Guardian*, 17 July.

Porter, M. (2006), 'The Boy Can't Help It', *Evening Standard*, 23 May.

Porto, M. P. (2005), 'Political Controversies in Brazilian TV Fiction: Viewers' Interpretations of the Telenovela Terra Nostra', *Television and New Media* 6: 342–59.

Prasad, R. (2002), 'Silent Voices', *Guardian*, 23 October.

Press Association (2003), 'Corrie's Boys Wake Up to Gay Love', *Guardian*, 24 September.

Propp, V. I. (1968), *Morphology of the Folk Tale*, Austin, TX: University of Texas Press.

Purnell, T. (1995a), '£250,000 for Close TV Secret', *Daily Mirror*, 30 March.

Purnell, T. (1995b), 'About That Patio Beth', *Daily Mirror*, 3 February.

Quinn, A. (2006), 'Research Evidence and Media Bias: Reflections on a 1980s Dispute', *Media, Culture and Society* 28:457–65.

Radway, J. (1984), *Reading the Romance: Women, Patriarchy and Popular Literature*, Chapel Hill, NC: University of North Carolina Press.

Rasmussen, J. and B. Hoijer (2005), *Media Images of Mental Illness and Psychiatric Care in Connection with Violent Crimes: A Study of Dagens Nyheter, Aftonbladet and Rapport*, Orebro: Orebro University.

Redmond, P. (1985), 'Brookside: a Socially Realistic Twice-Weekly Drama', *European Broadcasting Union Review* 6: 39–42.

Revely, A. (1997), 'Soap Tackles Stigma of Schizophrenia', *British Medical Journal* 314: 1560.

Rogers, E., P. Vaughan, R. Swalehe, N. Rao, P. Svenkerud and S. Sood (1999), 'Effects of an Entertainment-Education Radio Soap Opera on Family Planning Behavior in Tanzania', *Studies in Family Planning* 30: 193–211.

Roscoe, J. (2001), 'Big Brother Australia: Performing the "Real" Twenty Four Seven', *International Journal of Cultural Studies* 4: 473–88.

Rose, D. (1995), 'When DIY Turns out to Mean Dead in Yard', *Observer*, 29 January.

Schizophrenia Home Page (1997), 'Living with Schizophrenia: EastEnders TV Program Covers Schizophrenia', accessed March 2006, available at www.schizophrenia.com/newletter/697news50.html.

Schlesinger, P. (1987), *Putting 'Reality' Together: BBC News*, London: Routledge.

Schlesinger, P. (2006), 'Is there a Crisis in British Journalism?', *Media, Culture and Society* 28: 299–307.

Schlesinger, P., G. Murdock and P. Elliot (1983), *Televising Terrorism*, London: Comedia.

Schlesinger, P., R. E. Dobash, R. P. Dobash and C. K. Weaver (1992), *Women Viewing Violence*, London: BFI.

Schudson, M. (1993), 'The Sociology of News Production Revisited', in J. Curran and M. Gurevitch (eds), *Mass Media and Society*, London: Edward Arnold, pp. 141–59.

Seale, C. (2002), *Media and Health*, London: Sage.

Seiter, E., H. Borchers, G. Kreutzner and E. M. Warth (1989), *Remote Control: Television, Audiences and Cultural Power*, London: Routledge.

Shapiro, D., D. Meekers and B. Tambashe (2003), 'Exposure to the "SIDA Dans La Cité" AIDS Prevention Television Series in Côte' d'Ivoire, Sexual Risk Behaviour and Condom Use', *AIDS Care* 15: 303–14.

Sharp, R. (2006), 'The Prodigal's Return', *Observer*, 23 July.

Sieff, E. M. (2003), 'Media Frames of Mental Illnesses: The Potential Impact of Negative Frames', *Journal of Mental Health* 12: 259–69.

Signorielli, N. (1993), *Mass Media Images and Impact on Health*, Westport, CT: Greenwood Press.

Skuse, A. (2002), 'Vagueness, Familiarity and Social Realism: Making Meaning of Radio Soap Opera in South-East Afghanistan', *Media, Culture and Society* 24: 409–27.

Skuse, A. (2005), 'Voices of Freedom: Afghan Politics in Radio Soap Opera', *Ethnography* 6: 159–81.

Smith, R. (2000), 'Have You No Shame?', *Guardian*, 26 October.

Sontag, S. (1991), *Illness as Metaphor*, London: Penguin.

Soothill, K., B. Francis and E. Ackerley (1998), 'Paedophilia and Paedophiles', *New Law Journal* 148: 882–3.

Spigel, L. (2004), 'Entertainment Wars: Television Culture After 9/11', *American Quarterly* 56: 235–70.

Standard Reporter (2002), 'Paedophile Spoof Draws More Viewers', *Evening Standard*, 14 May.

Stempel Mumford, L. (1995), 'Plotting Paternity: Looking for Dad on the Daytime Soaps', in R. C. Allen (ed.), *To Be Continued: Soap Operas Around the World*, London: Routledge, pp. 164–84.

Sutcliffe, T. (1993), 'Domestic Troubles', *Independent*, 1 May.

Sutcliffe, T. (2006), 'Clooney a Big Hitter in Celebocracy', *Independent*, 9 May.

Taylor, S. (1995), 'All Human Life is Here: How Soaps Help Solve Our Own Little Dramas', *Daily Mirror*, 11 April.

Teeman, T. (2005), 'Serial Killers', *The Times*, 12 February.

Tibballs, G. (1998), *Total Brookside*, London: Ebury Press.

Todorov, T. (1977), *The Poetics of Prose*, Oxford: Blackwell.

Tuchman, G., A. Daniels Kaplan and J. Benet (1978), *Hearth and Home: Images of Women in the Mass Media*, New York: Oxford University Press.

Tufte, T. (2001), 'Entertainment-Education and Participation: Assessing the Communication Strategy of Soul City', *Journal of International Communication* 7: 25–50.

Tulloch, J. (1990), *Television Drama: Agency, Audience and Myth*, London: Routledge.

Tulloch, J. (2000), *Watching Television Audiences: Cultural Theories and Methods*, London: Edward Arnold.

Tulloch, J. and A. Moran (1986), *A Country Practice: 'Quality Soap'*, Sydney: Allen and Unwin.

Tunstall, J. (1993), *Television Producers*, London: Routledge.

Turner, G. (2005), 'Cultural Identity, Soap Narrative, and Reality TV', *Television and New Media* 6: 415–22.

Turow, J. (1989), *Playing Doctor: Television, Storytelling and Medical Power*, Oxford: Oxford University Press.

Valaskivi, K. (2000), 'Being a Part of the Family? Genre, Gender and Production in a Japanese TV Drama', *Media, Culture and Society* 22: 309–25.

van Zoonen, L. (2004), 'Imagining the Fan Democracy', *European Journal of Communication*, 19(1): 39–52.

van Zoonen, L., J. Hermes and K. Brants (1998), 'Of Public and Popular Interests', in K. Brants, J. Hermes and L. van Zoonen (ed.), *The Media in Question*, London: Sage, pp. 1–6.

Wahl, O. F. (1995), *Media Madness: Public Images of Mental Illness*, New Brunswick, NJ: Rutgers University Press.

Wahl, O. F. (2003a), 'Depictions of Mental Illnesses in Children's Media', *Journal of Mental Health* 12: 249–58.

Wahl, O. F. (2003b), 'News Media Portrayal of Mental Illness', *American Behavioral Scientist* 46: 1594–600.

Westcott, S. (2002), 'Stop this Soap Sex Orders TV Watchdog', *Daily Express*, 10 May.

Wilson, C., N. Raymond, J. Coverdale and A. Panapa (1999), 'Mental Illness Depictions in Prime-Time Drama: Identifying the Discursive Resources', *Australian and New Zealand Journal of Psychiatry* 33: 232–9.

Winston, B. (2000), *Lies, Damned Lies and Documentary*, London: BFI.

Yorke, J. (2002), 'EastEnders: Faith, Morality and Hope in the Community', speech given at the Bishops' Conference for Clergy and other Ministers in the Diocese of St Albans, 4 September, accessed 20 May 2006, available at www.bbc.co.uk/pressoffice/speeches/stories/yorke_stalbans.html.

Index